When Legal Worlds Overlap:
Human Rights, State and Non-State Law

The International Council on Human Rights Policy wishes to thank the British Department for International Development (DFID), the German Federal Ministry for Economic Cooperation and Development (BMZ) and the German Agency for Technical Cooperation (GTZ), the Dutch Ministry of Foreign Affairs, the Norwegian Ministry of Foreign Affairs, the Swedish International Development Co-operation Agency (SIDA), the Swiss Agency for Development and Cooperation (SDC), the Ford Foundation (New York), the Catholic Agency for Overseas Development (CAFOD) (United Kingdom), and an anonymous donor, for their financial support. The contents of this report do not necessarily reflect the views or policies of the donors.

When Legal Worlds Overlap:
Human Rights, State and Non-State Law

CONTENTS

GLOSSARY

Adat	customary laws in Indonesia
Aksakal	elders with customary authority in Kyrgyzstan
Barangay	non-state justice mechanisms in parts of the Philippines
Bii	customary legal authorities in parts of pre-Soviet Central Asia
Bulubulu	ritual apology and recompense in Fiji
Casa de Justicia	legal service centres in Colombia
Dhimmi	non-Muslim minorities or majorities who, provided they paid a tax to the Muslim state or ruler and accepted certain legal disabilities, were granted state protection and permitted to continue to practice their religion and to be governed by separate personal laws
Dina	customary dispute and conflict resolution mechanism body in Madagascar
Diya	blood money and retribution payments derived from interpretations of Shari'ah
Get	a written consent to being divorced, required for the validity of a divorce in Halachic Jewish law which prohibits divorce against the will of the spouse
Jirga or shura	tribal council in parts of Afghanistan and Pakistan
Kaikuli	a customary payment from the husband to the wife which is held in trust by the husband (Sri Lanka)
Kastom	customary law in the Solomon Islands
Kris	Romani dispute resolution mechanism
Lok adalat	a quasi-judicial, alternative dispute resolution mechanism established by act of Parliament in India
Mamzer	illegitimate Jewish child who is forbidden to marry a Jew for ten generations
Mehr	dower
Millet system	the Ottoman Empire's system of distinct personal laws for various religious communities
Musalihat anjuman	literally, 'forum for problems', an alternative dispute resolution mechanism established by law in Pakistan

Nyaya panchayats	village panchayats granted some judicial powers under 1950s legislation in India
Panchayat	customary decision-making forum in the Indian subcontinent
Rido	clan and interkin group conflicts among the Maranao and Maguindanao Muslims in the Philippines
Riwaj	customary law among the Pathan in Pakistan and Afghanistan
Rondas campesinas	neighbourhood or night watch peasant patrols with some adjudicative functions, found in some Latin American countries (especially Peru)
Shalish	informal adjudication of civil and criminal disputes by local notables in Bangladesh
Talaq	unilateral divorce initiated by a Muslim husband
Xeer	Somali customary law

ACKNOWLEDGEMENTS

The International Council on Human Rights Policy (ICHRP) is grateful to all those who made possible the successful completion of this project, in particular: Cassandra Balchin, Research Consultant, who also led the drafting of this report; Yüksel Sezgin and Kirsty Gover who authored Working Papers for the project; Matthew John, supported by Anuj Bhuwania, who prepared background research papers; and the Project Advisors: Prof. Anne Griffiths, Imrana Jalal, Dr. Celestine Nyamu-Musembi, Gita Sahgal and Prof. Franz von Benda-Beckmann.

In addition, the ICHRP is very grateful to the following individuals who gave their valuable time to attend the First Expert Meeting and subsequent Research Workshops, comment on a draft of this report, discuss the project, or shared material or information with the Council: Abdullahi An'-naim; Karima Bennoune; Judith Beyer; Chetan Bhatt; Julian Burger; Claude Cahn; Kamala Chandrakirana; Sylvia Chirawu; Mark Davidheiser; Marie-Benedicte Dembour; Christoph Eberhard; Sally Engle Merry; Raquel Y. Fajarado; Julio Faundez; Miranada Forsyth; Yash Ghai; Stephen Golub; Lisa Gormley; Kirsty Gover; Anne Griffiths; Pena Guzman; Manfred O. Hinz; Sara Hossain; Robert Husbands; Jean Jackson; Mathew John; Christina Jones-Pauly; Helene Maria Kyed; Leslie Lois; Hallie Ludsin; Vivek Maru; Ingrid Massage; Juliane Neuhaus; Enyinna Nwauche; Celestine Nyamu-Musembi; Chidi Odinkalu; Mireya Maritza Pena Guzman; Faustina Perreira; Bishnu Raj Upreti; Gita Sahgal; Yüksel Sezgin; Dina Siddiqi; Rachel Sieder; Shannon Speed; Rodolfo Stavenhagen; Gila Stopler; Franz von Benda-Beckmann; Sohail Akbar Warraich; Marcus Weilenmann; Lynn Welchmann; Richard A. Wilson; Gordon Woodman.

The ICHRP is also grateful to the following interns who provided research and other assistance for the project: Steve Ako Tanga; James Douglas; Sandra Oyella; and Tom Sanderson.

Vijay Kumar Nagaraj, Research Director at the ICHRP, directed and managed the project.

INTRODUCTION AND OVERVIEW

WHY EXAMINE PLURAL LEGAL ORDERS?

This report is written for human rights advocates and policy-makers who find themselves in contexts where a specific dispute or subject matter is governed by multiple norms, laws or forums that co-exist within a single jurisdiction. Plural legal orders occur in numerous circumstances: for example, where different family laws apply to specific ethno-cultural groups, where customary dispute resolution mechanisms operate without state sanction, where non-state legal orders (such as chiefs' courts) are officially recognised, or where quasi-state legal orders (such as alternative dispute resolution mechanisms) are established.

Given the concerns surrounding the failure of most state legal systems to ensure effective access to justice, particularly for marginalised and vulnerable communities, a range of actors – using a range of arguments – have encouraged or demanded the introduction or recognition of plural legal orders. These claims in turn have led legal and human rights organisations, but also other actors, to express concern at the human rights implications of recognising and extending forms of legal plurality.

When Legal Worlds Overlap: Human Rights, State and Non-State Law aims to provide human rights and other actors with tools that will enable them to evaluate whether a plural legal order is likely to enhance access to justice, and to identify human rights risks that are associated with the plural legal order in question. While it is widely recognised that plural legal orders generate many human rights conflicts and dilemmas, discussion of them has generally created more heat rather than light. This is no doubt partly because, though a large body of research exists on the subject, drawing on law, anthropology, sociology, political science, and development and environment studies, surprisingly little specific work has focused on their human rights impact. Besides, theoretical and conceptual discussions have seldom connected with experiences of human rights practice in plural legal contexts. The aim of the report is therefore to lay the groundwork for a more careful and inclusive discussion of the issues involved, with the aim of improving practical policy responses on the ground.

It must be said at the outset that this task is not straightforward. Plural legal orders exist in every part of the world and in all types of political systems. They vary enormously in jurisdiction, procedure, structure and degree of autonomy. Numerous interrelated factors influence their evolution including colonialism; the state's need for legitimacy; the quality, reach and relevance of official legal systems; conflict and post-conflict reconstruction; respect for diversity, multiculturalism and identity politics; privatisation or reduction of public expenditure in the justice sector; other forms of intervention by donor and international development agencies; etc.

Plural legal orders also engage significant political and economic interests. In a resource-hungry world, claims to jurisdiction over land, water and other natural resources are often entangled with issues of customary usage and indigenous peoples' rights, and trigger many conflicts between these groups and national and international economic interests. Other commercial and political interests are also involved, such as control over land for tourism, military use or urban development. States and development agencies allocate millions of dollars in aid to justice sector reforms that influence the introduction or recognition of legal plurality. Ethno-cultural and religious communities, minorities and majorities, also represent vital political constituencies. Internationally too, culture has become a flashpoint with the result that plural legal orders lie at the heart of many current human rights debates, especially those regarding gender equality, and minority and indigenous peoples' rights. The subject both defies easy generalisation and arouses strong emotions.

The boundaries between the wide range of actors concerned with plural legal orders – human rights activists and policy-makers, donor and multilateral aid agencies, governments, social and political movements, legal professionals and scholars – are not watertight and this report therefore addresses all those who are generally concerned with the protection and promotion of human rights in the context of plural legal orders, rather than a specific category of actors.

The report adopts a resolutely interdisciplinary approach. It touches on a wide variety of themes including human rights principles and standards, the rights of indigenous peoples and ethnic or religious minorities, gender equality, citizenship, the rule of law, governance, decentralisation, aid programmes, globalisation and fundamentalisms. It also draws on experiences from many different contexts to reflect the diverse character of plural legal orders and is rich in examples.

The report contributes to the discussions on plural legal orders in four ways:

- It identifies some important misunderstandings and false dichotomies that have made coherent discussion of plural legal orders particularly difficult (and which similarly undermine the understanding of how religious, indigenous, and gender rights actually interact). (Chapters I to IV)

- It sets out the human rights issues that need to be addressed in the context of plural legal orders. (Chapters V and VI)

- It examines some specific policy challenges, notably those that occur in the context of recognition of non-state legal orders; recognition of cultural diversity in law; and justice sector reforms. (Chapters VII to IX)

- It offers a practical approach – some principles and a framework of questions – that human rights advocates and policy-makers can use as a guide when they work in plural legal contexts. (Chapters X and XI)

The paragraphs below name some of the themes that are discussed in the report's four parts. Readers should take note that each chapter ends with a summary of key issues, highlighted in grey.

THE CONCEPTUAL LANDSCAPE

Much of the debate regarding plural legal orders is characterised by polarised presumptions that disregard the complexity and variety of local situations. While recognising that cultural differences are significant and real to people, the report underlines the complexity of the relationship between law and culture and that culture is a dynamic process, which is socially and politically contested. Plural legal orders lie at the centre of this contestation with both state and non-state actors mobilising law and culture towards ends that can be either inclusive or exclusive.

From a human rights perspective, the report notes that the simple presence of plural legal orders makes plain that state law is not the only relevant and effective legal order in people's lives. At the same time, the state remains central to a human rights analysis of plural legal orders because it is the primary duty-bearer in relation to human rights.

In addition, not all justice claims can be resolved through law and many languages of justice are available to people. It needs therefore to be understood at the start that human rights lie within, rather than outside, the universe of normative systems and culture. People are bearers of both culture *and* rights, and recognition of rights does not imply rejection of culture. On this basis, the report rejects the view that universalism and cultural relativism are "alternatives between which one must choose once and for all". Instead, it suggests that much can be learned from how local struggles for justice have appropriated universal general principles of human rights in their own contexts.

Human rights standards and instruments contain much that is relevant to plural legal orders, but there are important gaps. For example, the 2007 UN Declaration on the Rights of Indigenous Peoples offers little guidance on how indigenous and national legal systems are to work together effectively in accordance with human rights standards, even though it introduces a qualitatively different approach in recognising the collective right of indigenous peoples to maintain their legal and judicial systems.

The fragmentation of international human rights law is a particular problem. Human rights standards relevant to plural legal orders have developed furthest in respect of indigenous peoples and minority rights, but this work has occurred largely without reference to standard-setting on other matters, notably culture and gender equality.

The report suggests that fragmentation, combined with a "gender blindspot" and the influence of religious fundamentalisms on standard-setting, have encouraged the emergence of approaches that seek to 'balance' gender equality against the rights to culture or religious freedom. This false dichotomy is an analytical trap, notably for women's human rights.

It highlights the misleading distinction between 'minor' and 'major' criminal and civil matters. In many instances, human rights standards call for limiting the jurisdiction of non-state legal orders (customary law or religious courts) to 'minor' matters, typically areas of family law. Yet these have major human rights consequences. It suggests that human rights actors need to give family law far more attention.

The report goes on to question certain presumptions about non-state legal orders. It notes first that the line between state and non-state legal orders is blurred rather than rigid, and that they influence one another. Just as state law does not exist in isolation but is affected by cultural and political preferences, non-state law is not necessarily always 'traditional', but is subject to contemporary influences and may be created by processes that are internally or externally facilitated.

Second, compared with the state system, non-state legal orders are not always quicker, cheaper, more accessible, more inclusive, focused on restorative justice, or more effective in resolving local disputes.

Third, support for non-state legal orders is not universal. In many instances, people want more rather than less of the state.

Further, the report notes that the way both state and non-state systems are used is often gendered, and may reflect social or economic compulsion rather than a normative preference. Rushing to replace state systems that enjoy little legitimacy with non-state mechanisms (or vice versa) may make little difference if analyses of 'choices' between state and non-state legal orders leave issues of power unexamined.

THE HUMAN RIGHTS IMPACTS

The area of family law is most likely to be governed by plural legal orders, because controlling family and intimate relationships is central to the preservation of collective cultural identity. The report raises the question as to why it has come to be largely accepted, even in human rights circles, that family law may be culturally particular rather than subject to universal norms.

The relative absence of family law from human rights discourse is one reason why international standards have not adequately addressed plural legal orders as a human rights issue. The standards do not provide tools that identify and address violations that arise from jurisdictional confusion and their limitations are especially evident where the state order legitimises plural family laws based on ethno-religious frameworks that tend to have particularly adverse consequences for women.

The report highlights a range of negative human rights consequences that can result from plural legal orders. It does not say that plural legal orders are necessarily harmful, and cites cases where non-state legal orders can be a positive influence. However, in many cases plural legal orders precipitate certain negative human rights outcomes as a result of their structure.

In particular, the subordination of rights to a regime based on (religious or other) identity can cause discrimination and inequality before the law. The confusion over personal and subject matter jurisdiction or the application of law, common to plural legal orders, may result in abuse of power, reduced human rights protection, and impunity. Those who are poor or otherwise marginalised can be seriously disadvantaged, because they lack resources to navigate the complicated jurisdictional and procedural arrangements that are characteristic of plural legal orders.

The weaknesses of the formal system are indeed real, but when states recognise non-state legal orders or alternative dispute resolution mechanisms, there are also concerns that they may offer diluted due process guarantees and other procedural protections, and thus violate rights and restrict access to justice. In addition, separate civil law regimes for minorities can obscure substantive and institutional problems within those regimes, or they may become so 'politically sensitive' that reform is very difficult.

Further, official recognition of non-state legal orders can undermine democratic processes and human rights freedoms in other ways. It may confer power on unelected leaders, or reinforce hegemonic or majoritarian interpretations of custom; it may actually undermine plurality, if identity-based laws segregate society in ways that reinforce ethnic and religious fundamentalisms.

POLICY CHALLENGES

The report focuses on three key areas of policy: the issue of recognition of non-state legal orders; the issue of recognising cultural particularities in law; and donor-funded justice reform programmes.

Recognition, incorporation, and decentralisation are ways by which a non-state legal order may become part of a pluralised state legal order. All involve questions of: normative content; jurisdiction (over territory, issues and persons); authority (who has it, who bestows it, and how); adjudicatory process (procedure); and enforcement of decisions. If a plural legal order is to operate smoothly, all these elements need to be defined clearly – but this is rarely achieved.

It suggests that, from a rights perspective, decisions to recognise or incorporate a non-state legal order, or devolve powers to it, must take into account not only the *outputs* of a non-state legal order but also the authority and autonomy of its *processes*.

Recognition presents numerous conceptual challenges and policy dilemmas. Claims to recognition based on religious, minority ethnic or indigenous identities each have distinct legal and socio-historical foundations. They are ontologically different and the justification for recognising a claim in one dimension cannot be transferred automatically to another. In addition, what exactly is being recognised or incorporated? Is it a 'thing', a claim, a process, an institution, or a combination of these? If culture is understood to be a dynamic human endeavour, it becomes clear that recognition is not just a technical matter but deeply political in character.

The incorporation or recognition of customary law presents particular challenges. One approach is 'translation', which attempts to find precisely equivalent rules or institutions that can be recognised or incorporated, but which is not always possible in practice. A different approach is to recognise customary laws without elaborating their content but this also raises questions about the state's adherence to human rights standards. The report notes that calls to recognise the 'customary' do not always imply a retreat into the past: they may legitimate present and future political claims. Such calls are often associated with claims to 'authenticity'. These are not only reminiscent of colonialism, but have policy and human rights implications: how is 'authenticity' and 'expertise' established and thereby whose knowledge and power is privileged.

The second policy area also raises dilemmas. The demand to recognise cultural particularity in law is based on the principle of universal equality but, by definition, it implies acknowledging and giving status to something that is not universally shared. In addition, those who demand recognition of their cultural diversity may themselves prove intolerant of other differences and pluralities (notably of women, sexual and religious minorities or atheists). Further, recognition by a state that is considered to be alien and inequitable can erode the non-state authority's legitimacy. Finally, when state recognition requires the formalisation of custom, this may block the dynamic evolution of customary laws and the internal political contestation that drives it.

Further difficulties arise when state law is based on ethno-religious identities or when the state recognises identity-based non-state legal orders. In such cases, an individual's multiple identities become legally fixed or formalised. This creates an unrealistic expectation that people will act as "undifferentiated citizens in the public sphere" but express "distinct cultural or religious identities in the private domain of family and communal life", though it is not clear where the *private* ends and the *public* begins. The report suggests that one way around this difficult question is an approach that does not validate rights claims only on the basis that claimants have a shared culture or belong to a community, but in terms of the "legitimate interests of the members of the group", because cultures are not "moral entities to which we can owe obligations of fairness". Another helpful approach is to assess how recognition of cultural diversity in law affects both intra and intergroup rights in practice.

To protect against violations of rights in an identity-based regime, the provision of an option to exit the community is a necessary but insufficient guarantee against the violation of rights in a plural legal order, not least because the option may not be accessible to some individuals. Overall, justice in a multicultural context, and state facilitation of dialogue between and within communities, must take into account differences in social, economic and political power and how a given plural legal order affects each of these. The report leans towards the view that the obligation to accommodate and support a minority culture cannot and should not be absolute, just as the preference to advance a majority culture cannot and should not be unlimited.

Donor-funded justice reform projects, the third policy area considered, frequently promote non-state legal orders or alternative dispute resolution mechanisms. While some justice sector aid has facilitated constitutional development and helped transform justice systems, it has also suffered from weaknesses. Many programmes lack a sound research base and may be underpinned by poor scholarship resulting in inconsistent, incoherent or unrealistic policies.

In addition, many donor institutions do not apply human rights principles consistently, especially when they fund or design decentralisation projects and alternative dispute resolution mechanisms. Poor consultation, and the absence of meaningful local participation and effective monitoring and evaluation, have undermined the human rights impacts of some programmes. Donor projects are often uncoordinated and agendas may even mutually conflict, leading to unintended consequences and preventing learning from successful initiatives.

WAYS FORWARD

Notwithstanding their limitations, existing human rights standards do offer scope for effective engagement with plural legal orders. For example, the prohibition on discrimination is absolute, and no cultural defence is admissible with regard to violence against women.

Human rights instruments also provide approaches, for example, to understand the complexities of identity and the internal diversity of culture, which rise above a 'balancing' approach. A great deal can be learned from the way human rights principles have been used by regional and national courts to address violations associated with plural legal orders and cases where rights apparently conflict.

The report supports the view that any recognition of cultural difference in the form of plural legal orders must first assess: actual human rights impacts on inter and intragroup equality; the proportionality of any restriction on rights caused by such recognition; and whether the cumulative effect of the proposed measure would be to create a qualitatively new level of discrimination.

With regard to recognition of indigenous peoples' customary law or justice mechanisms, a functional rather than a categorical approach is more likely to produce positive human rights outcomes. The report suggests a four point approach: avoid a single all-purpose definition of 'customary laws and practices'; aim to secure all basic human rights for every member of the community; deal with internal stresses and difficulties within the community that are due to external forces; and avoid establishing distinct and possibly conflicting systems of law that will generate inequities and inefficiencies.

The further development of human rights standards is desirable in several areas. These include: the meaning and practical application of due diligence; family law; the allocation to different jurisdictions of 'minor' and 'major' disputes; and due process standards in the context of civil disputes governed by non-state legal orders that have a measure of state recognition.

With regard to the recognition of indigenous peoples' legal orders (and indeed all non-state legal orders), more national research and transnational sharing of experience is required on whether and how such recognition contributes to or obstructs, progress in human rights. The report also highlights the value of cooperation between those working on different aspects of rights - on women's rights, minority ethnic and religious rights, indigenous peoples' rights, sexual orientation, etc., as well as between those working nationally and internationally. Such cooperation is an urgent imperative for the development of more congruent human rights standards across different areas.

The report concludes by outlining some guiding principles for a human rights engagement with plural legal orders. The final chapter also proposes a framework that may assist human rights advocates and other actors to grapple with the complex challenges generated by existing or proposed plural legal orders. The framework poses a sequence of main and subsidiary questions that enable practitioners to interrogate the merits of demands to introduce, preserve or reform a plural legal order. (For the full framework, see Chapter XI.)

A NOTE ON METHODOLOGY

The project began with the drafting of a concept note based on preliminary research by the ICHRP. An expert meeting in January 2008 discussed and debated the note. The research team then prepared an Approach Paper, which, following further consultation, led to the finalisation of the Project Design.

In addition to a wide-ranging survey of literature from academic and non-academic sources, two background papers were prepared as part of the initial research. Subsequently, the ICHRP commissioned two research papers. The first was a comparative study of legal pluralism with respect to indigenous peoples' rights in the area of adoption and membership in Australia, Canada, New Zealand and the United States;[1] the second was a comparative assessment of personal status laws in Egypt, India and Israel.[2]

Two research workshops in late 2008 provided further opportunities to develop the research. They brought together experts from different regions and included legal anthropologists, sociologists, international human rights lawyers, human rights activists in local and international organisations, development consultants and political scientists.

The report draws from, and refers to, a large body of published and unpublished work, both academic and non-academic, as well as to the experiences and insights of activists and advocates. Much of this literature is field-based research by scholars, activists and policy analysts. The participation of several of the authors of such studies in the two Research Workshops enabled the ICHRP to build on, and in some cases deepen the insights of, their work and findings. The report cites some studies repeatedly, because they highlight a range of relevant issues. The many references in the text should be read as illustrations, taken from one context to throw light on a point of analysis that the report found applies more generally. Where several illustrative examples are cited, the intention is to indicate the range and variety of contexts to which the analysis applies; they are not exhaustive listings.

A range of experts from different regions and disciplines commented on the first draft of this report. It has benefited significantly from their feedback and suggestions. The draft report was also made publicly available on the website of the ICHRP for comment and review.

---

1   Gover, 2008b.

2   Sezgin, 2008.

PART ONE

THE CONCEPTUAL LANDSCAPE

I.   PLURAL LEGAL ORDERS: PREMISES, DEFINITION AND CONTEXTS

PREMISES: WHERE WE START

Given the contentious nature of debates relating to plural legal orders, and the immense variety of possible perspectives, it is important to indicate some starting premises:

- All societies are, in one way or another, legally plural. Every country and jurisdiction will reflect one or more of the broad variations of plural legal orders listed overleaf. Within this potentially vast discussion, this report prioritises those forms of plurality which have featured less in human rights analysis despite their serious rights implications, or which are particularly pertinent to discussions of cultural diversity.[3]

- There is much that can be learned from legal-anthropological and sociological perspectives in the process of developing a human rights perspective on plural legal orders.

- International human rights standards are relevant and important to any discussion of plural legal orders and the protection of rights. At the same time, the report recognises that using this framework presents many challenges and that other frameworks can also contribute to equality and justice.

- Given the centrality of the state and state law as the primary guarantors of human rights, the state remains central to the discussions in the report. Nevertheless, the report recognises that in some contexts states are failing or absent, that not all states are the same, and that states respond differently to their human rights obligations.

- Human rights are an incomplete project in that standards and their content are continuously evolving, as actors in the global South and North and activists at all levels contribute to their development. Their evolution at local and national level (especially as a result of engagement with national constitutions and laws) often exceeds or pre-empts the development of international standards.

---

3   This report does not deal with all forms of legal plurality. It does not cover military tribunals, anti-terrorist or Speedy Trials courts, ombudsman's offices, truth and reconciliation mechanisms, or mechanisms established under international humanitarian law. For a discussion of some of these see Mungoven, 2001. Nor does it cover pluralities and human rights related to conflicts in private international law; for a discussion, see Warraich and Balchin, 2006 and Fournier, 2005. Finally, plurality in the law should not be confused with the variety of specialised areas of law and internal differentiation found in most larger state justice systems (e.g., labour, criminal, taxation, family law), or with the different types and levels of courts (e.g., employment tribunals, lower courts, appeals courts, etc.).

- The *content* of culture, custom, tradition and religion changes over time and space, and is contested, both internally and with respect to other cultures. Being contested, culture, custom, tradition and religion relate to structures of power and are undeniably political.

- Although contestations regarding culture lie at the heart of many debates about plural legal orders, and certainly at the heart of some of the most heated discussions of international human rights standards, plural legal orders are not exclusively about culture, custom or religion. Issues of poverty and alienation, or privatisation and concerns about protecting scarce state resources, are also powerful influences.

- Finally, since the evolution of legal orders, both state and non-state, reflects the dynamics of power, debates about plural orders cannot be divorced from an analysis of relationships of power between and within the state and society. Given the manipulation of plural legal orders by powerful state and non-state interests, national and international power imbalances, and structural inequalities at the level of family and community, are central to any discussion of human rights and plural legal orders.

PLURAL LEGAL ORDERS: WHAT ARE THEY?

'Legal orders' may be understood as the norms, rules and institutions formed by a society or group of people to ensure social stability. They usually describe what is right and how to act, and what is wrong and how not to act; and the remedies for and consequences of such actions. Plural legal orders arise when a specific dispute or subject matter may be governed by multiple norms, laws or forums that co-exist within a particular jurisdiction or country.

> On the ground, there can sometimes be a confusing array of alternatives. For example, if a member of a peasant community in the Department of Ayacucho, Peru, is involved in a dispute, she can resort to the authorities of her own peasant *comunidad*, to the local Justice of the Peace, to an NGO-based Rural Centre for the Administration of Justice, or to the state courts.[4] The plurality arises not just from the multiplicity of forums but also because each forum has different underlying values and will take a different approach to addressing the dispute.

Plural legal orders: basic categories

Plural legal orders are found in every part of the world, North and South, and in all types of political systems, democratic as well as authoritarian. As a starting point and at the risk of simplification, below are some basic categories. Their great variation is discussed later.

---

4   Faundez, 2003, p. 40.

1. A legal order having no state sanction exists parallel to state law

This form is found in all countries, and includes dispute resolution mechanisms such as those run by: street committees in Brazil; animist or Christian religious authorities in Chinese villages; Shari'ah Councils in Britain; tribal *jirgas* in Afghanistan and Pakistan; caste *panchayats* in India; Romani *kris*; customary water management bodies in Tanzania; and paramilitary groups during the conflict in Northern Ireland.

2. The state legal order is plural

- Within the formal system, family and some property matters are governed by different laws for different religious or ethnic communities, whereas most matters (usually criminal, employment, commerce, taxation) are governed by laws applicable to all. This form of plurality is particularly common in the Middle East, North Africa, South Asia and parts of South-East Asia.

- Indigenous peoples' legal orders are recognised as law. Generally found in countries with large indigenous populations (especially in Latin America, Scandinavia and South Asia, as well as states such as Canada, the United States, Australia and New Zealand).

- Geographically or administratively distinct areas have different state laws. In Pakistan's Federally Administered Tribal Areas (FATA) bordering Afghanistan, the 1901 Frontier Crimes Regulation applies rather than the Pakistan Penal Code. Similarly, federalism results in murder attracting the death penalty in some states in the United States but not others, and provincial autonomy laws render whipping legal in Aceh but not elsewhere in Indonesia.

- Concurrent jurisdiction exists within state law, so that a case may be heard under different laws providing for very different processes or outcomes. For example, in Israel, maintenance cases may be heard under religious or a general civil law.

3. Quasi-state legal orders are established, or the state recognises or incorporates non-state legal orders

- Under alternative dispute resolution (ADR) reforms, the state establishes quasi-formal mechanisms (such as India's *lok adalats*, Pakistan's *musalihat anjumans*, and Brazil's Special Criminal Courts).

- State courts enforce privately arbitrated agreements, such as agreements between businesses under *lex mercatoria*, or the private religious arbitration conducted by Jewish and Muslim organisations under Britain's 1996 Arbitration Act.

- In the course of decentralisation, the state incorporates parts of a non-state legal order into the state system at the lowest level of governance. Mozambique has recognised 3,651 'community authorities' under Decree 15/2000 since 2002, including 'traditional leaders' and 'secretaries of suburban quarters or villages', who have responsibilities in relation to policing, taxation, justice enforcement, rural development, etc. Similar examples may be found in China, India, the Philippines, and much of Africa south of the Sahara.

- Norms or institutions from non-state orders are included in the main body of the formal legal system. In Canada, aboriginal justice practices, including mediating peacemakers, are sometimes integrated into certain provincial courts. Examples include the Tsuuu T'ina Peacemaking Court in Alberta, and the Gladue Court (the first urban Aboriginal court) in Toronto.

Examples of plural legal orders challenge a number of presumptions. Although the state is the focus of much of the discussion regarding plural legal orders, the first category in the scheme above indicates that a legal order that is not part of the state legal system and is not recognised by the state, can be as or more important in people's lives than state laws. Not all plural legal orders result from action by the state or 'community authorities'; other non-state bodies such as local non-governmental organisation (NGO) law centres, peoples' committees, and even multilateral agencies are also major actors. Legal orders that operate outside the state legal order are not always 'traditional'. For example, communities of urban slum dwellers in Colombia and South Africa have set up street committees to deal with local crime; NGOs in Sierra Leone offer mediation by paralegals; and powerful political parties may set up their own dispute resolution forums.[5]

Considerable variation occurs within each of the broad categories of plurality in state legal orders; most relates to questions of jurisdiction and choice of forum and/or law. For example, in Lebanon, each of the 18 state-recognised religious communities has its own court with exclusive jurisdiction over laws governing matters of family, marriage and succession. In India and Bangladesh, different religious communities have their own personal laws (some codified and some not) that govern many aspects of marriage and family, though all cases are heard in a unitary court system. In Malaysia, a person's religious identity automatically determines which law governs his or her family disputes, whereas in Cameroon a person is free to choose whether family matters are governed by customary laws or by general civil law which is open and applicable to all. Under the 1923 Treaty of Lausanne, Muslims in Thrace, Greece, may choose to use Muslim laws for certain matters.

---

5   The Hindu fundamentalist political party, the Shiv Sena, in Mumbai, India, is an example – see Eckert, 2005.

Where indigenous people's legal orders are recognised by the state (referred to as Special Indigenous Jurisdictions in some Latin American countries), the range of issues covered by these systems varies widely. Some cover all disputes, while the mandate of others is very specific (in Scandinavia, for example, it is limited to reindeer herding). Certain systems have jurisdiction over non-members, but many (as in Venezuela) do not. How far indigenous peoples develop their own legal orders also varies. For instance, Native American tribes in the United States have their own courts which range "from tradition-based systems with little or no written rules or codes to systems that mirror Courts in the Federal and State systems".[6]

Another area of variation is a vital issue for human rights: whether the plural system is subject to some overarching national standards. For example, Colombia's Constitutional Court is mandated to settle conflicts between the rulings of the indigenous legal order and constitutional standards, and in South Africa customary law, to be recognised, must conform to constitutional principles. In Zambia and Zimbabwe, by contrast, customary law is exempt from an obligation to conform with the Constitution.

The degree to which appeals are permitted raises an additional issue of standards, with respect to procedure and constitutional guarantees of fundamental rights. Some ADR and privatised justice mechanisms (such as arbitration) allow few or no grounds for appeal. In the case of multiple family law systems, the extent to which the appeals process is plural varies. Where systems merge is often the point at which fundamental rights can be accessed. In Sri Lanka and Syria, for example, separate appellate courts hear the first appeals, but further appeals proceed within the unitary system. Notwithstanding the theoretical extent of a community's legal autonomy under plural legal orders, in practice the state may exercise considerable control, as in Israel, where the state controls seemingly autonomous religious legal orders by determining court budgets and appointments.

The above paragraphs demonstrate that no form of plural legal orders is 'typical'. A plural legal order may or may not have a basis in culture and tradition. The state may or may not recognise legal plurality, and individuals may or may not be permitted to choose the law that is applicable to them. Moreover, certain contexts defy simple categorisation. For example, in conflict zones where the state is largely absent it becomes hard to label existing legal orders in relation to the state. Somali customary authorities applying *xeer* are by default the only legal order in much of the country. A very different example is that of the Kyrgyzstan *aksakal* (Elders') courts whose status and relationship to the state order has shifted repeatedly since their creation in 1993, from being part of the judiciary to being a local self-governance structure.

---

6   www.ntjrc.org/tribalcourts/basics.asp.

Legal pluralism

In discussing all of the above, this report draws heavily on a large body of scholarly research on legal pluralism, which includes anthropological and socio-legal scholarship.[7] Legal pluralism covers "diverse and often contested perspectives on law, ranging from the recognition of differing legal orders within the nation-state, to a more far reaching and open-ended concept of law that does not necessarily depend on state recognition for its validity".[8] According to a legal pluralist perspective, a 'plural legal order' is a situation in which diverse legal orders are "superimposed, interpenetrated, and mixed".[9]

From the late 1970s some scholars began applying the concept of legal pluralism to non-colonised societies, notably in the advanced industrial countries of Europe and the United States. Legal pluralism expanded "from a concept that refers to the relations between the colonizer and colonized to relations between dominant groups and subordinate groups, such as religious, ethnic, or cultural minorities, immigrant groups, and unofficial forms of ordering located in social networks or institutions".[10] In fact this was a return to the concept's roots because what is widely regarded as the first modern study of legal pluralism, written at the beginning of the 20th century, focused on an eastern province of the Habsburg Empire, where besides the central legislator in Vienna and a centralised judiciary, an independent customary law existed that was more important than state law.[11]

If European scholarship on the subject is no more than a century old, it is clear that societies have been legally plural for many centuries. As Tamanaha describes it, the legal terrain of Western Europe in "the mid-to-late medieval period was characterized by a remarkable jumble of different sorts of law and institutions, occupying the same space, sometimes conflicting, sometimes complementary, and typically lacking any overarching hierarchy or organisation. These forms of law included local customs (often in several versions, usually unwritten); general Germanic customary law (in code form); feudal law (mostly unwritten); the law merchant or *lex mercatoria* – commercial law and customs followed by merchants; canon law of the Roman Catholic Church; and the revived roman law developed in the universities. Various types of courts or judicial forums coexisted: manorial courts, municipal courts, merchant courts, guild courts, church courts, and royal courts.... The mid through late Middle Ages thus exhibited legal pluralism along at least three major axes: overlapping

---

7   For a discussion on legal pluralism see Griffiths, 2002. See also Griffiths, 1986; Merry, 1988; Dupret, 2007; Benda-Beckmann *et al.*, 2009.

8   Griffiths, 2002, p. 289.

9   de Sousa Santos in Dupret, 2007, p. 9.

10   Merry, 1998, p. 872.

11   Ehrlich in Gunther, undated.

bodies of law with different geographical reaches, coexisting institutionalized systems, and conflicting legal norms within a system".[12]

The idea of legal pluralism helps clarify that state law is not the only relevant and effective legal order in people's lives, especially for dispute resolution. It draws attention as well to transnational and globalised means of developing, interpreting and enforcing law, including international human rights law. Notwithstanding its richness and complexity, the idea of legal pluralism presents some difficulties, which arise partly from the different purposes for which it is invoked.[13] In addition, while legal pluralism often presumes some decentering of the state, the state remains central to a human rights analysis of plural legal orders. This is because states are the primary duty-bearers in relation to human rights guarantees that arise from regional and global treaty obligations; they have a duty to protect and exercise due diligence and take action when non-state legal orders violate human rights, and to prevent violations from occurring in the first place.

POLICIES AND CONTEXTS THAT GIVE RISE TO PLURAL LEGAL ORDERS

The state's need for control and legitimacy

Throughout history, empires have faced the same basic challenge: how to project colonial authority over vast territories containing hostile or indifferent populations. Colonial rulers adopted various strategies to ensure state control, many of which contributed, with different effects, to the strengthening of plural legal orders.

For example, classical Muslim[14] statecraft acknowledged the concept of the *dhimmi* – non-Muslim minorities or majorities who, provided they paid a tax to the Muslim state or ruler and accepted certain legal disabilities, were granted state protection and permitted to continue to practice their religion and to be governed by separate personal laws. The Mughal empire in the Indian subcontinent largely followed this model, as did the Ottoman empire in parts of North Africa, Eastern and Central Europe and the Caucasus (where it was called the *millet* system). Both empires granted a degree of legal and judicial autonomy to a wide range of religious communities.

---

12   Tamanaha, 2008, p. 5.

13   Griffiths, 2002, p. 289.

14   The terms 'Muslim' and 'Islamic' are often mistakenly used interchangeably. In this report we use 'Muslim' to signify the laws and practices of Muslims. 'Islamic' refers to that which conforms to, or is mandated by the principles of Islam. The sheer diversity of family laws in Muslim contexts indicates that Muslims themselves often disagree as to which interpretation of family law conforms with the principles of Islam.

British rule preserved or extended a similar legal segregation across much of Asia and Africa, particularly in family law. The policy was more a result of colonial pragmatism rather than any particular privileging of religion. Because it was politically expedient to placate local patriarchal landed elites, custom – rather than religion – was recognised as the primary rule governing property ownership and control in parts of the Indian subcontinent. Enhancing the power of chiefs over their people was similarly a key element of Britain's colonial strategy of ruling by proxy in much of Africa.[15] In some cases colonial authorities introduced forms of local rule which did not previously exist, or made existing systems more authoritarian. This was true for the tribal *jirga* system in parts of Afghanistan and Pakistan.[16] In addition to creating or re-organising non-state legal orders, colonial governments also reinforced plurality in the formal system. British colonial rulers, for example, perceived the volatile tribal frontier districts bordering Afghanistan as a perpetual threat to the stability of the Empire and under the guise of non-interference in the ancient *riwaj* (customs) they introduced the infamous Frontier Crimes Regulation 1901, which was designed to ensure British control by empowering a loyal local elite. Largely preserved by the post-colonial Pakistani state, this form of plurality with its origins in the colonial impulse to control is today being used to enhance state control in the context of the 'war on terror'.

The 19th century Russian colonisers in Central Asia permitted the continuation of 'customary law' as they understood it in order to placate communities and where possible co-opt them. Under a 1868 decree, customary courts of *bii* could continue to decide what the Russian administration considered 'minor' issues (although now subject to annulment by the colonial authorities), while the Russian courts dealt with serious offences such as murder.[17]

In contrast to the British common law approach, which perhaps was naturally more inclined to recognise custom, French colonial theory preferred the republican concept of a citizenry bound by a common civil and criminal code. In practice, nevertheless, French colonial rule was also characterised by the recourse to chiefs and other 'traditional' or kinship-based authorities to help administer colonial territories.[18] For instance, in parts of the former Ottoman Empire colonised by the French, the Ottoman *millet* system was preserved, with family laws based on religious affiliation, but the wider civil and criminal systems introduced were based on the Napoleonic Code. In Senegal customary, Muslim and Christian laws also prevailed alongside the civil code.[19] When they left

---

15 Maru, 2006, p. 435. In contrast, the Portuguese did not codify customary law or grant the courts of chiefs official status in the Lusophone colonies.

16 Sarwar, 2004.

17 Beyer, 2006.

18 Gellar, 2006, p. 6.

19 Joireman, 2001.

Indonesia, similarly, the Dutch bequeathed a civil code but also a legal system that, in general, draws significantly both on Islam and *adat* (customary laws).

Statutory and institutional segregation – in terms of race, ethnicity and location – is the most significant colonial legacy, retained across large parts of the post-colonial world.[20] This segregation often entailed 'codification of native law' in a manner that both ossified customary systems that had been more fluid and consolidated boundaries between communities, arguably facilitating the colonial 'divide and rule' approach. In many cases post-colonial states in Africa did not alter the basic edifice of colonial law.[21] This was also true of countries in the Middle East, South Asia and parts of South-East Asia, where legal religious segregation has remained in force well after independence, especially in family law. In many instances, the recognition of customary law in colonial and post-colonial states was prompted by the need to legitimise state authority and extend its penetration on one hand, and on the other to "make the legal system more 'authentic', in order to create a better fit between society and its norms".[22]

However, many post-colonial governments did abolish, ban or severely curtail the judicial (and often administrative and political) powers of chieftaincies after independence.[23] Abolition reflected efforts to legitimise and consolidate the power of the new nationalist elite. In Mozambique and Tanzania, the legal or judicial power of chiefs was substituted by popular justice and party cells. However, in post-conflict Mozambique, the state gained much-needed legitimacy by presuming to identify 'true' chieftaincies in the course of a decentralisation programme. This was prompted by acknowledgement that the former ban on chiefs had failed and the ruling party needed the political weight of chiefs to counter the political opposition (Renamo).[24] Similarly, in states such as Canada and New Zealand, Aboriginal or indigenous legal systems are also being recognised as a means to improve or repair state legitimacy.[25] Even the authoritarian, centralised Chinese state has found it necessary in practice to recognise the dispute settlement arrangements of the nomadic communities in Eastern Tibet.[26] In sum, states are likely to try to enhance the power and legitimacy of their own law by taking advantage of the 'greater popular legitimacy' of customary law.

---

20   Mamdani, 1996.

21   See for example Chanock, 1985; Mamdani, 1996.

22   Sezgin, 2003, p. 13.

23   Kyed and Buur, 2007.

24   Buur and Kyed, 2006, p. 8.

25   Gover, 2008b.

26   Pirie, 2005.

The state legal order is alien, inadequate, irrelevant, or withdraws

Many communities across the world often view the state legal order as distant, inadequate, irrelevant or alien, leading to situations in which non-state legal orders flourish.

Colonial policies of assimilation produced legal orders that were foreign to the population, whose non-state legal orders continued to flourish underground in response. In contrast to the British, French and Dutch colonial projects, the Spanish in Chile and Argentina brutally subordinated and segregated indigenous cultural and legal institutions. Similarly, 19th century Scandinavian political authorities invoked theories of cultural hierarchy to impose legal regimes and take control of traditional Saami land, water and natural resources.[27] In the Soviet Union, too, social engineering goals required uniform codes across the republics but this faced considerable opposition in parts of Soviet Central Asia.[28] Similarly, "[i]ndigenous law was not wiped out by Peruvian law. On the contrary, it showed a remarkable vitality, adaptability, and legitimacy. The injustice of the Peruvian legal system only served to reinforce indigenous law".[29]

Far from disappearing under the rule of urban-based authoritarian nationalist regimes, non-state legal orders flourished in the rural areas of post-colonial Africa.[30] In contexts ranging from Somalia to indigenous populations in settler states, the continued recourse to non-state orders has been a means of resisting the state.[31] Also, state laws may not have been seen as adequately addressing issues such as the practice of witchcraft or perceptions of affront to family honour. Finland's Gypsy community routinely obstructs state efforts to intervene in and mediate blood feuds, and state punishments carry no stigma.[32] Elsewhere, state procedures are simply inadequate: thirty percent of cases in Afghanistan's Kunduz region lacked written documentation or had other technical problems that made it impossible to follow normal legal procedures.[33]

In some situations the state tactically encourages the flourishing of plural legal orders. Sometimes the driver for such reforms is economic. Neoliberal policies designed to save state resources have led to the privatisation of justice and

---

27   Ahrén, 2004, p. 81.

28   Tokhtakhodjaeva, 1995, p. 51.

29   Drzewieniecki, 1995, p. 29.

30   Kimathi, 2005, p. 6.

31   Le Sage, 2005, p. 9; Charters, 2003, p. 23.

32   Grönfors, 1986, p. 108.

33   Barfield, 2006, p. 3.

quasi-formal mechanisms such as *aksakal* courts in Kyrgyzstan and ADR systems in Europe, South Asia and Latin America.[34]

The state's apparent withdrawal can be deceptive and may conceal other political motives. During the civil conflict in Guatemala in the 1980s, the country's military governments undermined an already weak judiciary, strengthening extra-judicial mechanisms that involved extreme levels of violence.[35] On the other hand, according to Palestinian feminists, the Israeli state preserves different family laws for the Arab minority as a means to perpetuate that community's social and economic backwardness.[36]

Contemporary factors that contribute to the emergence of plural legal orders

Plural legal orders are often a result of conflict or a legacy of post-conflict processes of reconstruction, as in the Democratic Republic of Congo, Mozambique, Namibia, Nepal, Sierra Leone, Somalia and Sri Lanka.[37] In some cases, multiple non-state legal orders co-exist with the remnants of a state order. In Afghanistan, the 2001 Bonn Agreement referred to the need to rebuild the post-war Afghan domestic justice system in accordance with "Afghan legal traditions" – a phrase that the UN Assistance Mission in Afghanistan vaguely elaborated to mean "the customs, values and sense of justice acceptable to and revered by the people of Afghanistan. Justice, in the end, is what the community as a whole accepts as fair and satisfactory in the case of dispute or conflict, not what the rulers perceive it to be".[38] However, this formulation led to significant confusion because in many areas it was not clear what the 'law' was or which law was actually applicable, leading to an almost inevitable flourishing of legal plurality.

Plural legal orders are also sometimes introduced in an attempt to prevent conflict by developing a new social contract, between the state and its citizens or between different groups of citizens. This was done, for example, in Guatemala, the Solomon Islands, the Philippines, Indonesia and South Africa. Both in Latin America and to a lesser extent in settler states such as Australia, Canada, New Zealand and the United States, indigenous legal orders were recognised as part of a nation-building exercise which in turn reflected the state's acknowledgement that it is necessary both to respect diversity and

---

34   Pirie, 2005; Sohail Akbar Warraich, presentation at ICHRP workshop; Macaulay, 2005.

35   Sieder, 2008, p. 7 (page number as in manuscript on file).

36   Rouhana, 2006.

37   See Kyed and Buur, 2007, regarding Africa.

38   UNAMA in Wardak, 2004, p. 333.

correct injustices associated with historical subjugation. In Bolivia and Ecuador, the recent recognition of indigenous legal orders was the result of the greater presence and voice of organised indigenous interests within government.

The transnationalisation of law (the imposition or import of legal concepts) certainly contributes to the emergence of plural legal orders. Transnationalisation is not uniquely a North-South process, and nor does it necessarily advance equality (for example, Taqi Usmani, a Pakistani judge known for his conservative views, played an influential role in drafting a regressive Muslim family law proposal in South Africa). Nor is transnationalisation of law a new phenomenon – it was a pillar of imperialist systems. Nevertheless, its spread has accelerated markedly since the mid-1980s, and human rights are very much involved.[39] In its application of human rights law, a state is influenced not only by other states and multilateral bodies but also by non-state actors such as transnational corporations and international human rights NGOs.[40] In a similar way, European Union law has deeply transformed the national law of member states. Indeed, in today's porous states it can be difficult to separate what is local and what is not.[41] Many attempts to secure rights illustrate what Keck and Sikkink call a 'boomerang effect'; when local actors participate in transnational advocacy networks that bring pressure to bear on states 'from below' and 'from without'.[42]

Multicultural policies in Australia, Britain and Canada have also used 'community' as a means of governing ethnic and religious migrant-origin minorities. Arguably, the emergence of demands to recognise 'community' laws, and a government's willingness to consider such demands, are unsurprising outcomes of such policies. Identity politics are an important related contemporary factor: they have become prominent particularly since the end of the Cold War and often take the form of religious and ethnic fundamentalisms or cultural chauvinism. Based on their vigorous assertion of 'difference', proponents demand political and legal recognition from the state – often in the name of human rights. In Canada and Britain, for example, Muslim fundamentalist groups have called on the state to recognise the authority of forums that apply highly conservative interpretations of Shari'ah.

Identity politics can also strengthen legal orders that operate completely outside the state system. In Fiji, following the 1987 coup by ethnic Fijians against an Indo-Fijian government, resurgent Fijian cultural nationalism has made it more difficult to criticise the misuse of traditional apology and reconciliation practices (*bulubulu*) in the case of rape.[43]

---

39   Sieder, 2008.

40   Michaels, 2005, p. 1211; Günther, undated.

41   See Benda-Beckmann *et al.*, 2009.

42   Keck and Sikkink in Sieder, 2008, p. 3 (page number as in manuscript on file).

43   Merry, 2006, p. 125.

International financial institutions (IFIs), such as the World Bank, and bilateral and multilateral agencies and intergovernmental agencies such as the United Nations Development Programme (UNDP), have increasingly focused their access to justice programmes on strengthening the informal justice sector. 'Legal empowerment' is considered to be integral to development, especially within a 'good governance' framework and in the context of decentralisation programmes. At the heart of this approach is an understanding that development and reform of legal services must include, among other things, a focus on "counseling, mediation, negotiation, and other forms of nonjudicial representation" including alternative dispute resolution and non-state legal orders.[44]

Some analysts consider that the emergence of certain forms of identity politics is linked to the rise of free-market neo-liberalism.[45] Economic policies can also be driver for plural legal orders, especially as economic actors have a significant influence on justice systems particularly because the establishment of the rule of law is seen as a necessary step towards successful privatisation and market-oriented economic reforms.[46] The UN-sponsored Commission on Legal Empowerment, for instance, recommends the liberalisation of the justice sector, and recognition of non-state legal services and informal justice systems.[47]

Ultimately, numerous interrelated factors usually contribute to the preservation, introduction or strengthening of plural legal orders in a given context. This complicates analysis. Serbs that remained in UN-administered Kosovo, for example, continued to operate courts that ran parallel to UNMIK (the UN administration in Kosovo) and answered directly to Belgrade. Among many reasons for this were lack of access to UNMIK services due to conflict-related limitations on freedom of movement; the geographical distance to the UNMIK structures; a lack of trust and perceptions of discrimination; the state's failure and unwillingness to integrate Kosovan Serb institutions; and the absence of a comprehensive strategy for addressing issues of difference and diversity.[48] The case of Israel illustrates the degree to which plural legal orders may be influenced by numerous factors that can also shift over time. The architect of the Israeli state, David Ben-Gurion, supported the establishment of Druze religious courts to "foster among the Druze an awareness that they are a separate community *vis-à-vis* the Muslim community".[49] Further, by officially prohibiting

---

44   Golub, 2003a. See also USAID, 2007.

45   Stopler, 2007, p. 4.

46   See for example www.adb.org/Documents/Periodicals/ADB_Review/2006/vol38-1/privatization-reform.asp.

47   Commission on Legal Empowerment, 2008. This is discussed in greater detail in Chapter VIII.

48   OSCE, 2007.

49   Firro in Sezgin, 2008, p. 8.

mixed marriages between members of different religious communities, the Israeli state utilised the old *millet* system both to guarantee the homogeneity of its Jewish population, and prevent the Druze, Christian and Muslim Arab communities from forming an overarching Arab or Palestinian identity.[50] However, as ultra-Orthodox Jews acquired greater political influence (to a point where secular political parties are unlikely to come to power without the support of religious parties), preserving Israel's plural legal order has become a matter which even apparently dominant secular parties can scarcely question.[51] Thus, a plural legal order designed to control personal status and shape identity has evolved into a nation and state building project that is difficult to reverse.

---

50   Sezgin, 2008.

51   Ibid.; Stopler, 2007.

SUMMARY

Plural legal orders arise when a specific dispute or subject matter is governed by multiple norms, laws or forums that co-exist within a particular jurisdiction or country. For example, such as when different family laws govern different ethno-cultural groups or when customary dispute resolution mechanisms operate without state sanction or a non-state legal order, such as chief's courts, is officially recognised by the state, or a quasi-state legal order is established such as an alternative dispute resolution mechanism.

There is considerable variation within each of the broad types of plural legal orders in terms of personal and subject matter jurisdiction, procedure and structure, and whether the plural system is subject to any overarching national standards.

Plural legal orders are found in every part of the world and in all types of political systems. They usually arise as a result of one or more of the following interrelated factors: colonialism; the state's need for legitimacy; the weakness or irrelevance of the state legal order; conflict and post-conflict reconstruction resolution; respect for diversity, multiculturalism and identity politics; privatisation or reduction of public expenditure in the justice sector; and, specific forms of intervention by donor and international development agencies.

The idea of legal pluralism helps clarify that state law is not the only relevant and effective legal order in people's lives. Nevertheless the state remains central to a human rights analysis of plural legal orders because it is the primary duty-bearer in relation to human rights guarantees.

II.   GOING BEYOND COMMON PRESUMPTIONS ABOUT LAW, CULTURE AND HUMAN RIGHTS

The way we think about human rights changes the way we 'do' human rights:[52] this point can be applied to many of the ideas that are central to this report. For example, if human rights in the context of plural legal orders are presumably trapped in binaries (such as modern and traditional, or universalism and cultural relativism), then discussion will fail to reflect the complexity of human rights practice or the ways in which plural legal orders are experienced on the ground, and rights protection may be weakened as a result. As discussions about concepts are not just a matter of academic interest but have outcomes in terms of human rights practice, this and the next two chapters examine the conceptual landscape of plural legal orders in some detail.

Many presumptions about concepts associated with plural legal orders need to be interrogated. This chapter starts by discussing the centrality and power of law. Then, since the report prioritises plural legal orders in the context of cultural diversity, it discusses the relationship between law and culture and whether presumed cultural differences, such as those based on religion and ethnicity, necessarily generate plural legal orders. Finally, it considers some constructive ways of thinking about human rights in the context of cultural differences.

THE LIMITS AND POWER OF LAW

Many, if not all the issues that manifest themselves as legal problems either cannot be conclusively solved through legal routes or require broader political and development measures. For example, some argue that in South Africa the Witchcraft Suppression Act of 1957 (as amended in 1970 and 1999) has led to vigilantism against those accused of witchcraft and is a failure of law.[53] However, the proposed legal solution of permitting customary procedures to deal with witchcraft practice would mean allowing people (mostly women) to be identified as witches and then divorced, fined or banished for a 'crime' that is inherently impossible to prove. Both ways rights violations will continue and therefore solutions must lie in areas other than law. Similarly, recognising indigenous peoples' right to their own legal arrangements may address some access to justice problems but cannot alone remedy ingrained structural racism. Some non-legal solutions to rights violations can be truly important: a legal aid centre in Colombia responded to high levels of domestic violence, partly linked with high male unemployment, by devising an informal affirmative action programme that provided men jobs in local businesses.[54]

---

52   Nyamu-Musembi, 2002, p. 8.

53   Ludsin, 2003, p. 109.

54   Faundez, 2003, p. 46.

It is recognised that effective reforms relating to non-state legal orders must be accompanied by governance reforms, and that socio-political factors such as community mobilisation, links between justice-seekers and civil society organisations, and rigorous codes of ethics, are important to the defence of rights in the context of decentralisation.[55] The failure of state and non-state legal orders to provide justice is often due to wider national and international development problems, including trade inequalities that consume development resources or impede their flow. Where the law works as an instrument of exclusion rather than inclusion because it disregards or discounts the knowledge and experience of the marginalised, some ask whether it is even appropriate to press for more of the same (e.g., improved access to justice programmes).[56]

The inadequacies of a purely legal approach have led some to suggest that human rights Treaty Bodies should require states to enable communities to address discriminatory customs themselves, perhaps by supporting and facilitating consultation and dialogue.[57] Indeed, Aboriginal title claims in Australia are now more frequently settled by political negotiation than by judicial pronouncement. This shift has occurred because there is growing recognition of the *on-going* law-making capacities of indigenous legal systems.[58]

Nevertheless, the significance and power of law cannot be dismissed. "The power of law as well as its attraction and danger lie in its ability to create and impose social reality, meanings and values, and eventually to make them appear natural and self-evident and thus uncontested. In other words, the dual aspect of law enables the rulers to govern not only by rule *of* law (e.g., by means of the administration and the judiciary) but equally by rule *by* law by creating social reality and meanings which are considered self-evident."[59] This power is what lies behind demands for the recognition of diverse kinds of norms as *law*.

THE RELATIONSHIP BETWEEN CULTURAL DIFFERENCES AND LAW

Cultural differences are most apparent in different understandings: of right and wrong, good and evil, and appropriate and inappropriate personal and public

---

55   See Kimathi, 2005; World Bank in Byrne *et al.*, 2007, p. 19.

56   This question is discussed in detail in Danardono, 2006, pp. 2-3, based upon but also critiquing Smart, 1989.

57   See Charters, 2003, p. 22. It is not clear *who* the state would support and fund to participate in such consultations.

58   Anker in Gover, 2008b. See also McNeil in Gover, 2008b, p. 12. A World Bank study on multiple legal systems, *Cambodia: Legal pluralism and equity: some reflections on land reform in Cambodia: 2008* also notes how the poor tend to resolve land conflicts through political rather than legal means: http://siteresources.worldbank.org/INTJUSFORPOOR/Resources/J4PBriefingNoteVolume2Issue2.pdf.

59   Pradhan, 2007, p. 3.

conduct; of what constitutes social harmony, and what to do when harmony has been disrupted or people deviate from given norms; and of who has the right to decide such questions. The ways in which such rules are made and enforced – whether by state, non-state or international institutions – are intimately connected to patterns of power that shape social and political institutions and interpersonal relations in general. In addition to the extent that cultural norms shape rights, privileges and responsibilities, and frame many dimensions of personal and social life, they can have significant human rights consequences.

It may appear obvious that cultural differences are likely to produce a plurality of legal orders, as competing ideas of right and wrong – or rights and duties – require different adjudication and enforcement mechanisms.[60] However, this relationship between culture and law is not entirely straightforward or automatic. Two legal systems based on the same religion or custom may differ, across countries and over time, because neither are monolithic or internally consistent. For example: "To say that there is only one normative realm within Roman Catholicism and merely a single set of norms would be a denial of the lived experience of many married Catholic couples. More than that, it would be to deny the role the believer plays in constituting his or her own faith. Reconciling the values, principles and canons of one's religion with other sources of knowledge and experience is the challenge that confronts every Catholic."[61] The same is true of Islam. The Maldives has operated a moratorium on the death penalty since 1953, whereas other Muslim-majority states actively apply the death sentence, but to a varying range of crimes. As for custom, research on customary practices affecting women's rights in Pakistan found significant variations *within* each of the main ethnicities, not only between them.[62]

Even where 'religious' or 'customary' authorities are involved in dispute resolution, this does not necessarily mean religion or custom is the primary framework invoked. Pirie records that Buddhist monks settled feuds between Buddhist eastern Tibetan nomads – but did so without reference to Buddhist morality.[63] Further, shared norms may not necessarily always be invoked. During a dispute hearing observed by Faundez in a Peruvian Rural Centre for the Administration of Justice, though both parties and panel members belonged to the same Quechua-speaking community, decisions were based "on equitable principles that could have been equally effective had they been invoked before a state court".[64]

---

60   For example, Nina and Schwikkard, 1996, who believe there is a relatively linear relationship between cultural and legal plurality: the latter emerging when a community has alternative notions of justice and establishes its own 'laws'.

61   Macdonald and McMorrow, 2007, p. 40.

62   Balchin, 1996.

63   Pirie, 2005, p. 17.

64   Faundez, 2003, p. 33.

Cultural difference is also not just a question of state versus non-state orders. Formal state law is itself rarely monolithic or internally consistent, even within specific jurisdictions. For example, in India polygyny is legal for Muslims under state-recognised Muslim laws, but is not so for Indians governed by other laws recognised by the state. Attempts to draw a strict distinction between 'religious' and 'secular' laws can also be unhelpful. For instance, Britain's current Marriage Act, considered to be a secular law, exempts Jews and Quakers and, despite some evolution, remains profoundly influenced by Christian concepts of marriage.

Ultimately, understanding the link between cultural difference and law means understanding the important distinctions between social location, identity and values, which are all too often conflated.[65] To illustrate, for a non-religious or a believing feminist Israeli, all of Israel's 14 separate family law regimes are arguably normatively similar because they all claim divine inspiration and sanction, and appear as different manifestations of the same patriarchal, ideologically conservative set of norms.

At the same time cultural differences are real to people and cannot be reduced to political positions. At some intangible level, people of the same ethnicity or religion do recognise shared cultural norms.

Given the difficulties in identifying where one set of norms begins and another ends, and how this relates to law, the Australian Law Reform Commission (ALRC), in a pioneering study on indigenous customary law, opted to analyse the relationship between law and culture on a spectrum rather than in terms of distinct blocks. At one end, the ALRC noted that an Aboriginal person may commit an offence against the general criminal law, which may be categorised as 'non-customary', and at the other end he may commit an 'offence' that is entirely 'customary'. In between, there may be "offences against the general criminal law which may be categorised as 'non-customary' but which may be very disruptive of community life, with the result that members of his community would like some say in the way in which the offender is dealt with. Some offences may breach both the general criminal law and Aboriginal customary laws".[66]

If culture and cultural differences are considered uncritically, in minority rights discourses for example, the effect is often to mask intergroup injustices. In Israel, both Orthodox Jews and Arab Muslims are minorities, but the realities of redistribution and political participation mean that the rights of the latter are

---

65   For example, that a person is born Indian and biologically female does not mean they necessarily identify as such, and if a person identifies as a transsexual British-Indian it does not necessarily mean they will vote Labour or Conservative. The distinctions are discussed by Yuval-Davis, 2006.

66   Australian Law Reform Commission, 1986, para. 679.

far more vulnerable. Stopler therefore argues that forms of multiculturalism that privilege cultural or ethnic difference *a priori* can obscure significant power disparities, and economic and political discrimination.[67]

Though the mobilisation of law and culture in support of power is nothing new, the rise of identity politics has brought new threats. In a 2006 report to the UN General Assembly, the Secretary-General expressed concern that the "[t]he politicisation of culture in the form of religious 'fundamentalisms' in diverse… religious contexts has become a serious challenge to efforts to secure women's human rights".[68] This said, it is also important to bear in mind Sahgal's warning that these tendencies (and the nature of their political ambitions) may well have little relation to "traditional religious formations (which may be patriarchal and oppressive but are not necessarily fundamentalist)".[69] One should not mistake one for the other, even if the two may often converge.[70] Bhatt traces how in Britain the new emphasis on religious identity has led to the formation of selective community histories that efface past secular anti-racist struggles that were opposed to prioritising ethnicity, culture and religion as dominant markers of communal identity.[71]

Both internationally and nationally, religious fundamentalist groups have successfully campaigned to promote conservative norms in the legal sphere.[72] At times, this is articulated through "strategic secularism"; in other words, "religious activism tends to strategically insert secular justifications in its defence of a religious worldview".[73] Examples include the co-option of the language of human rights, especially minority rights. Sunder rightly asks: "When religious fundamentalists can deploy global capital, the Internet, and democracy to work in their interest, why assume they cannot appropriate human rights law in their favour, as well?"[74]

---

67   Stopler, 2007, p. 311.

68   Bennoune, 2007, p. 373 quoting UN doc A/61/122/Add.1.

69   Gita Sahgal, 2006, p. 2.

70   The Association for Women's Rights in Development (AWID) project on Resisting and Challenging Religious Fundamentalisms has produced a publication which, among other issues, examines the distinctions between fundamentalists and conservatives: www.awid.org/eng/About-AWID/AWID-News/Shared-Insights-Women-s-rights-activists-define-religious-fundamentalisms.

71   Bhatt, 2006, p. 106.

72   AWID, 2008a, 2008b; Vaggione, 2005, p. 244.

73   Vaggione, 2005, p. 243.

74   Sunder, 2005, p. 904.

Speaking about human rights and culture

> "We agree on these rights, providing we are not asked why.
> With the 'why' the dispute begins."[75]

As the language of human rights gains global currency, questions increasingly arise as to their relationship with other normative systems and other languages of justice. Do these sit *within* human rights, more or less comfortably *alongside*? Or do they inevitably *clash* with human rights? Can lessons be learned from the ways human rights advocates translate universal standards into localised practices? Certainly, human rights are not the only language of justice available to the peoples of the world and they need therefore to be positioned within, rather than outside, the universe of normative systems.[76] This enables us to see human rights as a system that is constantly contested and shifting.

While many may argue that there is no universal understanding of what 'human rights' mean in practice, none can dispute the fact that they are a powerful idea that mobilises individuals and groups across the world to press specific claims, especially against the state.[77] Abdullahi An-Na'im concludes that human rights must remain a shared frame of reference for otherwise one is left with "cultural hegemony at home and imperialism abroad".[78]

In analysing universality, it is also strategically important not to conflate the empirical with the normative. For example, slavery was practised in most parts of the world but this did not make it permanently or globally acceptable. Noting that "if those who formulated and/or fought for human rights would have waited for their universal existence, they would probably still be waiting", Benda-Beckmann calls on human rights analysts and advocates to acknowledge openly that human rights are a political project, and affirm their moral and political preferences.[79] A review of European and American history reveals that "an important blind spot in human rights discussions" is that the real point of

---

75   French philosopher Jacques Maritain in response to a question as to how people with such different ideological persuasions agreed on a draft list of rights for the Universal Declaration of Human Rights in Leary, 1992, p. 123.

76   HRC General Comment No. 22, paragraph 8, appears to hint at just such a relationship between human rights and normative plurality: "The Committee observes that the concept of morals derives from many social, philosophical and religious traditions; consequently, limitations on the freedom to manifest a religion or belief for the purpose of protecting morals must be based on principles not deriving exclusively from a single tradition."

77   Sieder, 2008, p. 2 (page number as in manuscript on file).

78   An-Na'im, 1999, p. 60.

79   Benda-Beckmann, 2009, p. 17 (pagination as in unpublished version).

difference is not so much "between 'Western human rights' and 'Third World cultures' but between different laws and cultures within states".[80]

It is important to recognise that people are bearers of both culture *and* rights, and that recognition of rights does not imply rejection of culture. Universalism and cultural relativism "are not alternatives between which one must choose, once and for all; one should see the tensions between the positions as part of a continuous process of negotiating ever-changing and interrelated global and local norms".[81] To a large extent, the tension is between the formulation of universal general principles and their application in particular circumstances and contexts.

On the one hand, the international human rights framework recognises a universal right to culture, for example in the Universal Declaration on Human Rights (UDHR), Article 27 of the International Covenant on Civil and Political Rights (ICCPR), and the UN Declarations on Minorities and more recently Indigenous Peoples. On the other, 'culturalist' assertions that invoke tradition, language, religion, ethnicity, locality, tribe or race, and affirm the centrality of group difference to justice claims, have been a defining feature of a 'post-socialist condition'.[82] Many of these assertions use a vocabulary of human rights – for example to assert claims to language, education, employment, land rights, self-determination, etc. Yet these same assertions may serve the political ends of religious fundamentalisms and those who advance them may deny equal rights to women or homosexuals, wish to suppress religious dissent, or adopt other positions that are antithetical to the letter and spirit of human rights.

Merry has identified a misreading of culture in these processes, noting that the UN Treaty Bodies' "tendency to see culture as a problem is enhanced by their commitment to a model of legal rationality, an idea that is incompatible with celebrating local cultural complexity".[83] She describes in detail the unhelpful approach of the CEDAW (Convention on the Elimination of Discrimination against Women) Committee regarding the Fijian practice of *bulubulu*. Rather than address the particular problem in Fiji (that *bulubulu* was being used to persuade prosecutors to drop rape charges and magistrates to mitigate sentences), the Committee demanded to know whether the custom had been abolished altogether. This left no space for discussion of the practice of *bulubulu* and its possible merits, and created a false rights-culture dichotomy.[84]

---

80 Ibid., pp. 9-12 (pagination as in unpublished version).

81 Cowan, Dembour and Wilson, 2001, p. 6, usefully propose three ways of looking at the rights and culture relationship: rights *versus* culture; rights *to* culture; and rights *as* culture.

82 Fraser in Cowan, Dembour and Wilson, 2001.

83 Merry, 2003, p. 30.

84 Merry, 2006, p. 118.

Claire Charters suggests that, when human rights mechanisms address cases that present an apparent rights-culture or universalism-relativism dilemma, they should instead require states to facilitate dialogue *within* the relevant ethno-cultural group, enabling the group's members to address the issue themselves.[85] Similarly, intra as well as inter and crosscultural dialogue are widely advocated as the way forward. Multiculturalism for instance is seen as recognising that "universal values are emphasized in a variety of different ways in different cultures and that they are all worthy of respect".[86] However, a major challenge for all such processes is to take into account social inequalities within and between dialoguing groups if they are to avoid replicating them; the participation of marginalised groups within a community must be facilitated proactively and in ways that go beyond tokenism. Care must also be taken to ensure that 'reform from within' is not seen as a panacea that leads to reduced support for other means of bringing about change.[87]

A constructive understanding of the relationship between human rights and culture may also be advanced by recognising the various ways in which globalised human rights have been appropriated and used for social struggles locally. Human rights activists work "at various levels to negotiate between local, regional, national and global systems of meaning", translating "the discourses and practices from the arena of international law and legal institutions to specific situations of suffering and violation".[88] Continuity and change in the relationships between human rights, other normative orders and law has also to be viewed in the context of globalisation, a "process [which] consists of a great number of chains of interaction in which legal forms are reproduced, changed and hybridised".[89] Globalised human rights discourses are also carried by the media and NGOs, bypassing state administrations. Today it has become difficult to pinpoint when something is transnational in origin and when local. Frequently, what are referred to as 'global' are in fact "often circulating locals",[90] with "local cultures contesting the universal, expressing it, participating in its development".[91]

---

85   Charters, 2003, p. 22.

86   An-Na'im and Deng, 1992; Raz in Twinning, 2007 p. 19. See also Yrigoyen Fajardo, 2004 in the context of effective development of Special Indigenous Jurisdiction in some Andean countries. See also Mouffe, 2007 for a discussion of Arendt's idea of moving from antagonisms (strict dichotomies) to agonisms, the negotiation and recognition of differences and tensions as a result of plurality.

87   For a discussion of the impact of development policies that privilege reform of religion 'from within' see Balchin, 2003, pp. 40-47; and Balchin, 2007.

88   Merry, 2006a, p. 40.

89   Benda-Beckman and Benda-Beckman, 2006, pp. 63-64.

90   Merry, 2006, p. 14.

91   Kennedy, 2006.

For example, Mednicoff describes in some detail how human rights advocates in Tunisia debated the adaptation of human rights language into what he calls the local Arab-Islamic context. When the Tunisian League of Human Rights (LTDH) was framing its Charter in 1985, a question arose regarding the right to change one's religion. To avoid implying that the LTDH supported apostasy it used the phrase 'the right to *choose* religion'. The Tunisian government emphasised the human rights versus Islam debate in order, apparently, to weaken the LTDH, then the most powerful non-governmental political force in the country; but the LTDH survived by managing to reconcile Arab-Muslim identity and international human rights discourse.[92]

These approaches recognise culture as dynamic and internally contested: "Culture in this sense does not serve as a barrier to human rights mobilisation but as a context that defines relationships and meanings and constructs the possibilities of action".[93] It is equally vital to recognise "the extent to which the human rights project is itself a cultural one", and to avoid implying that human rights represent "modernity and law, a culture-free zone" since "modernity is also a cultural system".[94] Ultimately, although their advocates can claim that human rights in their contemporary form derive ethical strength from their universal appeal, as a "language of insurrection" this universalism is constantly shot through and exceeded by contextuality and social rootedness. The challenge then is how to operationalise this rooted universality through the application of international human rights standards.

---

92   Mednicoff, 2005, p. 84.

93   Merry, 2006, pp. 8-9 and 222.

94   Merry, 2003.

SUMMARY

Many issues that manifest themselves as legal problems cannot be conclusively solved through legal routes and require broader political and development measures. Nevertheless, the significance and power of law as an instrument of exclusion as well as inclusion cannot be dismissed because the "attraction and danger of law lies in its ability to create and impose social reality, meanings and values".

Cultural differences are presumed to produce a plurality of legal orders, because competing ideas of right and wrong – or rights and duties – require different adjudication and enforcement mechanisms.

However, the relationship between culture and law is not straightforward. Two laws based on the same religion or customary order may differ, across countries and over time, because neither is internally monolithic. Culture is not static but is part of a dynamic process of social and political contestation. At the same time, cultural differences are real to people and cannot be reduced to diversity in political positions.

Though the mobilisation of law and culture in support of power is nothing new, the rise of identity politics has brought new threats especially in the form of religious fundamentalism.

Human rights are not the only language of justice available to the peoples of the world and they need therefore to be positioned within rather than outside the universe of normative systems. People are bearers of both culture *and* rights, and recognition of rights does not imply rejection of culture. Universalism and cultural relativism "are not alternatives between which one must choose, once and for all".

A constructive understanding of the relationship between human rights and culture is advanced by recognising the various ways in which universal general principles of human rights have been appropriated in local struggles for justice through application in particular circumstances and contexts.

III. HUMAN RIGHTS STANDARDS AND PLURAL LEGAL ORDERS

This chapter considers the treatment of legal plurality in certain key human rights texts and human rights bodies. It highlights the complexities and challenges that legal plurality, and the demand for it, poses to human rights principles, practice, mechanisms and instruments. It discusses some of the most relevant standards set out in human rights instruments and their interpretation by human rights bodies. It then underscores some major concerns with respect to legal plurality: focussing on the fragmented and uncoordinated development of standards; and the problem of 'balancing' rights, especially sex equality and religious freedom. In addition, it also points to the problem of addressing human rights concerns that arise due to the structure of plural legal orders; the human rights system's difficulties in speaking about culture; and, the lack of substantive clarity and direction in standard-setting.

LEGAL PLURALITY IN HUMAN RIGHTS TEXTS AND MECHANISMS

The human rights framework does not recognise 'plural legal orders' as a distinct area of policy, yet the subject touches many areas of human rights law, including minority and indigenous peoples' rights, women's rights, right to freedom from discrimination, the administration of justice, and fair trial and right to equal treatment before the law, among many others. Human rights benchmarks that are relevant to plural legal orders can therefore be found across the spectrum of standards: in the major Covenants and Conventions, as well as in Declarations, General Comments from the Treaty Bodies, Observations from the Treaty Bodies regarding country reports, and the work of UN Special Procedures. Further contributions come from regional instruments (such as the African Charter and Declarations) as well as via case law before regional courts (like the European Court of Human Rights and the Inter-American Court), and national case law.

Support for plural legal orders is most visible in the area of indigenous peoples' rights. The 2007 UN Declaration on the Rights of Indigenous Peoples (a non-binding standard), appears to introduce a qualitatively different approach to legal pluralism within the human rights context, notably in Articles 4, 5 and 34. Article 4 provides for exercise of the "right to autonomy or self-government in matters relating to their *internal* and local affairs..." (emphasis added). Article 5 affirms the right of indigenous peoples to maintain and strengthen their distinct political, *legal*, economic, social and cultural institutions (emphasis added). Article 34 states that: "[I]ndigenous peoples have the right to promote, develop and maintain their institutional structures and their distinctive customs, spirituality, traditions, procedures, practices and, in the cases where they exist, juridical systems or customs, in accordance with international human rights standards."

Further, the Declaration's first Article notes that "[i]ndigenous peoples have the right to the full enjoyment, as a *collective* or as individuals, of all human rights and fundamental freedoms" (emphasis added). This appears to go beyond the 1993 UN Declaration on the Rights of *Persons* Belonging to National or Ethnic, Religious and Linguistic Minorities (emphasis added), whose Article 3, for example, refers to the exercise of rights by minorities "individually as well as in community with other members of their group". Arguably, this formulation perceived communities as the sum of rights-bearing individuals, whereas the formulation in the Declaration on Indigenous Peoples treats collectives as qualitatively distinct entities.[95]

Prior to these developments, Articles 8 and 9 of International Labour Organization (ILO) Convention 169 (1989), Concerning Indigenous and Tribal Peoples in Independent Countries, obliged signatory states to recognise indigenous laws "where these are not incompatible with fundamental rights defined by the national legal system and with internationally recognized human rights".[96]

Additionally, the UN Special Rapporteur on the situation of human rights and fundamental freedoms of indigenous peoples has made several observations establishing a clear link between the enjoyment of human rights by indigenous peoples and diversity within the legal system.[97] Noting that "in many countries, a monist conception of national law prevents the adequate recognition of plural legal traditions and leads to the subordination of customary legal systems to one official legal norm",[98] the Rapporteur notes that "legal pluralism appears to be a constructive way of dealing with diverse legal systems based on different cultural values".[99] In his report on Guatemala, for example, the Rapporteur suggests that one reason why indigenous people do not enjoy effective access to justice is "non-acceptance of indigenous law and customs by the official legal institutions of a national state".[100] The Rapporteur's critique of a "monist conception of national law", at the cost of ignoring indigenous people's "own concept of legality",[101] emphasises the existence and importance of multiple legal traditions.

---

95   The new Bolivian and Ecuadorian Constitutions also recognise this distinction. That the Declaration is seen as a non-binding standard does not diminish its importance.

96   The Convention entered into force in 1991 and has so far been ratified by 19 countries.

97   See for example Stavenhagen, 2004b.

98   Ibid., para. 54.

99   Ibid., para. 67.

100   Ibid., p. 2.

101   Ibid., para. 54.

The Declaration on the Rights of Persons Belonging to National or Ethnic, Religious and Linguistic Minorities[102] was not as far reaching and explicit on this matter as the Declaration on the Rights of Indigenous Peoples. Nevertheless, Article 4 provides that: "States shall take measures to create favorable conditions to enable persons belonging to minorities to express their characteristics and to develop their culture, language, religion, traditions and customs, except where specific practices are in violation of national law and contrary to international standards".[103]

A 2006 UN General Assembly Resolution called on states "to ensure that their political and legal systems reflect the multicultural diversity within their societies ...".[104] In a similar vein, the European Court on Human Rights has observed that "there could be said to be an emerging international consensus amongst the Contracting States of the Council of Europe recognizing the special needs of minorities and an obligation to protect their security, identity and lifestyle, not only for the purpose of safeguarding the interests of the minorities themselves but to preserve a cultural diversity of value to the whole community".[105]

The UN Human Rights Committee (HRC) in its General Comment No. 32[106] recognises the existence of legal plurality insofar as it holds that Article 14 of the ICCPR (on the right to fair trial) applies "where a State, in its legal order, recognizes courts based on customary law, or religious courts, to carry out or entrusts them with judicial tasks". It also sets certain important standards and calls on states to ensure that "such courts cannot hand down binding judgments recognized by the State" unless certain requirements are met. These include:

i. proceedings before such courts are limited to minor civil and criminal matters;

ii. proceedings meet the basic requirements of fair trial and other relevant guarantees of the Covenant;

iii. the guarantee under Article 14(1) "is violated if certain persons are barred from bringing suit against any other persons such as by reason of their

---

102 Adopted by General Assembly resolution 47/135 of 18 December 1992.

103 However, the direction of current demands to recognise the rights of religious minorities tends to be framed in ways that overlook the entitlements to protection of both atheists and dissidents within the minority.

104 General Assembly Resolution 60/167 (2006) Human rights and cultural diversity.

105 As articulated in the Court's Grand Chamber decision in *D.H. and Others vs. the Czech Republic* (Application no. 57325/00), decision of 13 November 2007, in Cahn, forthcoming.

106 General Comment on the Right to Equality before Courts and Tribunals and to a Fair Trial, U.N. Doc. CCPR/C/GC/32 (2007).

race, colour, sex, language, religion, political or other opinion, national or social origin, property, birth or other status"; and

iv. the judgements of such courts are "validated by State courts in light of the guarantees set out in the Covenant and can be challenged by the parties concerned in a procedure meeting the requirements of Article 14 of the Covenant".

In addition, the HRC notes that the above principles are "notwithstanding the general obligation of the State to protect the rights under the Covenant of any persons affected by the operation of customary and religious courts". Significantly, the General Comment explicitly specifies that "procedural laws or their application that make distinctions" based on race, colour, sex, language, religion, political or other opinion, national or social origin, property, birth or other status or "disregard the equal right of men and women" to guarantees set forth in Article 14, not only violate the right to equality before the courts and tribunals but may also amount to discrimination. Regional international law follows a similar pattern. For example, the African Commission on Human and People's Rights has held that "traditional courts are not exempt from the provisions of the African Charter relating to fair trial".[107]

Other UN Treaty Bodies have also engaged with legal plurality. In its observations on the United Arab Emirates, for example, the Committee on the Rights of the Child expressed concern that "discrepancies may occur between Shariah court decisions and decisions of other types of courts in the State party".[108] The CEDAW Committee has probably encountered legal plurality most often, however, because of its focus on family law. In a statement on the 25th anniversary of CEDAW's adoption, the Committee observed that "the co-existence of multiple legal systems, with customary and religious laws governing personal status and private life and prevailing over positive law and even constitutional provisions of equality, remains a source of great concern".[109]

In 2009, the UN Human Rights Council created a new Special Procedure Mandate of Independent Expert on Cultural Rights. The mandate of the Independent Expert includes identifying the best practices in the promotion of cultural rights at the local, national, regional, and international levels, and identifying possible obstacles to the promotion and protection of cultural rights and to submit proposals and/or recommendations to the HRC on possible actions in that regard. The broad field of 'cultural rights' is closely related to

---

107   Mungoven, 2001, p. 22.

108   UAE CRC/C/15/Add.183.

109   Statement to commemorate the 25th anniversary of the adoption of the Convention on the Elimination of all forms of Discrimination against Women, 13 October 2004: www.un.org/womenwatch/daw/cedaw/cedaw25anniversary/cedaw25-CEDAW.pdf.

indigenous, ethnic and religious minority rights. It is inevitable that this important new mandate will involve discussion of plural legal orders.[110]

While the creation of the mandate is potentially meaningful in terms of advancing a human rights discussion on plural legal orders, in a parallel and more worrying development, the HRC adopted a resolution on defamation of religion that "underscores the need to combat defamation of religions by strategizing and harmonizing actions at local, national, regional and international levels through education and awareness-raising".[111] The resolution raises serious concerns because it could be used to "effectively place the tenets of religion in a hierarchy above the rights of the individual" and "be used to silence progressive voices who criticize laws and customs said to be based on religious texts and precepts".[112]

KEY ISSUES ARISING FROM INTERNATIONAL STANDARDS ON PLURAL LEGAL ORDERS

It is in the nature of international human rights standards to be generalised and open to interpretation. This reflects two aspects: first, the negotiating compromise in the development of the standard; and second, the need for flexibility of application in specific contexts. Nevertheless, with respect to plural legal orders, human rights standards leave important gaps in clarity and direction. The fragmented and uncoordinated development of standards creates additional problems, particularly in regard to indigenous and minority rights, gender equality and the right to culture. This is also reflected in the problem of 'balancing' these rights.

First, there is a need for greater substantive clarity and direction in the standards. It remains unclear, for example, how indigenous and national legal systems can work together effectively in accordance with international human rights standards. This raises two questions: first, whether and how indigenous and national legal orders can be harmonised; and second, whether and how indigenous legal orders and international standards can be harmonised. Is Article 34 of the Declaration on the Rights of Indigenous Peoples (see above) to be read as indicating that, in all cases of conflict between them, it is desirable

---

110   There is also an on-going campaign by feminist organisations for the creation of a Special Rapporteur on laws that discriminate against women, which would equally have a strong focus on the human rights impacts of plural legal orders. www.equalitynow.org/english/wan/beijing10/rapporteur_en.html.

111   The non-binding text, proposed by Pakistan on behalf of Islamic states, with a vote of 23 states in favour and 11 against, with 13 abstentions: Resolution 10/22 on 10/22. Combating defamation of religions www2.ohchr.org/english/bodies/hrcouncil/docs/10session/edited_versionL.11Revised.pdf.

112   www.wluml.org/english/newsfulltxt.shtml?cmd[157]=x-157-564223.

that international human rights standards should prevail over an indigenous justice system? If so, to what extent would the indigenous system remain *indigenous*? On the other hand, if indigenous systems are to retain control over the development of indigenous legal orders, how would failings and problems within indigenous justice systems be resolved? How would evaluations be made and by whom?

Second, the standards indicate that certain human rights issues are 'minor' legal matters, which threatens the indivisibility of human rights. For example, the HRC affirms in General Comment No. 32 that states must ensure that the jurisdiction of customary law or religious courts be limited to 'minor' criminal and civil matters. Yet, matters that are usually classified as 'minor' (typically areas of family law, such as desertion by the husband, divorce, maintenance, inheritance and succession, and domestic violence) often have serious human rights consequences. Moreover, it is often extremely difficult to distinguish what is defined 'from the outside' as minor or civil, from what is severe or criminal. For local users, these are often interlinked and hard to separate.[113]

Third, HRC General Comment No. 32 also states that judgements by customary and religious courts should only be recognised by the state if they meet the basic requirements of fair trial. But this is an insufficient guarantee because fair trial and due process guarantees have been shaped largely to address criminal cases and are not tailored to deal with civil and family matters, which are the main preserve of customary and religious legal orders.

Fourth, while human rights standards have proved useful in highlighting the discriminatory *content* of customary and religious family laws, they have not provided tools for identifying and preventing violations that arise because of the *structure* of plural legal orders. For example, standards can be applied to evaluate the provisions of customary laws and a general civil law that operates in parallel but they have less to say about rights violations that occur because more powerful actors can 'forum shop' between different state-recognised laws.

Fifth, many Treaty Body recommendations regarding customary or religious laws are imprecise. For instance, the Committee on the Elimination of Racial Discrimination advised Ghana to attempt to achieve "a balance in practice" between statutory law, common law and customary law[114] without any guidance as to how this feat was to be achieved or indeed what constituted such 'balance'. Similarly, the HRC called on Gambia to "ensure domestic laws (including decrees) and customary law, as well as Shariah, are interpreted and

---

113   Comments by Helene Maria Kyed; on file at ICHRP.

114   Concluding observations of the Committee on the Elimination of Racial Discriminations: Ghana 02/06/2003. CERD/C/62/CO/4, para. 13.

applied in ways compatible with ICCPR"[115] without spelling out what this means in practical terms. To some extent, the general nature of such recommendations regarding customary or religious laws results from the difficulties of speaking about culture in a nuanced manner. The Treaty Bodies evaluate developments in numerous countries (not all of which are within their range of expertise) in a short time and are thus unable (even if willing) to account for the complex and fluid nature of culture. Moreover, since some reporting states invoke 'culture' as a general defence, Committee members understandably treat it with some scepticism.

Fragmented and uncoordinated development of standards

There is concern that different areas of international law are fragmenting "into a number of self-contained regimes",[116] each of which is developing in parallel without taking into account the other.[117] Human rights standards relevant to plural legal orders have developed most in respect of indigenous peoples and minority rights. However, these standards appear to be developing largely without reference to standard-setting on other matters, notably culture and gender equality.[118]

A report of the UN Special Rapporteur on violence against women (2007) alerts us to the uncoordinated development of standards. The Rapporteur criticised the shortcomings of the (then Draft) Declaration on Indigenous People on the grounds that "it remains unclear, for instance, what legal recourse, if any, an indigenous woman would have, who is confronted with a discriminatory decision issued by a male-dominated community council that exercises indigenous peoples' 'right to autonomy or self-government in matters relating to their internal and local affairs'". [119]

---

115   Para. 16, CCPR/CO/75/GMB (HRC, 2004).

116   Report of the Special Rapporteur on the right to food, Olivier De Schutter, Addendum, Mission to the World Trade Organisation (25 June 2008), A/HRC/10/5/Add.2, 2 February 2009, para. 34.

117   For a wider discussion on fragmentation see the work on the International Law Commission on "Risks ensuing from the fragmentation of international law".

118   This is contrast to developments in some national jurisdictions, discussed further in the report.

119   A/HRC/4/34, 17 January 2007. The Declaration does not mention or refer to CEDAW. This is especially relevant considering the observation of the Special Rapporteur on indigenous peoples in an earlier report that there are "discriminatory practices against women within their own communities, such as forced marriages, the practice of giving children away to other families, frequent domestic violence, child rape, dispossession of property, limited access to land ownership and other forms of male patriarchal domination. For the most part, women are unable to take these abuses before the courts and when they do they experience a lack of sympathy and fierce pressure from the family and community". A/HRC/4/32, 27 February 2007, para. 71.

The absence of coordination has a long history. For example, the 1981 Declaration on the Elimination of All Forms of Intolerance and of Discrimination Based on Religion or Belief failed to mention CEDAW or that freedom of religion should contribute to ending sexism (as well as racism and colonialism, both of which the Declaration does mention). In the context of increasing efforts by religious fundamentalisms to influence international human rights standards and roll back standards on women's human rights, the need to address such fragmentation acquires added significance.[120]

A brief survey of standards on gender equality indicate that it is a non-derogable right, including in the context of culture, tradition and religion, which is particularly relevant to a discussion of plural legal orders. Under Article 4(2) of the ICCPR, any derogation from, or suspension of, rights must not involve discrimination on grounds of race, colour, sex, language, religion or social origin. Paragraph 9 of the HRC's General Comment No. 24 (which discusses reservations to the ICCPR and its Optional Protocol) clarifies that no reservations to Article 2(1) are acceptable, owing to the preemptory nature of the norm.[121] Articles 2(f) and 5(a) of CEDAW specify that states have a responsibility to end discriminatory cultural practices. Other relevant texts include HRC General Comments Nos. 22 on freedom of thought, conscience and religion and 28 on equality of rights between men and women, and the CEDAW Committee's General Recommendation No. 19 on violence against women. Paragraph 5 of HRC General Comment No. 28 notes that "States parties should ensure that traditional, historical, religious or cultural attitudes are not used to justify violations of women's right to equality before the law and to equal enjoyment of all Covenant rights". Further, in paragraphs 9 and 21 the HRC affirms that it cannot be argued that a woman's right to freedom from discrimination is a lesser right than any other in the ICCPR, and that ICCPR Article 18 cannot be used to justify discrimination against women on grounds of freedom of thought, conscience and religion.[122] It has thus been argued that, where practices undermine women's opportunity to define the content of 'culture', states have an obligation to take protective measures against such practices, given that Article 15 of the International Covenant on Economic, Social and Cultural Rights (ICESCR) provides for a free-standing individual right to culture.[123] While discussing ICCPR Article 27 on minorities, HRC General Comment No. 28 (paragraph 32) calls on states to report on how they are addressing cultural or religious practices *within* minority communities that affect the rights of women.

---

120   AWID, 2008b.

121   Article 2(1) of the ICCPR states: "Each State Party to the present Covenant undertakes to respect and to ensure to all individuals within its territory and subject to its jurisdiction the rights recognized in the present Covenant, without distinction of any kind, such as race, colour, sex, language, religion, political or other opinion, national or social origin, property, birth or other status."

122   Bennoune, 2007.

123   Cook and Kelly, 2006, p. 44.

The CEDAW Committee has reiterated that custom and culture are no defence in cases of violence – a principle that also applies to informal community forums and customary laws recognised by state law, although this appears to be restricted to criminal abuse.[124]

The problem of fragmentation sometimes creates an artificial need to 'balance' rights, and not just with respect to women's human rights, and pose a number of real-life dilemmas for rights advocates and legal professionals. The Colombian Constitutional Court's ruling in Decision T-523 (1997) is illustrative of one such dilemma with respect to standards on indigenous peoples' rights to culture and the prohibition on torture, cruel and inhuman treatment. The Court was considering a case in which an indigenous person accused of murder argued that, among other procedural grounds, the punishment (sixty lashes, banishment from the community and loss of political rights) handed down by indigenous legal authorities went beyond the mandate granted under the country's Special Indigenous Jurisdiction regime. However, the Constitutional Court disagreed and ruled that the sentence handed down was within the competence of indigenous legal authorities as it was in keeping with the traditional indigenous practice of the community in question. While some criticised the sentence as sanctioning torture and cruel and inhuman treatment, others defended it on grounds of both indigenous legal autonomy and a culturally-specific understanding of punishment and sentencing. The Court took the view that the manner in which whipping was to be carried out in this particular case and its objectives meant that it did not run counter to the prohibition on corporal punishment, torture and cruel and inhuman treatment in the Colombian Constitution.[125]

In addition to the issue of application of standards particular to a culture in sentencing, the case, at least indirectly also raises the question of whether someone from an ethno-cultural group that enjoys a degree of legal autonomy has the right to access a universally acknowledged human rights standard that may be contrary to that of her own community? Whipping is clearly not permissible under human rights law especially the Convention against Torture and Other Cruel, Inhuman or Degrading Treatment or Punishment (CAT). Further, the assertion that human rights standards are *per se* not intercultural is somewhat weak; CAT, for example, was a result of extensive deliberations by experts, governments and states from varied political and cultural backgrounds and adopted by the UN General Assembly by consensus, and has been ratified by 146 countries to date. In fact, in another case (T-349, 1996) the Colombian Constitutional court itself acknowledges the right to freedom from torture as one around which there is a real intercultural consensus.

---

124   See for example, Albania 02/12/2004 CCPR/CO/82/ALB, paras 10-12.

125   For more on these cases and Colombian (and related) jurisprudence, see for instance, Yrigoyen Fajardo 2004; Jackson 2008. See also Guzman, 2003 and Assies, forthcoming.

In the context of such punishments, it is also often argued, for example, that whipping may be more acceptable when 'balanced' against several years spent alienated from the community in dehumanising prison conditions that also violates a range of human rights. However, the implied argument that inhuman prisons justify whipping or even that whipping is somehow less inhumane when committed by some communities threatens to undermine the basis of human rights and represents, at best, a moral relativism that questions a shared sense of human dignity.

'Balancing' rights: non-discrimination, sex equality, culture and freedom of religion

In 1991, Sullivan noted the international human rights system's continued reluctance to prioritise women's human rights and its preference instead to 'balancing' gender equality and right to culture/religious freedom.[126] It should be a matter of concern that nearly two decades later, and the passage of several new standards that protect women's rights, the criticism still rings true. National courts have similarly been preoccupied with the issue. In India, for example, constitutional litigation over several decades has failed so far to show how rights should be 'balanced' in the context of Article 44 of the Indian Constitution (which pledges to establish a Uniform Civil Code), the continued existence of multiple family laws framed with reference to religion, and Article 15 (which protects against discrimination on the basis of, among others, religion or gender).[127] Nor is 'balancing' a problem only in relation to gender. It arises in the context of broader intragroup rights, such as the rights of religious dissidents, atheists, Lesbian, Gay, Bisexual, Transgender, Queer, Questioning and Intersex (LGBTQI) persons, and other marginalised groups whose human rights are adversely affected by assertions of intergroup rights.

Why then are difficulties of 'balancing' so frequently raised in human rights discussions of plural legal orders, especially (but not only) in the context of family laws and personal status (such as membership of tribes)?

Sullivan traced the problem of 'balancing' partly to a 'gender blindspot' due to "male domination of policy and law-making processes and inadequate international scrutiny of the breadth and depth of the constraints imposed by religious law on women's equality".[128] While progress was made during the mid-1990s, a decade later feminist analysis is concerned at a growing rollback in

---

126 Sullivan, 1992, p. 811.

127 For example, see *Gurdial Kaur* AIR 1968 Punjab 396; *Dr. Abdur Rahim Undre vs. Smt. Padma Abdur Rahim Udre* AIR 1982 Bom 341; *Naresh Chandra Bose* AIR 1956 Calcutta 222 (224); *Mahfooz Ali Khan* AIR 1980 Allahad 5 (7); *H. Syed Ahmad* AIR 1958 Mysore 128 (131); *Danial Latifi Union of India* 2001 (7) SCC 740.

128 Sullivan, 1992, p. 811.

this sphere[129] which is to a significant extent connected with the re-emergence of identity politics, especially religious fundamentalisms. Many of these promote monolithic visions of culture, and conflict with the vision of rights advanced by advocates of women's human rights, for example, which has gathered strength over the same period.

Additionally, international human rights law "offers minimal guidance on the practicalities" of resolving conflicts that arise between the right to sex equality and freedom of religion.[130] This weakness applies perhaps equally to conflicts between sex equality and the rights of indigenous peoples and minorities. Human rights case law indicates how difficult it is in practice for national policy-makers to take a nuanced approach to culture and human rights.

Paragraph 3 of the Human Rights Committee's General Comment No. 22 (on ICCPR Article 18),[131] as well as regional human rights law (such as the *Rafeh* case or *Leyla Sahin vs. Turkey*[132]) distinguish between the non-derogable right to freedom of thought, belief and religion, and the right to manifest such beliefs. Human rights analysis suggests that the right to manifestation or expression of religion or other beliefs is trumped by the right to freedom from gender discrimination.[133] This perspective is supported by paragraph 8 of the HRC's General Comment No. 22, which notes with regard to limitations on religious practices that: "States parties should proceed from the need to protect the rights guaranteed under the Covenant, including the right to equality and non-discrimination under the Covenant, including the right to equality and non-discrimination on all grounds specified in articles 2, 3, and 26."

Although distinguishing between freedom of religion and belief and the freedom to express these has some value, a number of questions remain. First, given they are experienced as a unified whole in people's daily lives, to what extent is it possible in practice to unravel the two? While it is simpler to separate the religious from the non-religious, it is much harder to apply the

---

129   AWID, 2008a, 2008b.

130   Bennoune, 2007, p. 404.

131   "Article 18 distinguishes the freedom of thought, conscience, religion or belief from the freedom to manifest religion or belief. It does not permit any limitations whatsoever on the freedom of thought and conscience or on the freedom to have or adopt a religion or belief of one's choice. These freedoms are protected unconditionally, as is the right of everyone to hold opinions without interference in article 19.1. In accordance with articles 18.2 and 17, no one can be compelled to reveal his thoughts or adherence to a religion or belief."

132   *Leyla Sahin vs. Turkey* App. No. 44774/98 (Eur. Ct. H.R. Fourth Section June 29, 2004), affirmed by the Grand Chamber 10 November 2005. This case upheld the ban on headscarves in educational institutions in Turkey.

133   Bennoune, 2007, p. 397. See also Cook and Kelly, 2006; Raday, 2003; Sullivan, 1992.

distinction to those who have religious beliefs but do not wish to be coerced regarding specific aspects of their religion or religious practice. Second, when providing examples of 'manifestations of religion' that can potentially be limited (paragraph 4), the HRC's General Comment No. 22 does not mention family or personal status laws based on religion. Yet these are perhaps the most obvious manifestation of religious belief and one of the most intensely contested within religious communities.

In contrast to the quite significant body of human rights case law that can, at some level, be read in terms of rights *versus* culture, comparatively few cases address the problem of those who wish to remain within an ethno-cultural community to which they belong but also wish to reject some of its discriminatory norms.

The *Lovelace* case appears to address this problem.[134] Sandra Lovelace, a Maliseet Indian in Canada, had married a non-Indian and left the reservation. Following her divorce, she sought to return to live on the reservation. However, under section 12(1)(b) of the Indian Act she had lost her rights and status as an Indian by marrying a non-Indian; Indian men who married non-Indian women did not face the same consequence. The Human Rights Committee decided that the most relevant claim was under ICCPR Article 27, relating to the rights of minorities. Lovelace was "ethnically Maliseet" and had been absent on account of marriage "only for a few years". The HRC ruled that the Indian Act was discriminatory because it denied Lovelace her right to culture. The ruling led to the repeal of many gender discriminatory provisions in Canada's Indian Act.[135]

Lovelace, while important, leaves some questions unanswered. The HRC specifically addressed the case as a minority rights issue, leaving unclear its applicability to women who are not members of a minority but experience discrimination on account of their culture. The HRC found that denying Lovelace's status as an Indian was neither reasonable nor necessary to preserve the identity of the tribe, which might appear to have solved the problem of whether a group right to culture is superior to the individual right to non-discrimination. Regrettably, the HRC chose to sidestep this controversial point by noting in paragraph 16 that "it is not necessary, however, to determine in any general manner which restrictions may be justified under the Covenant, in particular as a result of marriage, because the circumstances are special in the present case". The 'special circumstances' were that Ms Lovelace was in fact no longer married to a non-Indian; the decision is therefore of questionable relevance

---

134 *Lovelace vs. Canada* (30 July 1981), Com No 24/1977, CCPR/C/13/D/24/1977, UNHRC.

135 UN Doc. Supp. No. 40 (A/38/40) at 249 in Banda and Chinkin, 2004, p. 7. Unfortunately, the amendments did not go far enough, resulting in continuing gender discrimination in the Act. See: *McIvor vs. Canada* (Registrar of Indian and Northern Affairs), 2009 BCCA 153.

in situations where indigenous or minority women seek to retain rights to their culture while remaining married outside their tribal or ethno-cultural group.

In conclusion, despite providing some clear directions, international human rights standards and jurisprudence leave some significant gaps in standard-setting with respect to plural legal orders. These gaps are filled by the politics of interpretation. This returns us squarely to the point made earlier, that at its heart the human rights project is a political one. A final example illustrates that political preferences rather than religious or cultural imperatives influence acceptance of human rights standards. Algeria, Bahrain, Egypt, Lebanon, Thailand, Tunisia (until recently this also included Turkey) maintain reservations, and India a declaration with respect to Article 16 in CEDAW that mandates equality in the family in respect of marriage, divorce, childcare responsibilities, etc. At the same time, none of these states filed reservations with respect to Article 23(4) of the ICCPR, which makes broadly equivalent provisions for equality in family life.[136] Is a convention that explicitly secures rights specifically for women more sensitive politically than one that secures more 'general' human rights? Another paradox is generated by the reservations that some countries, for example, Bahrain, Egypt, Lebanon and Morocco entered to Article 2 of CEDAW, which binds states to take all appropriate measures to pursue the elimination of sex-based discrimination, but not to articles with equivalent provisions in the Convention on the Rights of the Child (CRC).[137] In effect, these states promise rights to girls which are subsequently denied when they become adults.

---

136   Abiad, 2008.

137   Ibid.

SUMMARY

Though the human rights framework does not recognise 'plural legal orders' as a distinct area of policy, the subject touches many areas of human rights law. Human rights benchmarks relevant to plural legal orders can therefore be found across the spectrum of standards.

The 2007 UN Declaration on the Rights of Indigenous Peoples appears to introduce a qualitatively different approach to plural legal orders within the human rights context by treating collectives as qualitatively distinct entities and by emphasising the right to indigenous legal institutions.

With respect to plural legal orders, human rights standards leave important gaps in clarity and direction. It remains unclear, for example, how indigenous and national legal systems are to work together effectively in accordance with international human rights standards. Instead, political preferences are what determine how national policy fills these gaps.

Human rights standards call for limiting jurisdiction of customary law or religious courts to 'minor' criminal and civil matters. Yet, matters that are usually classified as 'minor' (typically areas of family law) have major human rights consequences. Moreover, it is often extremely difficult to distinguish what is defined 'from the outside' as minor or civil, from what is severe or criminal. For local users, these are often interlinked.

Fair trial and due process guarantees have been shaped largely to address criminal cases and are not tailored to deal with civil and family matters, often the preserve of plural legal orders.

Human rights standards are useful in highlighting the discriminatory content of customary and religious family laws, but do not provide tools for critiquing violations that arise out of the structure of plural legal orders such as jurisdictional confusion.

There is concern that different areas of international law are fragmenting "into a number of self-contained regimes", each of which is developing in isolation. Human rights standards relevant to plural legal orders have developed most in respect of indigenous peoples and minority rights. However, these standards appear to be developing largely without reference to standard-setting on other matters, notably culture and gender equality.

Standards on gender equality indicate that it is a non-derogable right, including in the context of culture, tradition and religion, which is particularly relevant to a discussion of plural legal orders. The problem of fragmentation also creates an artificial dilemma about how to 'balance' rights, and not just with respect to women's human rights.

The international human rights system continues to attempt to 'balance' gender equality and the right to culture/religious freedom. This is in part due to a 'gender blindspot' but is also connected to the active engagement of religious fundamentalisms at the international level, which promotes monolithic visions of culture that conflict with the vision of rights advanced by advocates of women's human rights.

Although distinguishing between freedom of religion and belief, and the freedom to express these is important, this does not resolve all the questions that arise when implementing policy on the ground. A growing body of international, regional and national case law provides contextualised lessons in how to address all these challenges.

IV. UNDERSTANDING NON-STATE LEGAL ORDERS

This chapter examines the complex relationships between state and non-state legal orders as well as between non-state legal orders themselves, and goes on to review some popular generalisations and presumptions about the nature of non-state legal orders.

Labels commonly used to describe the subject matter of this chapter include informal justice mechanisms, community or local justice systems, traditional authorities, folk law, parallel or supplementary justice systems, non-state justice and security systems, etc. No single label accurately captures this diverse universe. For the purposes of this report we use the term 'non-state legal orders' to indicate that these are norms and institutions that tend to claim to draw their moral authority from contemporary to traditional culture or customs, or religious beliefs, ideas and practices, rather than from the political authority of the state. We use 'legal' to acknowledge the fact that these norms are often viewed as having the force of law by those subject to them.

Any discussion of this subject must start by acknowledging that the search for justice, and ways to resolve disputes outside courts and the formal justice system, is a universal phenomenon. One study in Scotland indicates that a very small proportion of disputes involving justiciable issues actually end up in court.[138] Resnick, pointing to the growing shift away from courts in the United States and elsewhere, notes an increasing "privatisation of court-based processes across the docket".[139] Non-court processes can involve alternative dispute resolution mechanisms, including those sanctioned and established by the state, or mechanisms based on customary or religious norms and institutions or other private mechanisms. Many studies suggest that alternative, traditional or non-state systems manage and resolve a very large proportion of disputes and cases, especially in developing countries (see below).

The reasons for this are many. In most countries, significant economic, social, political, cultural, geographical, technological, knowledge and institutional barriers obstruct effective access to the formal justice system. These barriers are nearly insurmountable for those without resources or who face structural disadvantages, forcing them to rely on less formal, community or customary forms of justice and alternative dispute resolution mechanisms. Efforts to promote 'legal empowerment' are designed to address these barriers by assisting the poor to engage with the formal system while improving the accessibility and quality of non-state dispute resolution mechanisms. At the same time, this renunciation of the formal justice system can be a conscious choice, signalling a political or cultural preference, a presumed economic advantage, or an

---

138   Genn and Paterson, 2001.

139   Resnick, 2009.

otherwise positive cost-benefit analysis. The state's response to such behaviour varies, from degrees of tolerance to suppression, or recognition of such non-state mechanisms. Recognition is the subject of a subsequent chapter: here, we simply sketch the main elements of non-state legal orders.

CHARACTERISING NON-STATE LEGAL ORDERS (NSLOS)

When discussing NSLOs a number of caveats should be noted. First, as discussed in depth in the next section, a complex relationship often exists between state and non-state orders. While they may conflict, and often precisely for that reason, they influence and shape each other in many ways. The 'non-state' in NSLO is therefore not an impermeable boundary.

Second, it is important not to equate 'non-state' with 'traditional'. NSLOs are subject to contemporary influences and can be new institutions that are created by internally driven processes or as a result of external facilitation (such as donor-supported justice sector reforms). In Mexico, for instance, non-state authorities include civic-religious authorities and the new autonomous authorities formed since 1994 by pro-Zapatista communities.[140] Often, the 'new' in a claim to tradition actually "expresses claims of specific political groups to a new organisation of political and economic power, new norms of inclusion and exclusion, and new bases of legitimacy of state power"; the push for "institutionalisation of specific interpretations of tradition" may come "from the urban, well-educated elite".[141] In India, for example, those who promoted *lok adalats* (a quasi-judicial, alternative dispute resolution mechanism established by act of Parliament in India) stressed "their indigenous character and 'rich tradition', even though they have little resemblance to earlier institutions".[142] In Mozambique, the state embarked on an elaborate post-conflict process of identifying the true 'traditional' chieftaincies – a misnomer given that war, colonial impositions, and shifting identities and hierarchies, had deeply changed the country and its NSLOs.[143]

For similar reasons the term 'community leader' is often misleading. It assumes a higher degree of social integration of neighbourhoods than is often the case and a higher degree of authority than neighbourhood leaders necessarily

---

140   Castillo, 2002, p. 22.

141   Benda-Beckman *et al.*, 2002-2003, pp. 300-302.

142   Galanter and Krishnan, 2004, p. 798.

143   Buur and Kyed, 2006, p. 9. Numerous studies note how custom constantly shifts and many practices today labelled 'tradition' are in fact relatively recent developments, Weilenmann, 2007; Malzbender *et al.*, 2005; Höhne, 2007; USAID 2005b; Buur and Kyed, 2006. The notion of 'traditional' leadership as uncontested is also challenged by a new range of actors, such as militia leaders and secularised returned diasporic groups who reject 'traditional' authority: Le Sage, 2005.

hold. Their 'leadership' is often situational, and the 'community' often comes into being around particular issues.[144] When dealing with a 'community-based' system, it is therefore important to assess who precisely has membership, and even the extent to which 'the community' exists.[145] These questions, which are central to claims for recognition by non-state legal orders, are discussed further in Chapter VII.

Third, a clear line cannot always be drawn between popular justice (understood to be developed and controlled organically by end-users)[146] such as in the case of the street committees that emerged in 1980s South Africa, and "social cleansing and vigilantism"[147] as in the case of the Peruvian *rondas campesinas*.

Fourth, an overemphasis on the relationship between state and non-state law can hide pluralities *within* state law,[148] and also miss the immense variety of interactions between different NSLOs, overlooking human rights consequences in both instances. To understand post-conflict transition in the Solomon Islands, for example, it is vital to recognise that NSLOs can conflict, because multiple non-state orders coexist, each having legitimacy.[149] Menzies observes "that modern movements of significant numbers of people resulting in two (often conflicting) sets of customary laws coexisting in one place, with no traditional way of reconciling them" create more complications than the interaction between the formal (state) and informal (customary or non-state) systems of law.[150] During the conflict in Nepal, 'peoples' courts' forcibly replaced the informal traditional *panchayat* dispute resolution mechanism,[151] and in Malawi chiefs appear to have resisted pilot projects that introduced Church-based mediation because they felt this would diminish their power.[152] Elsewhere, as in the Philippines, Indonesia and Nigeria, women negotiate their way through multiple layers of Muslim and customary laws to secure better property rights and rights within marriage.[153]

---

144   Eckert, 2002, p. 13.

145   Uvin, cited in Mungoven, 2001, p. 36. See also Buur and Kyed, 2006 p. 14.

146   Nina and Schwikkard, 1996, p. 73.

147   Faundez, 2003.

148   Largely but not only in the area of family laws, discussed in detail in Chapter VI.

149   Menzies, 2007.

150   Ibid., pp. 9-10.

151   ICJ, 2008.

152   DFID, 2004.

153   Benda-Beckmann *et al.*, 2004; Fianza, 2006; WLUML, 2006.

Lastly, as some of the above examples illustrate, it is important to underline that NSLOs are actively produced by participants through political processes involving contestation and disagreement.[154]

THE COMPLEX RELATIONSHIP BETWEEN THE STATE AND NON-STATE LEGAL ORDERS

In all regions, examples can be found that show states engaging with non-state legal institutions in ways that deeply challenge the supposed separation between state and non-state legal orders. Very often in practice, state and non-state legal orders may be so intertwined that it is impossible to draw a clear line between what is 'state' and what is 'non-state'. At the same time, however, each may tend to represent themselves as *different* in order to claim distinct legitimacy or challenge the other's authority. In sum, they influence each other through a relationship characterised by a mixture of competition and collaboration. For human rights advocates this complicates the task of determining the responsibilities of different actors, and their culpability in case of rights violations, and making effective recommendations.

In many parts of the world, this blurring of the line between state and non-state is entwined with the history of colonialism. Numerous studies, particularly in Africa and Asia, note how colonial and post-colonial authorities shaped and reinvented 'traditional' authorities to serve political need.[155] Colonial powers, legal administrators in particular, significantly reshaped NSLO practices. They transplanted them into geographical areas where they did not exist, or into contexts they did not address; they created new 'traditional authorities', even new collective identities, to suit their agendas and purposes. Colonial (mis)readings of local cultures often caused the authorities to conflate ritual and political power holders and to institutionalise these tropes as 'customary law'.[156] 'Codifying native law' was central to the colonial project, and civil servants, priests, anthropologists, and others, frequently talked to elders, ritually important persons, and community leaders and chiefs, in order to *discover* or *give* law to the 'natives' that was in line with their often highly racialised principles of justice. Post-colonial states continue to bear the imprint of these initiatives. In post-colonial Mozambique and South Africa, the state's co-option of 'traditional' leaders has led to serious disputes regarding 'authentic chieftaincies'. In Latin America, the practices ranged from non-recognition, repression, and *de facto*

---

154   Gover, 2008a, p. 5.

155   See for instance Hobsbawm and Ranger, 1983; Chanock 1985; Mamdani, 1996. See also Buur and Kyed, 2006; Davidheiser, 2007; Malzbender *et al.*, 2005; and Sarwar, 2004.

156   Mamdani, 1996.

toleration, to co-option, as in Mexico where the state selectively legitimised certain norms and practices within indigenous communities.[157]

Today, non-state mechanisms are routinely employed by various branches of the state to facilitate state business.[158] In the Gambia, where even the police are known to question the value of the formal legal system, police officers delay procedures to allow non-formal peacemakers to intercede, make their own efforts to reconcile parties to a dispute, or refer cases to respected elders. Similar practices exist in Afghanistan, where many cases go through the complete cycle of court review only to be referred to NSLOs for final settlement. In Peru, the government continuously attempts to co-opt the *rondas campesinas* to further its political or military objectives.[159] Even in centralised China, local government authorities seek the assistance of imams in villages of Bao'an Muslims to implement marriage registration regulations.

Non-state legal orders invariably seek greater autonomy from the state. They challenge the state's monopoly on violence, and appropriate state sovereignty by redefining authority (at least at community level) as well as notions of what is law and its exceptions. Even here, however, non-state justice structures arguably assist the state order by expanding national resources for dealing with conflict, and reducing the burden for the state of maintaining social order.[160]

Research also demonstrates that the relationship is not one-way. "State and non-state law are mutually constitutive. Legal norms are the result of political processes and are subject to revision by the community that created them."[161] This too has a history, as in the Middle East, where, despite opposition between the two systems, "tribes and states have created and maintained each other in a single system, though one of inherent instability".[162]

The result is that non-state orders also use and shape the state order. In Botswana, chiefs sometimes make use of the common law, while in Afghanistan and Kyrgyzstan non-state adjudicators threaten to transfer cases to the formal system in order to bring parties to a compromise. In essence, they appropriate part of the state's power to enhance their own authority.[163] The appropriation

---

157   Castillo, 2002, p. 22.

158   Davidheiser, 2007, p. 11; Barfield, 2006, p. 2; Wang, 2006, p. 9; Faundez, 2003, p. 39. See also Malzbender *et al.*, 2005, p. 3 regarding water management disputes in South Africa.

159   Faundez, 2003, p. 39.

160   Nina and Schwikkard, 1996, p. 75.

161   Gover, 2008a, p. 37.

162   Tapper in Pirie, 2005, p. 10.

163   Griffiths, 1998; Beyer, 2007, p. 13.

of state authority by a non-state order can also be symbolic. In Kyrgyzstan, non-state *aksakal* adjudicators create what in popular imagination resembles a 'proper' court (certain seating arrangements, a book in which 'the law' is written, a table at which the *aksakal* panel sits) to elevate their authority, while in Mozambique both state officials and chiefs use each other's regalia and artefacts to sustain their standing.[164] At times it can be impossible to tell the two systems apart. In eastern Tibet and in Pakistan, members of the 'non-state' mechanism turn out to be local government authorities or elected officials, while in Afghanistan elected members of local provincial councils are increasingly treated as mediators between the formal and non-state systems.[165] Meanwhile, to end disputes, officials in the Philippines sometimes provide part of the compensation awarded by a traditional authority to a feuding party.[166] Who uses whom in such relationships can therefore become almost impossible to pinpoint. Despite the blurring of boundaries state and non-state legal orders ultimately remain distinct because the state and state law structure determines "the terms through which non-state actors introduce their laws into state practice".[167]

To complicate matters further, in many contexts the line between the state legal system and NSLOs is blurred *de jure*. In Mozambique, 'community authorities' have judicial and executive authority while national legislation also assigns them a role as representatives of rural communities.[168] In the Solomon Islands there is a fusion of *kastom* and state law.[169] Hernandez Castillo argues that, instead of positing indigenous and national law as two separate legal systems guided by distinct cultural logics, in Mexico it would be more accurate to speak of a "shared legal map onto which different, overlapping normative systems are traced in an interaction which necessarily affects the very substance of those legal systems themselves";[170] tradition is mobilised by both the dominator and the dominated.[171] With regard to the Special Indigenous Jurisdiction in Latin America, theoretically no 'clash' can arise because the state has ceded authority to an alternative jurisdiction; in fact, clashes however continue to occur over the practicalities of implementation.[172] Finally, the liberal state may acknowledge that other legal orders exist but deny them the status of 'law' (as in Australia),

---

164   Kyed and Buur, 2007, p. 21; see also Faundez, 2003, p. 47 regarding state-abandoned *barrios* in Colombia.

165   Pirie, 2005, p. 2; Shah, 1998; Barfield, 2006, p. 2.

166   Ragsag, 2006, p. 6.

167   Eckert, 2002, p. 17.

168   Buur and Kyed, 2006.

169   Menzies, 2007, p. 5.

170   Castillo, 2002, p. 20.

171   Ibid., pp. 20-24. Beyer, 2007, p. 16, makes precisely the same point for Kyrgyzstan.

172   Yrigoyen Fajardo, 2004, discusses several cases.

or subordinate such orders to the state's own law.[173] There is then arguably no 'clash', at least from the state's perspective, because conflict can only arise when the state *recognises* the other as 'law'. In other words, the perception of a clash depends on whose perspective is privileged.

Ultimately, the presumption that the state and NSLOs are always in collision, or necessarily in tension, arises first from a tendency to see state law as a normative order that exists in isolation, and second from failure to examine the contested nature of both state and non-state legal orders (as discussed above). Any contrast between NSLOs and state legal systems must transcend the "unhistoricized distinction between the traditional and the modern: the former oral and the latter codified; the former representing 'certain local values,' and the latter 'international human rights standards'".[174] As will be obvious from the discussions that follow, such stereotypes about NSLOs simply cannot be sustained.

CHALLENGES TO PRESUMPTIONS ABOUT THE DEMAND FOR NON-STATE LEGAL ORDERS

Demand for recognition of non-state legal orders and their incorporation into the formal framework is by no means universal. In Canada, a broad-based coalition of secular Muslims, atheists from a Muslim cultural background, and secularists within wider Canadian society, successfully resisted expansion of the use of privatised religious arbitration in family matters. In Fiji, judicial reluctance to apply severe penalties for rape, in the face of ethnic Fijian nationalism, and the increased use of *bulubulu*, led the local women's movement to mount a national campaign between 1988 and 1994 to make sure that informal processes did not undermine legal processes.[175] It is clear that in many instances people value state norms and want state institutions to be more active, not less.

For example, in some *barrios* in Bogotá, Colombia, and in the Pasargada shantytown in Rio de Janeiro, Brazil, when communities ignored by the state develop their own local conflict resolution mechanisms, they often mimic the norms and procedures of the official system.[176] *Aksakals* charged with delivering justice in rural Kyrgyzstan complain of being abandoned by the state. Meanwhile, survey and interview data from Ghana showed that, despite the flexibility and accessibility of alternative dispute resolution mechanisms, and the problems and delays associated with state courts, there was "a very strong

---

173   Michaels, 2005.

174   Email from Mahmoud Mamdani to M. Mohamadou, then Research Director, ICHRP, on file 19 December 1999.

175   Merry, 2006, p. 126.

176   Faundez 2003, p. 47 citing Cansel, 1999, pp. 161- 175 and Santos, 1977.

demand for authoritative and enforceable settlements which only the state could provide".[177] In Ghana "[t]he kind of justice offered by the courts is not as alien or inappropriate as many of its critics believe. Although litigants are infuriated by the delays caused by constant adjournments, they generally respect the way the judges deal with them and most are not excluded by language or other factors from understanding what is going on; this is particularly true of the more informal and flexible procedures which have developed in the Magistrates Court".[178]

The demand for state justice is also often gendered. As Barfield notes, informal systems of adjudication may be quite inaccessible to women, not only because they may lack direct access unfiltered by a male representative, but also because of the unwillingness of many informal systems – such as traditional Afghan *shuras* or *jirgas* – to consider family and matrimonial matters.[179] These are supposed to be handled by families in private, but the failure of non-state systems means that most of the civil caseload before the formal system (up to 80%) relates to divorce and family issues.[180] Whereas the overwhelming majority of people in a Peruvian study reported a preference to submit their disputes to the *rondas campesinas* rather than the official justice system, the exception was marital disputes where 50% would opt for the official system.[181] In contrast, after the Venezuelan Justices of the Peace system was set up in 1995 to resolve disputes between neighbours, some 95% of the cases it received reportedly involved domestic violence.[182]

Processes of societal change can also increase the value accorded to state systems. In Côte d'Ivoire, where the formal system recognises customary laws and courts, people are increasingly turning to state rather than customary and informal courts due to increased urban migration and the subsequent breakdown of traditional community structures. Relational systems of justice inevitably fail if social debts cannot ever be repaid. There may also be generational differences in perception: younger and more educated South Africans feel it is the state's role to deliver clean water to all citizens, in contrast to the self-financed and self-regulated water supply system managed by local traditional leaders.[183]

Too rarely analysts ask why non-state legal orders that have been recognised or formalised have failed. In 1950s India, *nyaya panchayats* (modelled on the

---

177   Crook in Byrne *et al.*, 2007, p. 17.

178   Crook in Byrne *et al.*, 2007.

179   USAID, 2005a, p. 13.

180   Barfield, 2006, p. 1.

181   Faundez, 2003, p. 25.

182   Macaulay, 2005, p. 103.

183   Malzbender *et al.*, 2005, p. 2.

traditional village *panchayats* but with some judicial powers) were established as alternative dispute resolution mechanisms to provide localised justice especially for the rural poor, but in little more than a decade they were moribund. "It is not clear whether they withered away because they lacked the qualities of the traditional indigenous tribunals or because they displayed them all too well."[184]

Often criticism of the state legal system is confused with problems arising out of social attitudes for which the state legal order cannot be held solely responsible. In one study by a Pakistani women's organisation, Simorgh, the large majority (76%) of women victims of violence who had taken their cases to court categorically stated that they would never approach the court again, whatever the circumstances; one interviewee stated: "No, death is better."[185] Is this rejection of the state system due to its faults or due to societal pressures against women acting autonomously in public, or both? In reality, those on the margins of society are also on the margins of legal orders, state or non-state. Rushing to replace state systems that enjoy little legitimacy with non-state mechanisms (or even vice versa) may therefore make little difference if analyses of 'choices' between state and non-state legal orders leave issues of power unexamined.

The use of non-state legal orders may be a social or economic necessity or may be due to the inaccessibility of the state legal order, rather than reflect a normative or ethical preference. The tendency to confuse facts with aspirations perhaps arises because of a failure to interrogate in context the reasons why people act as they do. Numerous statements, particularly in donor documents, argue that *because* most disputes are resolved outside the state framework, reform must focus on promoting these institutions and "thereby better ensure that institutional reforms reflect demands of communities".[186] Yet high use of non-formal justice systems in rural areas does not necessarily mean that those systems are the best: it may simply mean that they are the only procedures that are accessible or available.[187]

UNPACKING NON-STATE LEGAL ORDERS: REVISITING POPULAR GENERALISATIONS

The sheer presence of non-state legal orders across the world – their visibility as a social fact – is a persuasive argument for engaging with them. "In Sierra

---

184   Galanter and Krishnan, 2004, p. 793.

185   Zia, 2002.

186   See for example, World Bank, 2007, p. 3; Wardak, 2004, p. 337; Commission on Legal Empowerment of the Poor, 2008, p. 63; Wojkowska, 2006, p. 31.

187   Kimathi, 2005, p. 17.

Leone about 85 percent of the population fall under customary law. Customary tenure covers 75 percent of land in most African countries, affecting 90 percent of land transactions in Mozambique and Ghana", while the British Department for International Development (DFID) "estimates 80% of cases in developing countries are lodged, managed and resolved by alternative, traditional or non-state justice systems".[188] However, 'fall under' and 'covered by' are elusive in meaning. Does this mean NSLOs are the only legal system accessible, and that people choose or have no choice but to be governed by them? It is occasionally acknowledged that such statistics must be interrogated: "poor people's preference for using [NSLOs] may reflect the weaknesses of the formal justice system, and does not necessarily indicate satisfaction with the systems themselves."[189]

Just as it is necessary to examine more closely the extent and reasons for their 'coverage' of people's lives and disputes, it is also vital to avoid simplistic characterisations of NSLOs. It is important to stress that the objective of the discussion that follows is not to suggest that formal legal systems are problem-free: arbitrariness, corruption, bias, discrimination and many such shortcomings have been noted in state legal systems as well. The primary objective is to highlight that many of the generalisations about the nature of non-state legal orders in current international policy documents are not as well founded as they may appear. Restorative justice is not universal across all NSLOs. For instance, among the Finnish Roma, avoidance (self- or externally-imposed exile) is seen as the only proper way to end a feud. Moreover, the supposedly non-adversarial approach of informal systems does not always lead to peace.[190] One tribal feud in Pakistan began in 1990 and claimed 200 lives, although as many as eight *jirgas* were convened, while in Mindanao in the Philippines *rido* feuding is the most common source of violence (more so even than armed conflict with the state) and has led clans to form private armies. In Madagascar, summary executions have been carried out on the basis of decisions by the *dina*, a traditional dispute and conflict resolution customary body.[191] In contrast to the stereotype that NSLOs produce consensual outcomes, coercion is a common feature.[192] Punishments by Maoist 'people's courts' in Nepal entailed cruel, inhuman or degrading treatment, while vigilante style neighbourhood security networks in Africa, and 'citizen justice' in Guatemala, have often carried out cruel punishments or premeditated lynchings. Participation is not always voluntary: in the Philippines and Eastern Tibet, bringing parties to the

---

188 Byrne *et al.*, 2007, p.15; Ragsag, 2006. See also Wojkowska, 2006, p. 12.

189 DFID, 2004, p. 3.

190 Sarwar, 2004; Ragsag, 2006.

191 UN Human Rights Committee, CCPR/C/MDG/CO/3 11 May 2007.

192 ICJ, 2008, p. 23; Kimathi, 2005, p. 15; Sieder, 2008, p. 20 (page number as in manuscript on file).

negotiating table often requires social pressure and argument, cajoling and implied threats.[193]

- NSLOs are not always based on the idea of privileging the collective.[194] Customarily, 'government' in the Solomon Islands was identified as an individual person. Among the nomads of Eastern Tibet, affront is conceptualised as an act committed against the individual (even if it later requires a collective response).

- NSLOs are generally presumed to be less expensive and more accessible than formal state courts, but this is not always the case.[195] For example in Mozambique it is common for adjudicators (as in many other parts of the world) to receive payments from all parties to the dispute for hearing cases. These costs can be significant if cases are heard several times or if people take their case to different non-state authorities.[196] Though NSLOs are stereotyped as 'compensation based', users often refer to these as 'fines'; in other words they perceive them as punitive. Fines among Peruvian indigenous communities are often heavy; the payment following a murder that related to straying animals in Eastern Tibet amounted to more than the family's entire wealth. Finally, as pointed out by the opponents of religious arbitration in family matters in Canada, costs are not always monetised and a potentially high social price must be factored into understandings of 'cost'.[197]

- Non-state systems are also credited with being quicker than state justice. Yet in Bangladesh, a *shalish* hearing may be complex, comprising many sessions over several months and is quicker only relative to an even slower formal court system.[198] In some countries in Latin America, where ADR-style mechanisms have been introduced for domestic violence cases, "the obligation to pass first through conciliation has the effect of dragging out these cases, exposing women to violence between hearings, achieving quite the opposite of the rapid, effective resolution for which such informalized justice was intended".[199] Moreover, speedy justice proceedings are not always just, and NSLOs are frequently criticised for shortcomings of due process.

---

193   Ragsag, 2006, p. 5; Pirie, 2005, p. 15.

194   Menzies, 2007; Pirie, 2005.

195   Faundez, 2003, p. 19; Maru, 2006, p. 437; Siahaan, 2006, p. 2; Pirie, 2005, p. 15; Menzies, 2007, p. 11; Amnesty International, 2002, pp. 13 and 32; Amnesty International, 2005, pp. 4-5; Rights and Democracy, 2005a, p. 6.

196   Helene Maria Kyed, comments at ICHRP Research Workshop.

197   Rights and Democracy, 2005a, p. 6.

198   Golub, 2002.

199   Macaulay, 2005, pp. 103–114.

- It is presumed that non-state legal orders are effective because the parties have shared norms, unlike the gap between community and state law norms. However, norms are not always shared and as a result NSLOs are not always more effective than state orders.[200] This is especially so in the case of intercommunity disputes, where there may be no shared norms on which to base adjudication and agreeing on an impartial adjudicator may be difficult. This is why eastern Tibetan nomads, for instance, are forced to rely instead on the Chinese state. Traditional dispute resolution may be irrelevant where armed political groups or warlords ignore customary norms and operate with impunity, as in Afghanistan and in many African conflicts. Issues of effectiveness also arise given that NSLOs may lack the power to enforce decisions against elites.[201]

- Non-state systems do not always accommodate normative diversity and are not always representative. In parts of the Philippines, *barangay* local non-state justice mechanisms are dominated by lowland Christians and sometimes fail to take account of Muslim or indigenous values (even if some Muslim customs are recognised in the *barangay* regulations), leading to conflicts and misunderstandings.[202] Claims that NSLOs are more 'representative' ignore the fact that women and younger men are commonly absent – as they are in Nigeria's customary law, in water management councils in Tanzania (even though users are mostly women), or in Kyrgyzstan's *aksakal* courts.[203] One also has to question precisely which 'people' benefit: in Somalia, minorities such as Bantus and Arabs are "heavily discriminated against" in *xeer* decision-making.[204] The legitimacy that NSLOs are accorded on account of their claim to be 'of the people' also needs to be questioned.[205] The primary founder of the first Peruvian *rondas campesinas* was in fact "a prosperous peasant who was also *teniente-gobernador* (police) in the locality" not an impoverished peasant alienated by the state.[206] The stereotype that 'community' or 'traditional' leaders know the local area and people intimately clearly no longer applies in contexts such as Somalia and Afghanistan where entire areas have been depopulated by conflict.

---

200 See for example Pirie, 2005, p. 23; Menzies, 2007; Kimathi, 2005, p. 9.

201 Barfield *et al.*, 2006.

202 Tachibana, 2006, p. 13.

203 This is not to ignore the fact that the formal system can be equally unrepresentative of gender and other kinds of diversity.

204 Le Sage, 2005, p. 36.

205 Buur and Kyed, 2006; Faundez, 2003, p. 23; Eckert, 2002; NCWD, 2005; Beyer, 2007; Kimathi, 2005, p. 9; Höhne, 2007, p. 167; Galanter and Krishnan, 2004, p. 813.

206 Faundez, 2003.

As the examples above suggest, there is no overwhelming evidence to suggest that enhancing legal plurality through NSLOs is necessarily the most effective solution to the problem of lack of access to justice.[207] However, it is also true that non-state legal orders have shown a remarkable tendency to grow, survive and adapt in various, often positive, ways.

• A study of 5,000 Justices of the Peace (a traditional community justice mechanism in Peru that now enjoys a degree of official recognition) noted that, following training in gender sensitivity, Justices were much less willing to insist on conciliation and more willing to use sentencing powers in cases of domestic violence.[208] Faundez confirms this, observing that, while "there's no question that there's strong gender bias in most N[on] S[tate] J[ustice] S[ystems] in rural Peru ... there has been a marked move toward gender equality in recent years in those systems".[209] He credits the training provided by NGOs in departments such as Ayacucho and Cajamarca for much of that progress, as well as the increase in dialogue between community groups and state officials from organisations such as the Office of the Ombudsperson (*Defensoría del pueblo*).

• The *shalish* has in some areas of Bangladesh been reshaped into a system that adheres to some basic standards of equality and due process in resolving disputes and conflicts. In some forms of dispute resolution modeled on the *shalish*, women now play increasingly important, even central roles; the poor are both represented in decision-making and treated more fairly; clearer procedures have been adopted; etc. All these changes have contributed to the mechanism's effectiveness.[210] Similarly, Merry shows that *bulubulu* in Fiji can be discriminatory or protective of rights depending upon the sensitivity of the person administering the process and that a wide variety of new and evolving practices, with both positive and negative human rights outcomes, now fall under this umbrella term.[211] The Civil Resource Development and Documentation Centre in eastern Nigeria was able to negotiate the appointment of women as tribal chiefs, drawing both on the historical recognition in customary laws of women's rights to speak and to have group interests, and on the CRC and CEDAW.[212]

---

207   For a more detailed discussion on this see Chapter VIII.

208   Vega in Macaulay, 2005, p. 107.

209   *Alternative justice in Peru*, Web Story, April 16, 2003, at www.iadb.org/news/articledetail.cfm?Language= ENandartid=1982andartType=WS.

210   For details, see Wojowska, 2006, pp. 39-40.

211   Merry, 2006, p. 123.

212   Byrne *et al.*, 2007, p. 20.

- Maru describes in detail the paralegal programme of the NGO Timap for Justice in Sierra Leone.[213] Paralegals with training in human rights threaten to resort to the state system in order to encourage rights violators to agree to extra-judicial mediation. However, in a break with traditional mediation practices, Timap's paralegals refuse to mediate cases of rape and domestic violence, but pursue these cases through the state courts if the client wishes. A Swiss Development Cooperation report provides a useful summary of the initiative: it "has developed a creative, versatile model to advance justice, one which combines education, mediation, negotiation, organising, and advocacy. The efficacy of the Sierra Leonean paralegals is due in large measure to their knowledge of and association with the law and to the program's capacity to litigate in some cases, but also to their familiarity with the social milieu of their clients and the potential for fostering self-help and amicable resolutions. The program strives to solve clients' justice problems – thereby demonstrating concretely that justice is possible – and at the same time to cultivate the agency of the communities among which it works. The program uses a synthetic approach to Sierra Leone's dualist legal structure, engaging and seeking to improve both formal and customary institutions [...]. Common issues the community-based paralegals work on include domestic violence, child abandonment, corruption, police abuse, economic exploitation, abuse of traditional authority, employment rights, right to education, and right to health".[214]

- "In Somalia, the Danish Refugee Council held dialogues with over 100 elders and community leaders from five different clans living in the region, focusing on aspects of traditional *xeer* that were perceived to be ineffective in managing conflict or which seemed to contradict basic concepts of justice and fairness, as enshrined in both Shari'ah and international human rights standards. Community interests expressed during the dialogue included ensuring the protection of the accused, fair treatment of women, orphans and minority groups, and problems associated with *diya* payment, collective punishment and property rights. The participants issued a declaration modifying the local *xeer* and travelled throughout the region to disseminate the new laws. The declaration made particularly important changes to the *xeer* governing revenge killing and forced marriages of a widow to her dead husband's brother. According to a monitoring study, after five months the region experienced a 90% reduction in murder cases".[215]

- In Kenya, NGOs have helped to revitalise 'traditional' systems and support the emergence of alternative community-based systems.[216] Examples include an initiative by a group of women in Wajir district which led to the

---

213   Maru, 2006.

214   OSI in Byrne et al., 2007, pp. 27-28.

215   Wojkowska, 2006, p. 32.

216   Kimathi, 2005, p. 13.

formation of the Wajir Peace and Development Committee that now facilitates the resolution of disputes by interclan mediation. The initiative is linked into the District Security Committee, which deals with larger problems that may threaten peace in the area.[217] Also in Kenya, initiatives such as the 'peace elders initiative' in Laikipia district are working to make dispute resolution processes more inclusive by bringing in youth and women as 'elders'.[218]

- In Mexico, the Zapatistas were the first guerrilla movement in Latin America to advocate and prioritise gender demands in their political agenda. They asserted the right of indigenous peoples to form governments in accordance with their own normative systems, and the right of indigenous women to hold local posts of authority, inherit land and have control over their bodies.[219] Indigenous women's organisations sought "to find paths through which we may view tradition with new eyes, in such a way that will not violate our rights and will restore dignity to indigenous women. We want to change those traditions that diminish our dignity".[220] The San Andrés Accords signed by Zapatista commanders and Mexican government representatives committed the government to respect indigenous autonomy in the following terms: "Indigenous peoples have the right to free self-determination, and, as the means of their expression, autonomy from the Mexican government… to [a]pply their own normative systems in the regulation and resolution of internal conflicts, honouring individual rights, human rights, and specifically, the dignity and integrity of women".[221] Castillo describes how autonomous authorities have used reinvented tradition to provide indigenous women with more rights in instances of domestic violence than were available in national law.

These examples indicate that plural legal orders involving recognition of NSLOs need not necessarily be damaging to human rights. However, it is notable how frequently the same positive examples are cited across the literature – in sharp contrast to the diversity of examples showing negative human rights impacts. Moreover, positive examples rarely, if ever, seem to arise from jurisdictions that have parallel religion-based family law regimes, especially in those states where there is no 'neutral' civil law.

The extensive survey of academic and other documentation, undertaken for this project indicates that NSLOs are rarely, if ever, presumed to provide justice that is intrinsically and undeniably of a high standard. If anything, NSLOs tend

---

217 A video on the initiative, *The Wajir Story* is available for free download www.freespeech.org/videodb/ index.php?action=detailandvideo_id=10175.

218 Nyamu-Musembi in DFID, 2004, p. 11.

219 Castillo, 2002 and Speed, 2007.

220 Castillo, 2002, p. 3.

221 Ibid., p. 4.

to be particularly problematic in replicating, both normatively and institutionally, patterns of power imbalances within the community. This is especially true with respect to women's rights and participation but also with respect to other traditional markers of discrimination such as age, property holdings, beliefs, etc.

Most positive NSLO reform initiatives have been the result of multi-pronged approaches that aimed to: increase the knowledge and confidence of key actors in using a range of legal orders (international human rights standards, constitutional rights, state law, customary laws, etc.); strengthen group access to rights by changing the attitudes of elites and empowering the disadvantaged; and challenge structural discrimination through community participation. In almost every case, the role of non-state actors, particularly NGOs, and the state has been crucial. It is important to stress that rights guaranteed under the international human rights regime are not self–executing: they are made available to individuals only by way of their states.[222] In human rights terms, the state therefore has a central role to play as a guarantor of rights, and this is especially true when it comes to granting space and a role to non-state legal orders in a plural legal context, and overseeing their functioning within a framework of rights.

---

222   Bosniak, 2000.

SUMMARY

The search for ways to resolve disputes outside courts and the formal justice system is a universal phenomenon. However, certain presumptions about non-state legal orders need to be questioned.

Non-state legal orders have a complex relationship with the state: while they may conflict, they influence and shape each other in many ways; the line between the state and non-state legal orders is often blurred – in practice or even *de jure*.

The presumption that the state and NSLOs are necessarily in tension arises first from a mistaken tendency to see state law as a normative order that exists in isolation of the cultural and political preferences of its citizens; and second from failure to examine the contested nature of both state and non-state legal orders. Sometimes non-state orders are in conflict with each other.

The non-state is not necessarily traditional, is subject to contemporary influences, and can be created by internally driven processes or because of external facilitation. Use of both state and non-state systems is often gendered. As compared to the inadequate state system, non-state legal orders are not necessarily always quicker, cheaper, more accessible and inclusive, focused on restorative justice, or more effective in resolving local disputes.

Demand for recognition of non-state legal orders and their incorporation into the formal framework is by no means universal. In many instances, people value state norms and want state institutions to be more active, not less.

Those on the margins of society are also on the margins of legal orders, state or non-state. Thus, rushing to replace state systems that enjoy little legitimacy with non-state mechanisms (or vice versa) may therefore make little difference if 'choices' between state and non-state legal orders leave issues of power unexamined.

The use of non-state legal orders may be a social or economic compulsion or may be due to the inaccessibility of the state legal order, rather than reflect a normative or ethical preference. The tendency to confuse facts with aspirations perhaps arises because of a failure to interrogate in context the reasons why people act as they do.

PART TWO

THE HUMAN RIGHTS IMPACTS OF PLURAL LEGAL ORDERS

V. FAMILY LAWS – A CASE STUDY OF PLURAL LEGAL ORDERS

The first part of this report focused on covering the conceptual ground and opened several debates and issues relevant to plural legal orders. This section examines the human rights impacts of plural legal orders. This chapter discusses plural legal orders in the context of family or personal status law.[223]

Family or personal status law covers marriage and divorce, custody and guardianship, adoption, inheritance and succession.[224] Family law is a pertinent starting point to examine the human rights impacts of plural legal orders because it brings together a number of the issues discussed in preceding chapters. In addition, it is an area that is not only overlooked by most analyses of plural legal orders but also by human rights actors in general. The struggle for equality in the family and for reform of family law has largely been led by women's organisations. 'Mainstream' human rights organisations have been only marginally involved, despite the fact that marriage, divorce, custody, adoption, etc. have long been the subject of international legal regimes, some of which even predate the two basic human rights covenants.

International standards on equality in the family and family law in general go back to the Universal Declaration on Human Rights, but also include specific instruments such as the Convention on the Nationality of Married Women,[225] and the Convention on Consent to Marriage, Minimum Age for Marriage and

---

223   There is a tendency to confuse the terms 'personal status law' and 'personal law', largely due to historical and colonial influences. 'Personal status law' is generally only used for legislation regulating family matters. Under personal status law systems, by virtue of their birth or marriage (or conversion) into a particular state-recognised community, a person is subject to laws supposedly derived from that community's ethno-religious code. This term is specific to the Middle East and North Africa as well as certain West African states, all influenced by Ottoman and French colonial legal systems; it is not generally used for family laws in common law countries or where unitary civil codes apply to all citizens. 'Personal laws' on the other hand include not just family matters but *all* laws, including criminal and fiscal matters, applicable to a specifically defined group which are framed with reference to the group's religious code or ethnic identity. The confusion arises largely because in most countries where the law recognises the application of personal laws this is primarily in the sphere of family matters. Recent exceptions include the application of interpretations of Muslim laws in penal matters in Pakistan and Nigeria. Thus, for the sake of clarity and to use a term applicable to all legal systems, this report generally uses 'family laws' rather than 'personal status laws'.

224   The range of laws labelled 'family law' in any given state order varies. Variations are most common regarding maintenance, adoption and wills. Provisions regulating group membership (e.g., tribe or band membership), or detailing the personal status consequences of conversion, are closely related to family law.

225   Entered into force 11 August 1958.

Registration of Marriages (1962).[226] Subsequently, the ICCPR, in Article 23(4), addressed the issue of equality in marriage and family, while provisions such as the right to marry followed in the ICESCR. The adoption of CEDAW in 1979 largely reiterated (with some specific amplification) these rights to equality in marriage and family.[227] Article 16 of CEDAW places an obligation on states to take "appropriate measures to eliminate discrimination against women in all matters relating to marriage and family relations" and ensure equality between men and women in all matters relating to family and marital relations. Article 16 of CEDAW obliges state parties to ensure that men and women enjoy equal rights in: choosing a spouse and marrying only with their free and full consent; marriage and its dissolution; as parents, regardless of marital status, deciding on the number and spacing of their children; personal rights as husband and wife, including the choice of a family name; and property rights in the context of family, i.e. inheritance.

To date, more than 25 states have entered reservations to this Article. If one were to examine the record of states parties who have not entered reservations but whose practice is nevertheless at variance with Article 16, in effect a regime of *de facto* reservations, the number would be far higher. The number and sweeping nature of many of the reservations have prompted the CEDAW Committee to declare such reservations incompatible with the object and purpose of the Convention and as impermissible.[228] As already discussed in Chapter III, the fact that relatively fewer reservations have been made to ICCPR Article 23(4), which makes broadly equivalent provisions for equality in family life, indicates that policies regarding women's rights within the family are highly politicised.

WEAKNESSES IN STANDARD-SETTING

In a number of areas relating to family law in the context of plural legal orders, human rights standards either have limitations or have to date been narrowly interpreted. These limitations are especially visible where the state order provides for parallel family laws based on ethno-religious frameworks, or where non-state legal orders are incorporated into the state legal order in some form or other. Further, the principle of equality elaborated in CEDAW Article 2(f) is generally taken to mean discrimination in relation to men; there is no clear

---

226   Entered into force 1964.

227   The Convention on Consent to Marriage, Minimum Age for Marriage and Registration of Marriages 1962 (entered into force 1964), and the Convention on the Nationality of Married Women, (entered into force 11 August 1958).

228   According to the Committee "reservations to Article 16, whether lodged for national, traditional, religious or cultural reasons, are incompatible with the Convention and therefore impermissible and should be reviewed and modified or withdrawn". www.un.org/womenwatch/daw/cedaw/reservations.htm.

understanding and examination of the fact that parallel state orders establish inequalities between women of different communities.[229]

Another example is that most commentaries on due diligence and non-state legal orders concentrate on criminal law issues: they call for 'prosecuting the alleged perpetrators', or 'bringing them to justice' in fair proceedings, 'investigating abuse', and reparation, rehabilitation and redress. The violations of rights that result, for example, from situations where men use plural legal orders to their advantage in order to facilitate their access to the practices of polygyny or unilateral divorce is the focus of activism by women in numerous countries.[230] Yet the concept of due diligence has not so far been expanded to cover such violations of rights. This may partly reflect the practical and political limitations on how far the state can be held responsible for the actions of non-state actors.

Similarly, emphasis on the right to due process is useful to address violations of criminal law by non-state legal orders, but has limited application with respect to family law and pluralities within state family laws. First, even if due process standards are applied, they do not preclude the possibility that discriminatory outcomes will arise because of substantive differences in provisions across state-recognised plural legal systems. Second, the availability of a remedy or appeal mechanism offers insufficient protection, if social, political and economic factors prevent people from accessing them. Women invariably face this problem more than men and it is particularly prevalent in the case of alternative dispute resolution mechanisms such as Pakistan's *musalihat anjuman*, and mechanisms that enable private religious arbitration.

Commenting on the relatively weak development of human rights standards regarding family laws, Tibi argues that family law is an area that state and non-state actors, including human rights organisations, have come to accept as almost exempt from "the need for globally shared legal frameworks based on cross-cultural foundations".[231] In this area, it appears often to be accepted uncritically that rights need to be 'balanced',[232] especially the rights of the individual *vis-à-vis* the collective; and the right to sex equality *vis-à-vis* religious freedom, for example. The different standards applied to women's human rights and those of other groups needing protection is also reflected in national legislation. Whereas Costa Rica's 1998 Children and Adolescent's Code strictly prohibited conciliation in cases of domestic violence, for example, the criminal

---

229   Arguably, pluralities in state family laws equally lead to discrimination between men given that for example different family laws provide differential access to divorce or polygyny. However, by and large, men are more able to 'forum shop' and use these pluralities to their advantage rather than disadvantage.

230   'Forum shopping' in family law is discussed in greater detail below.

231   Tibi in Galanter and Krishnan, 2002.

232   Gita Sahgal, comments at ICHRP Meeting.

code of 1998 contradicts this by permitting conciliation between two adults in first offences carrying a maximum penalty of three years imprisonment.[233] This apparent exemption further underlines why the women's rights movement rather than the human rights movement have largely led agenda-setting regarding women's rights in the family. It may also partly explain why, as discussed in Chapter III, the past two decades have witnessed fragmentation and uncoordinated development in human rights standards that are of critical importance to plural legal orders.

Even where the question of women's rights to equality in the family have been raised, opportunities to link violence against women (VAW) to discriminatory family laws have been missed. For example, CEDAW General Recommendation 19 on VAW is silent on the role of family laws, and thereby overlooks forms of discrimination that may occur as a result of parallel family laws, which may also restrict remedies against violence. Similarly, Article 4 of the 1993 UN Declaration on the Elimination of VAW notes that violence against women cannot be justified on the basis of culture or tradition, but fails to discuss how ethno-religious plural family laws *as a system* may perpetuate gender discrimination.

In mid-2009, the CEDAW Committee started the process of developing a General Recommendation on the economic consequences of marriage and divorce. This is the first major initiative to set standards in family law in recent decades and it will be important to see whether it takes into account the human rights impact of plural legal orders.

THE RELEVANCE OF PLURAL LEGAL ORDERS TO FAMILY LAW

In every region, family matters are the area of law most likely to be governed by plural legal orders, yet they are commonly excluded, in practice, from the application of human rights standards. Has this 'state of exception' arisen because family law is somehow less important to state power? Policy discourse certainly tends to label family law as 'minor'. Typically, ADR mechanisms or non-state legal orders are permitted jurisdiction over 'minor' matters, often understood to include many aspects of family law along with petty criminal or other civil matters. However, this approach can distort human rights analysis of plural legal orders. Though maintenance disputes and at times even domestic violence are often regarded as 'minor' matters, lack of maintenance can lead to impoverishment with serious economic and social consequences, and domestic violence involves a significant threat to bodily integrity or even life. The 'minor matters' approach to family law also appears to create a distinction between 'major' and 'minor' human rights.

---

233   Macaulay, 2005, p. 110.

Additionally, family law is often 'relegated' to the private or communal sphere to be governed by religion or custom. For example, discussing the development of personal status laws in Israel, Sezgin traces how "Ben-Gurion's statist approach meant the primacy of concerns with defense and foreign affairs over such issues of 'low politics' as family, gender, education and the minor inconveniences of Sabbath and kosher observance".[234] He recalls that Ben-Gurion "explained his compromise as a question of priorities".

The relative obscurity of family law in mainstream human rights discourse contrasts with its importance to relations between the state and communities, where it becomes a matter of 'high politics'. Article 41 of Ireland's Constitution, which deals with the family, the special role of women and the sanctity of marriage, is a case in point. The family is recognised not only as the "natural primary and fundamental unit group of Society" but also as "a moral institution possessing inalienable and imprescriptible rights". The idea of family that is privileged is the patriarchal, heterosexual family. Article 41 also states that "by her life within the home, woman gives to the State a support without which the common good cannot be achieved", and places an obligation on the state to "ensure that mothers shall not be obliged by economic necessity to engage in labour to the neglect of their duties in the home".

Similarly, for communities, "women and the family often serve a crucial symbolic role in constructing group solidarity vis-à-vis society at large. ... [G]endered images of idealized womanhood become a focal point for an unprecedented spate of state vs. religion conflicts over foundational collective identity and basic citizenship questions".[235] Thus, control over family law, and by extension women's rights, is important to the power of state and non-state actors alike.[236] It is a field that is consequently highly politicised and remains the focus of demands for recognition of normative difference, especially by conservative community leaders. State recognition of demands for distinct family laws therefore needs to be seen less as a minor concession for the sake of national stability, and more as a conscious political strategy that has profound human rights implications.

As already discussed in Chapter III, India has long wrestled with the contradiction between its constitutional commitment to a uniform civil code and recognition of minority rights. In recent decades, family law has become a flashpoint for conflicts between religious extremists and secular political parties, within or outside government. In the now infamous 1985 *Shah Bano* case, the Supreme Court recognised that Muslim women had the same right to maintenance as other women and also commented that "[a] common civil code will help the

---

234   Sezgin, 2003, pp. 31-32.

235   Shachar, 2008, p. 592.

236   See Sezgin, 2003, p. 15 for a discussion of political-economic theory regarding the centrality of the family.

cause of national integration by removing disparate loyalties to laws which have conflicting ideologies".[237] The judgement was seen as inflammatory by some Orthodox sections of the Muslim community and led to violent protests, following which the Muslim Women's (Protection of Rights on Divorce) Act 1986 was enacted to overturn the effect of the judgement. The only piece of post-Independence legislation on Muslim personal law, it had the effect of denying to Muslim women a right, which they had enjoyed since colonial times (along with women of other communities) under the Criminal Procedure Code, to claim maintenance from their husbands following divorce. Since *Shah Bano*, promotion of a uniform civil code, advocated by some women's groups as a basic framework for ensuring equality in the family across all communities, has instead become a means for those aligned with the Hindu right-wing parties to attack religious minorities, and progress on family law reform for all communities has remained slow.

Family law in the context of plural legal orders is not uniquely about current demands for the recognition of cultural diversity. As already established in Chapter I, in much of Africa, Asia and the Middle East the state legal order has itself been plural since colonial times – typically where family laws are framed with reference to religion, ethnicity or culture. It is vital that analyses of plural legal orders pay sufficient attention to the human rights implications of such systems, especially where they are excluded from constitutional guarantees of non-discrimination, especially gender equality.

Of even greater immediate concern, perhaps, is the current trend towards what Shachar calls 'privatized diversity', which actually revolves not around demands to accommodate diversity within society's dominant institutions, but rather an opting out of them, an alternative to inclusion.[238] Several alternative dispute resolution programmes – justified in the name of recognition of cultural difference, or 'tradition', or because they are speedier – have in effect placed civil and family disputes that have a religious or cultural aspect outside the scope of the principle of equal citizenship. Arbitration should be of particular concern since it appears to have state approval but at the same time is a form of plurality that is least accountable to state regulation and human rights standards.

THE IMPACT OF PLURAL LEGAL ORDERS IN FAMILY LAW MATTERS

Although the rights of children and men are also negatively affected, the impact of plural legal orders in family matters falls disproportionately on women. For example, in countries with parallel family laws based on religion, including Islam, and that lack a 'neutral' civil law option, Muslim women are unable to

---

237   *Mohd. Ahmed Khan vs. Shah Bano Begum and others* AIR 1985 SC 945.

238   Shachar, 2008, p. 581.

marry non-Muslim men.[239] In Egypt, young Christian girls may be pressured into converting to Islam to circumvent age of marriage regulations.[240] Parallel family laws are often used by men to 'forum shop' to their advantage. In Sri Lanka, men married under the General Law have attempted to use conversion to Islam and the consequent right to polygamy as a means to circumvent the general law's restrictive divorce provisions.[241] Muslim men settled in Britain have attempted to use conflict of laws to avoid having to make substantial *mehr* (dower) payments on divorcing their wives.[242] In Senegal, the husband is required under the civil marriage law to state whether the marriage will be monogamous or polygamous, a choice for life. If he chooses the former but violates this by taking a second wife under religious or customary law, he may face minor criminal penalties but the second wife has no status under civil law and little protection of her rights. In Israel, a Jewish man who has not validly divorced his wife under Orthodox family laws can take a common law wife and have children by her with relatively few legal consequences. In contrast, a Jewish woman who remarries and has children without first obtaining a *get* (sanction of divorce from the husband) is seen as an adulteress and her children are labelled *mamzer* (illegitimate, and forbidden to marry a Jew for ten generations). Some Jewish husbands exploit their power to withhold the *get* to continue to dominate the lives of their former wives. In Pakistan, adultery by the husband is the main ground available for a Christian woman to seek divorce. But from 1979 to their amendment in 2006, Pakistan also had Islamised criminal laws that applied to *all* religious communities which provided for extreme punishments for sex outside of a valid marriage and for false allegations of sex outside of marriage. Divorce was in effect virtually impossible for Pakistani Christian women due to the interaction between Christian family law and Islamised criminal law.

Plural legal orders in family matters also lead to discrimination between different communities and inequality before the law. In Nigeria, several sections of the Federal Criminal Code 2004, and Section 16(2) of the Evidence Act, make discriminatory distinctions between women in customary, Muslim and Christian marriages in terms of whether or not they can institute criminal proceedings against their spouse, testify against the spouse, or be held criminally liable for conspiracy between spouses or for assisting the spouse to escape punishment.[243] All these differences stem from different concepts of marriage under various

---

239 The same does not apply to Muslim men marrying non-Muslim women (provided they are a *kitabiya* – belong to a revealed religion) since Muslim jurisprudence generally recognises such unions as valid. Malaysia is perhaps an exception, where the definition of a *kitabiya* is so restrictive as to make such marriages in practice impossible.

240 www.state.gov/g/drl/rls/irf/2003/24448.htm.

241 In Sri Lanka a long line of case law on the matter was only settled in 1996 with *Abeysundere vs. Abeysundere and Attorney General* SC Appeal No 70/96 1996.

242 *Ali vs. Ali* (1966) 1 All E.R. 897.

243 NCWD, 2005.

personal laws. In Singapore and Sri Lanka, the courts have debated whether or not Muslim couples (who are governed by parallel personal laws) have the same right to adoption available to couples from other communities. In India, until recently, only Hindus, Jains, Sikhs and Buddhists were allowed to formally adopt a child under the Hindu Adoption and Maintenance Act of 1956. Muslims, Parsis, Christians and Jews were subject to the Guardian and Wards Act of 1890, wherein the 'adoptive' parent was recognised only as the child's guardian until the age of 18.[244]

The right to marry and found a family and the right to religious freedom are also restricted by plural legal orders. For example in Israel, rabbinical authorities refuse to solemnise the marriages of individuals whose 'Jewishness' according to *Halachic* criteria is in question. Given that Israel has no civil marriage law, they are in effect banned from marrying in the country. According to some, well over 300,000 Israeli Jews are denied their most fundamental right to marry and establish a family within the country.[245] In systems where no 'neutral' civil law exists, couples may find it particularly hard to marry across religious-ethnic boundaries while retaining their right to their religious-ethnic identity.

More broadly, far from ensuring greater national harmony through recognition of diversity, in the context of rising identity politics and religious fundamentalisms, personal law regimes appear to have offered a space where lines of difference and exclusion can be hardened.

These are just some of the human rights implications of plural legal orders in the area of family and personal status law. Others appear as examples throughout this report as well as in the following chapter.

---

244   Members of all religious communities are now legally entitled to adopt under the Juvenile Justice Act of 2000 as amended subsequently.

245   Rosenblum and Tal in Sezgin, 2008, p. 11.

SUMMARY

Family law remains relatively invisible in mainstream human rights discourse even though issues of marriage, divorce, custody, inheritance etc. have long been the subject of international legal regimes, some predating the two basic human rights covenants. This is because state and non-state actors, including human rights organisations, have come to accept family law as almost exempt from "the need for globally shared legal frameworks based on cross-cultural foundations".

Meanwhile in most jurisdictions, family is the area of law most likely to be governed by plural legal orders. This arises from women's central role in reproduction and socialisation which means that control of women through the family is crucial to the preservation of collective identity.

The relative invisibility of family law in human rights discourse has contributed to the limitations and narrow interpretations of international standards as regards plural legal orders.

These limitations are especially visible where the state order provides for parallel family laws based on ethno-religious frameworks, or where non-state legal orders are incorporated into the state legal order in some form or other.

There is often an uncritical acceptance with respect to family law that rights need to be 'balanced' especially the rights of the individual *vis-à-vis* the collective; and especially the right to sex equality *vis-à-vis* religious freedom. Although the rights of children and men are also negatively affected, the impact of plural legal orders in family matters falls disproportionately on women.

VI. HUMAN RIGHTS IMPACTS OF PLURAL LEGAL ORDERS[246]

Access to justice is a basic human right which millions of people around the world do not enjoy. Are plural legal orders part of this problem, or part of its solution? Examining the real-life human rights outcomes of plural legal orders can help to resolve such questions, or can at least assist human rights advocates and policy-makers to understand where to look for answers. This said, few of the answers are easy, because additional challenges accompany every new approach.

Following on the preceding analysis of family and personal status laws, this chapter discusses in greater detail some of the human rights impacts that plural legal orders generate. These flow not just from the normative content of plural legal orders but from their structure. Though the two are admittedly not easy to separate, in some cases the structure of a plural legal order has significant human rights implications, especially for those who are disempowered.

This chapter focuses on contexts where the lines between the state and non-state legal orders are blurred and where the state legal order is itself plural. It seeks to broaden the debate by highlighting areas of rights violations that are generally given less attention in analyses of plural legal orders. The objective of this discussion is to highlight the fact that plural legal orders are structurally vulnerable to precipitating certain negative human rights outcomes and not to say that plural legal orders are always necessarily harmful; for instance, cases where non-state legal orders can have a positive influence on human rights are discussed elsewhere in the report.

DISCRIMINATION AND INEQUALITY IN LAW

Plural legal orders that are based on ethnic, religious, racial or other identities establish different standards for people with regard to the same issues or disputes. A major consequence of the subordination of rights to an identity regime is discrimination and inequality before the law. For example, in 1995 the minimum age of marriage for females in Sri Lanka was set at 18 years for all except Muslims, who are governed by the 1951 Muslim Marriage and Divorce Act (MMDA). The MMDA does not provide a clear minimum age of marriage for girls, meaning that they can be legally married at a much younger age. The Minister of Justice justified the exclusion of Muslims by referring to the need to "recognise adequately the different cultural traditions and aspirations of the Muslim community" and respect "a whole plethora of cultural traditions

---

246   Major parts of this chapter first appeared in a 2007 internal research report on parallel legal orders by Cassandra Balchin and Sohail Akbar Warraich for the International Secretariat of Amnesty International.

which enrich our land", arguing further that this position "embodies the essence of democratic traditions".[247] The Committee on the Elimination of Racial Discrimination has noted that Zimbabwe's dual legal system, in which the descendants of black people dying intestate inherit according to customary law while white people inherit according to general law, furthers racial discrimination. As a result, black women have fewer rights than white women.[248]

When the formal system excludes a geographical area from the ambit of general law, it can result in discrimination even in the enjoyment of political rights. For example, elections to Parliament by adult franchise only became possible in Pakistan's Federally Administered Tribal Areas in 1997 – a full 50 years after independence. Moreover, the members of Parliament returned from these areas have no say in legislation affecting their constituencies, since the Constitution concedes law-making powers for these areas to the President. Such plurality is not necessarily based on religion or tribal status, and can instead derive from presumptions about rural populations. In rural Mozambique, local government authorities are not democratically elected but are 'community authorities' who are administratively empowered.

Discrimination is also evident in the institutional operation of plural legal orders. In numerous countries with parallel family laws, women are excluded from acting as adjudicators in religious or customary courts, which have jurisdiction to apply such laws, whereas they may preside over courts hearing other civil or criminal law cases.

IMPLICATIONS FOR FREEDOM OF RELIGION AND BELIEF

In identity-based plural legal regimes a person's identity must be determined prior to determining the rights or remedies available to her. This process has significant social, political and legal implications and also bestows substantial power on those who preside over it. In Israel, for instance, a fusion of ritual power and judicial authority (in key civil matters) means that defining community boundaries is almost entirely in the hands of religious authorities such as the Orthodox Rabbinate. In consequence, those Jews whose 'Jewishness' according to Orthodox *Halachic* rules is in doubt (such as those who have migrated to Israel from Russia) are unable to access a full range of rights to marriage and family, in violation of international law. Similarly, following the 1974 Ordinance declaring Ahmedis in Pakistan to be 'non-Muslim', and in the absence of any general civil marriage law, case law has not decided under what law Ahmedis can be married or even whether marriages concluded before 1974 are governed by the Muslim Family Laws Ordinance (1961).

---

247   Sri Lanka, Hansard, vol. 101, no. 2, 20 September 1995, pp. 209-210.

248   Zimbabwe 28/03/96. CERD/C/304/Add.3, para. 13.

In Indonesia, interreligious couples have great difficulty finding a religious official willing to perform an interfaith marriage ceremony, yet a religious ceremony is required before a marriage is registered. As a result, some are forced to convert solely in order to marry.[249] Moreover, under Law No. 5/1969, the Indonesian government recognises only six religions (Islam, Catholicism, Protestantism, Buddhism, Hinduism and Confucianism[250]). Other spiritual traditions, such as animists and Baha'is, or indeed atheists, therefore find it impossible to register their marriages or their children's births because a recognised religion must be specified at the time of registration.[251] Apart from violating international standards on freedom of religion and belief, this violates Article 2 of the CRC, which prohibits discrimination against a child because of parents' religious identity, and Article 7 which guarantees children the right to an identity, including registration after birth.

JURISDICTIONAL CONFUSION, IMPUNITY AND LACK OF ACCOUNTABILITY

Plural legal orders provide wide scope for confusion over jurisdiction and the application of law. This is aggravated when mechanisms for addressing such uncertainties, never easy to design, remain unclear. In such cases, even constitutional protections may be inaccessible. Worse, they can increase litigants' costs, lead to abuse of power, weak law enforcement and impunity.

In the United States, the administration of criminal justice with respect to Native Americans is divided between Native American authorities, and State and Federal agencies, depending on the identity of the persons involved and the place and nature of the offence. In a 2007 report, Amnesty International noted that this jurisdictional maze creates conditions in which non-Native American men often have virtual impunity when they commit crimes such as rape against a Native American woman on tribal lands.[252] A similar problem occurs in Latin American Special Jurisdictions, where crimes committed by non-indigenous individuals in indigenous territories "usually result in no reparation at all", because the accused can claim not to be subject to the jurisdiction of the indigenous system but may also remain beyond the reach of the state.[253]

Native Americans in the United States also have weaker civil rights guarantees and protections with respect to their indigenous authorities than other citizens

---

249 www.state.gov/g/drl/rls/irf/2005/51512.htm.

250 Confucianism was added in 2000 by presidential decree No. 6/2000.

251 www.state.gov/g/drl/rls/irf/2005/51512.htm. In 1980 the Indonesian Council of Ulamas issued a *fatwa* declaring that Ahmadiyyah is not a legitimate form of Islam; so members of this sect face similar problems.

252 Amnesty International, 2007.

253 Yrigoyen Fajardo, 2004, p. 41.

of the United States enjoy with respect to the government. This is because, in *Santa Clara Pueblo vs. Martinez*,[254] the Supreme Court ruled that, under the 1968 Indian Civil Rights Act, Native American authorities were immune from suits in Federal courts.[255] The case was the result of a sex discrimination suit brought by a woman of the Santa Clara Pueblo against an ordinance passed by the Governor of Santa Clara. This Ordinance denied "membership in the tribe to children of female members who marry outside the tribe, while extending membership to children of male members who marry outside the tribe". The decision regarding jurisdiction meant that the sex discrimination aspect of the case was never heard on merit.

Indigenous people in countries with Special Indigenous Jurisdictions in Latin America frequently confront the problem of jurisdictional complexity. Questions of personal competence – who is governed by the Special Indigenous Jurisdiction – can be difficult to ascertain given that "in almost every country the communities are mixed, the migration rates are high and the inter-ethnic relations are frequent and complex".[256] The plural legal order that developed as a result of Colombia's Special Indigenous Jurisdiction has also resulted in conflicts over institutional jurisdiction and hierarchy. These have been exacerbated by the absence of systematic rules governing the establishment of jurisdiction, and seniority and authority in decision-making.[257]

In Pakistan, jurisdictional grey areas generated by different laws covering the same offences mean that police and magistrates have considerable power to decide whether a case is registered under Islamic or general penal provisions, making possible significantly different human rights outcomes.[258] Inevitably, allegations of corruption surface in this process. Indeed, even those who advocate legal plurality acknowledge the potential for corruption.[259]

Further, the scope of Pakistan's *musalihat anjuman* is not clearly defined, leading apparently to extensive encroachment on the formal system, especially in family law matters and cases of violence against women. In some contexts, problems

---

254   *Santa Clara Pueblo vs. Martinez*, 436 U.S. 49 (1978).

255   With the exception of cases seeking *habeas* relief in the context of alleged illegal detention by Native American authorities.

256   Yrigoyen Fajardo, 2004, p. 41.

257   Ibid.

258   A famous 1980s case in Pakistan involved the theft of a clock from a mosque. If the mosque was considered a 'closed place', then the case was to be heard under the Hudood Ordinances (1979) with extreme *hadd* punishments (amputation) possible and a different line of appeal available; otherwise the case was to be heard under the Pakistan Penal Code, with lighter possible sentences and ordinary lines of appeal.

259   Byrne *et al.*, 2007, p. 8.

arise because of overlaps in the membership of adjudicating bodies belonging to various legal orders. In eastern Tibet, official structures and tribal authorities largely coincide in some matters.[260] In a similar manner, in Bangladesh, chairmen of the local government head both ADR-style Conciliation Courts[261] and Arbitration Councils constituted under the Muslim Family Laws Ordinance (1961) (MFLO), with the result that it is frequently presumed that they have additional authority to adjudicate family matters, beyond the powers conferred under the MFLO Rules. Also in Bangladesh, the fact that some individuals are members of both formally-recognised *shalishes* and traditional *shalishes* has the result that they preside over matters such as sexual misconduct which are not part of the former's jurisdiction. In all the above cases, the overlapping membership of adjudicators or mediators can confuse them, and users, both about which office an individual is representing, and the terms of reference and jurisdiction of that office.

Justices of the Peace in Peru are unsalaried lay magistrates, elected by the community, with limited jurisdiction over matters such as debt, misdemeanours, alimony and certain cases of domestic violence. They often exceed their jurisdiction at the demand of local communities.[262] At the other end of the spectrum, some *rondas campesinas* members in Peru have been sentenced for usurping state authority (although acquitted on appeal), which demonstrates "the lack of intercultural procedural mechanisms for settling alleged excesses or possible violation of individual rights by the special indigenous community or patrol jurisdiction".[263]

Customary laws, whether applied by a formal or informal system, tend to be uncodified and rich in variation, even within the same ethnic group, which often generates inconsistent and confusing outcomes.[264] In Nigeria, customary laws "vary widely among different groups and are usually ambiguous in nature. They are consequently prone to subjective interpretation, inconsistent and circumstantial in their application".[265] While flexibility in law can be useful,

---

260 Pirie, 2005.

261 Although the Conciliation Courts are no longer functional, the laws establishing them have not been repealed nor has their status been clarified. The result is that many people presume they still exist or refer to later ADR-style arrangements as 'Conciliation Courts' as this is the terminology they are familiar with.

262 Faundez, 2003.

263 Stavenhagen, 2006, p. 11.

264 It is acknowledged that on its own, codification is not a guarantee of rights. While feminists in the Gulf States are currently demanding codification of family laws as a means to end uncertainties about their rights, for example, socially secure women in some northern Nigerian communities (like the Fulani and some Hausa) prefer Muslim laws to remain uncodified because they fear that codification would strengthen homogenising regressive trends in Muslim laws.

265 NCWD, 2005, p. 62.

as Amnesty International has noted, "unpredictability in the law can foster arbitrariness and injustice".[266] Within the formal system too, multiple laws governing the same issue can deny individuals the right to effective remedy when it is unclear whether federal or State-level law, or customary law, is superior. For example, Sections 21 and 22 of Nigeria's Child Rights Act (2003) void early marriage and fix the minimum age of marriage at 18 years, although the Act is silent on the status of children arising out of a child marriage. This contrasts with the Infants Law in Sokoto, Zamfara and Kaduna States, which "encourage child marriage and infant marriage settlements".[267]

UNDERMINING ACCESS TO JUSTICE AND DILUTING DUE PROCESS

The continued failures of formal systems of justice – their delays, procedural complications and the many problems of access they present for poor and marginalised groups in particular – are often advanced to justify the introduction or recognition of parallel regimes of alternative dispute resolution, or other forms of decentralisation of the justice sector. While the weaknesses of the formal system are indeed real, such measures often bring significant problems of their own.

Evidence suggests that decentralisation can operate *against* choice of forum and that introducing plurality may actually restrict access to justice. In Kyrgyzstan, citizens' options to apply to a legal institution of their choice have been reduced.[268] Since the police or courts now send issues regarded as 'minor' directly to the local *aksakal* court, without the consent of the claimants, people are forced to engage first of all with this institution if they want to have their cases considered by official organs at all.

India's *lok adalats* ADR mechanism illustrates how the presence of such an alternative can undermine the formal court system and access to justice through that system. Galanter and Krishnan suggest that the *lok adalat* system diminishes the supply of precedents and impede the development of tort doctrine and expertise responsive to India's new industrialised economy. They

---

266   Amnesty International, 2005b, p. 15.

267   NCWD, 2005, p. 56. Many other examples could be mentioned. Under Nigerian customary law, the minimum age of marriage is puberty. How this is assessed varies but the age set is generally 12 years for girls and 14 for boys. Numerous State-level laws exist, with different names and a slightly different purpose (the Withdrawal of Girls from School Act, the Child Marriage Act, the Age of Marriage Act, etc.). The Criminal Code in force in the Southern States prescribes 16 as the minimum age but exempts from criminal offence any man marrying under customary law (Amnesty International, 2005b, p. 25), while according to the NCWD, the Age of Marriage Law (Eastern Region,1956) provides for the annulment, with criminal penalties, of marriages concluded under the age of 16 (NCWD, 2005).

268   Beyer, 2007, p. 9 and comments at ICHRP Workshop.

also "consume scarce resources of money, personnel, attention, and energy. To persist on the *Lok Adalat* track without critical examination of its costs and alternatives strikes us as manifesting all unwarranted pessimism about the possibilities for court reform that truly enhances access to justice".[269]

Elsewhere, although the UN Capital Development Fund asserts that "Uganda has become a 'flagship' country for decentralization programmes in the Southern and Eastern Africa Region", others are deeply sceptical, warning that decentralisation in Africa "has produced more ambiguous results than its proponents suggest", and characterised Uganda as a case of "decentralization *without* human rights".[270] In Sierra Leone, staff at Local Courts (which apply customary law) lack training in the provisions of the Local Court Act of 1963, while their poor conditions of service have resulted in a 'pay oneself attitude'.[271]

Non-state legal orders that gain some form of recognition by the state system raise particular concerns regarding due process and procedural aspects that in effect threaten to limit access to justice. For example, in India the governing Legal Services Authorities Act of 1987 (amended in 1994 and again in 2002) permits *lok adalats* jurisdiction over "any matter" (S.19(3)), and allows them to devise their own procedures (S.22(2)), merely "guided by the principles of justice, equity, fairplay and other legal principles" (S.20(4)). As Galanter and Krishnan point out, rather than award in accordance with the law, the *lok adalat* is instructed to "arrive at a compromise or settlement" (S.20(3)) which, following the 1994 amendment, "shall be final and binding on all the parties to the dispute, and no appeal shall lie to any court against the award" (S.21(2)). In parallel, amendments in 2002 to the Indian Civil Procedure Code can be seen as allowing state courts to transfer a case to *lok adalats* without the consent of the parties, while Section 22D of the Legal Services Authority Act allows a *lok adalat* to rule on the merit of a case without the agreement of the parties.[272] The procedure was criticised by the Indian Bar Council and led to a major lawyers strike in 2002: it is far from resembling the model of consensual arbitration in minor matters that is usually supposed to characterise such structures.

Overall, ADR mechanisms currently being introduced under legal reform and access to justice programmes or through state recognition of non-state legal orders raise particular concerns regarding their contribution to improvements in access to justice. In Fiji, law enforcement officers have encouraged the use of *bulubulu* in addressing rape cases, which shifts responsibility from the offender to the kin group. This can undermine the individual rights of the

---

269   Galanter and Krishnan, 2004, pp. 807 and 829-830.

270   Oloka-Onyango, 2007, p. 2.

271   Amnesty International, 2006, p. 7.

272   Galanter and Krishnan, 2004.

victim to redress or compensation.[273] In Canada's Ontario province, and in Britain and elsewhere, the recognition of religious arbitration in family matters and other 'minor' civil matters has been resisted by several sections of civil society because it might provide a legal cloak to privatised justice, outside the framework of standard constitutional and human rights protections. In Afghanistan, where state courts rarely exercise their right to review privately arbitrated agreements (especially those involving marital disputes), and where customary law regarding women's rights in marriage is highly discriminatory, one Civil Law Officer (an official who has the responsibility to decide whether a case goes to court or mediation) admitted that, whereas 60% of cases should have gone to court, he sent only 20% and the remainder went to mediation.[274] Macaulay has examined in detail the justice outcomes both where the state recognises non-state legal orders (such as *rondas campesinas*) and where the state sponsors ADR-style conciliation (as in Brazil's Special Criminal Courts designed to fast-track domestic violence cases).[275] The *rondas* usually respond by securing a promise from the husband to stop the violence and from the wife to meet her household duties, implying acceptance of some fault on her part.[276] In Brazil's Special Criminal Courts, the majority of cases (90%) end at the first stage of conciliation, either because the woman is intimidated by the presence in court of her abuser, or because the judge has pressed forcefully for both sides to conciliate and to close the case.[277]

OBSTACLES TO EFFECTIVE DEVELOPMENT OF MINORITY RIGHTS

Separate civil law regimes for minorities can render substantive and institutional problems within these regimes invisible or so 'politically sensitive' that reform becomes very difficult. This is what happened in the case of Muslims in India, when the Supreme Court affirmed the equal right of Muslim women to maintenance (as discussed earlier above).

Indeed, where pluralities within the formal legal order are based on identity, removal of discriminatory content is often more difficult than when the system is unitary. For example, Section 55 (1)(d) of the Penal Code of Northern Nigeria actually permits wife-beating (termed the husband 'correcting his

---

273   Merry, 2006, pp. 123-124.

274   Barfield, 2006.

275   Macaulay, 2005.

276   Ibid., p. 17. Similarly, women in two *barrios* of Bogota, Colombia, especially resent the ideology of conciliation promoted by *Casas de Justicia* because they reaffirmed patriarchal patterns of domination. They claim, for example, that *Casas de Justicia* generally encourage female victims of domestic violence to continue living with their male partners who, for the sake of promoting harmony, are never punished: García in Faundez, 2003, p. 46.

277   Campos in Macaulay, 2005.

wife') in case the husband or wife is "subject to any native law or custom in which such correction is recognized as lawful".[278] Certain women therefore suffer discrimination both with regard to men, and with regard to women who are subject to other laws. Moreover, when discrimination is given a veneer of cultural legitimacy, reformers within a community often face the powerful threat of social ostracism or excommunication.

Separate legal orders for minorities can exclude them from the general development of standards and institutions. What may begin as an enabling initiative (recognising religious, ethnic or indigenous diversity) can have the effect of limiting rights. In the Gulf Co-operation Council (GCC) countries, a multiplicity of systems has allowed minority law to remain less developed and largely uncodified, which can "often lead to confusion regarding the rights of individuals and to a general lack of cohesion and standardization of rights".[279]

Sri Lanka's Muslim Marriage and Divorce Act (1951) gave Quazi Courts exclusive jurisdiction in financial matters relating to marriage (maintenance, recovery of *mehr*, and customary *kaikuli*) but no power to enforce decisions. To secure the execution of Quazi Court decisions, a woman has to turn to the ordinary courts. Finally, all monies recovered are paid to the Quazi, to be transferred onwards to the wife, which adds a further layer to the proceedings. As a result, Muslim women are obliged to litigate in multiple forums, multiplying their costs and the time required to secure justice. Moreover, Quazis are required only to be 'of good character' and do not need any formal legal training. In reviewing one case that illustrates their operational problems, the Board of Quazis noted that the case had been improperly adjudicated, that the issues were not properly framed, that inadmissible and irrelevant evidence was admitted, that procedure was not followed strictly, and that even the law was misapplied.[280]

In the Philippines, the PILIPINA Legal Resources Centre has highlighted gross under-resourcing of the Shari'ah Court system. In some instances, the court had no telephone, no court sheriff and employees shared the electricity bills.[281] Such under-resourcing is familiar to some Native American tribal authorities.[282] In short, in the name of ethnic, religious and indigenous freedoms, states may be neglecting (by design or default) their due diligence responsibilities.

---

278   Sec.55(1)(d) "Nothing is an offence which does not amount to infliction of grievous bodily harm hurt upon any person and which is done by a husband for the purpose of correcting his wife, such husband or wife being subject to any native law or custom in which such correction is recognized as lawful".

279   Amnesty International, 2005a.

280   *Thahir vs. Gani Noor*, 1954 4 MMDR 51.

281   Solamo-Antonio, 2003, pp. 51-52.

282   Amnesty International, 2007.

Reinforcement of Socio-Economic Inequalities

Plural legal orders are often complex to navigate, and understanding their jurisdiction, procedures, and the rights and liabilities they confer, is made even more challenging by the web of inter and intrainstitutional variations in rules and practices. Where social, political and economic disparities are wide, this complexity can greatly disadvantage those who are poor or otherwise marginalised, and can privilege those who are well-informed and better-off. As Odinkalu notes, this affords "the dominant indigenous elites of Africa a choice in both the forum and location of the justice process ... [It is] possible, for instance, for a powerful man to implausibly accept marital equality (under civil law) and reject gender equality (pleading customary law)".[283]

In post-conflict situations, where the lines between customary and formal legal norms are often blurred, leaders and elites are better positioned to leverage plural legal orders to their advantage because of their access to information and authority. For example, land rights and the wealth and power associated with them often accrue to people who are positioned to take them by force, or who profit from post-conflict reconstruction programmes.[284] Le Sage provides an eloquent description of the jurisdictional confusion that arises from the extreme plurality operating in Somalia: "[A]midst this confusion, the choice of applicable law in any given case is largely driven by two factors: first, where the self-interest of the stronger party to the dispute is served; and second, how a decision that will preserve security and peaceful inter-clan relations can be reached. These factors have limited the equality of all Somali citizens before the law, as well as the degree of protection that the legal system can offer on a personal basis, particularly when powerful clans, politicians or businessmen exercise direct influence over how cases are decided."[285]

Sieder notes that current trends to privatise, fragment and decentralise law enlarge the space for local autonomy on one hand, but on the other often aggravate existing inequalities and social exclusion.[286] She also warns that, where a (usually externally promoted) 'rule of law' emphasis officially sanctions 'semi-autonomous spheres' but fails to incorporate human rights concerns, the effect may be to encourage vigilantism by the powerful and ultimately generate a more fragmented and weaker rule of law.[287]

---

283   Odinkalu, 2006, pp. 157-158.

284   Lastarria-Cornhiel, 2005, p. 9.

285   Le Sage, 2005, p. 7.

286   Sieder, 2008, p. 21 (page number as in manuscript on file).

287   Ibid.

In Aceh, it is mostly the poor who are bound by the local Islamic legal system while the elite are able to negotiate between the local and national system.[288] Similarly, the support of indigenous elites for greater recognition of indigenous rights in Latin America cannot be divorced from the fact that they are often in a much better position to leverage such recognition to their own advantage.[289]

India's *lok adalat* system was widely seen as an initiative to take justice to the poor; but it seems rather to have been a case of poor justice. Galanter and Krishnan show that "many of the groups affected by the reform see in the compromise-oriented procedural rules a weakening of their rights guaranteed by the state. Those who are assumed to 'be' traditional do not accept the retraditionalisation of judicial procedures".[290] One study found that *lok adalats* that handled motor accident claims against large insurance or transport companies often organised their case load so that all cases against the same company came before the same panel – clearly a more convenient arrangement for the defendants.[291] Awards averaged Rs 14,758, compared to an average of Rs 48,376 in cases pursued through the courts.[292] Significantly, state-sponsored alternative forums already exist precisely for such claims: the Motor Accident Claims Tribunals were established to provide expeditious court hearings, free of fees, without a showing of fault; and the Arbitration and Conciliation Ordinance (1996) was designed to handle large claims involving large sums of money. This led Galanter and Krishnan to question the state's motives in promoting the *lok adalat* structure, which the Indian government has repeatedly legislated to confirm and strengthen, without proper monitoring or a participatory review.[293] In effect, *lok adalats* do not claim to deliver superior justice but merely deliverance from the problems of the formal system. At issue is the cost-benefit balance of using this alternative system – a balance that works differently for the socially disadvantaged. "[T]hose who are risk averse and unable to finance protracted litigation are the ones who have to give the discounts in order to escape these costs; those who occupy the strategic heights in the litigation battle are able to command steep discounts."[294]

Finally, when a state regulates matters that were previously left to the customary sphere, it can limit the rights of those who have a weaker public voice. For women in Rwanda, access to land was historically guaranteed through customary channels, even though actual ownership was customarily limited.

---

288   Siahaan, 2006.

289   Faundez, 2003; Itturalde, 1995; Sieder, 2008.

290   Galanter and Krishnan in Benda-Beckmann *et al.*, 2002-2003, p. 300.

291   Galanter and Krishnan, 2004, p. 802.

292   Ibid.

293   Ibid., p. 804.

294   Ibid., p. 809.

More recent formal titling and registration processes have been based upon state recognition of customary *laws* (which expressly exclude women from owning land) that trump customary *practice* (which allowed women a measure of access). Whereas women effectively lost a right they had, men gained a *new* right: the right to go before the formal apparatus of the state and trump informal claims to land.[295]

THE POLITICAL IMPLICATIONS OF LEGAL PLURALITY

The preceding discussion indicates clearly that plural legal systems are inextricably linked to a range of political claims and state practices that have significant human rights dimensions. Debates and conflicts regarding recognition of customary or religious law and the relative standing of different forums within a plural legal context can determine the contours of the justice system, to the detriment of human rights, often disadvantaging women.

When differences are recognised through legal plurality, the outcomes can cut both ways. In Syria, "legal pluralism in family law can be said to contribute to, and strengthen, the survival of Christian religious minorities. Yet, at the same time, legal pluralism contributes to, and strengthens, the boundaries between religious groups. These boundaries, furthermore, function in an unequal manner, both in terms of gender and in terms of religious affiliation. Men and women are not equally free to choose a spouse from another religious community. Muslim men are furthermore in a legally stronger position than Christian men".[296] The rigid boundaries that can result from identity-based laws can amount to a segregation that may strengthen socially and politically conservative identity-based politics, including religious fundamentalisms, and undermine human rights. In Pakistan, the establishment of the Federal Shariat Court (FSC) in 1980, with powers to examine laws for conformity with the injunctions of Islam, created uncertainty over the relative standing of the superior courts (FSC, High Court and Supreme Court), especially in relation to interpretation of laws involving reference to Islam and fundamental rights. This uncertainty compounded national political clashes regarding the supreme source of law, and disputes over several human rights matters (the rights of women especially relating to divorce, the rights of religious minorities, etc.), and rendered these arguments more vulnerable to swings in the national political mood.[297]

Kyed and Buur note in the context of Africa that: "[W]hen the justification for bolstering the role of traditional leaders is based on their legitimacy as acting in

---

295   Gray and Kevane, 1999, p. 24.

296   Rabo, 2005.

297   The dispute was particularly intense until 1992 when a five-member bench of the Supreme Court settled the matter in *Hakim Khan vs. Federation of Pakistan* PLD 1992 SC 595. See Warraich, 2004.

the name of discrete, self-contained local communities, there seems to be little scope for the development of an autonomous space."[298] At times, plurality in the formal legal system, or the recognition of non-state legal orders, can contribute to national political instability, prejudicing the realisation of human rights. For example, where a dominant ethnic group's customary law is recognised, it can serve to extend ethnic hegemony and exacerbate national conflict.[299] The recognition of African chiefs has had impacts far beyond the legal sphere, most notably in the political arena and on the distribution of resources. The recognition and strengthening of traditional leaders (mostly by donor agencies) in Malawi has actually undermined democratically elected local leaders,[300] while in South Africa the failure to demarcate clearly the powers and duties of elected councillors from those of traditional leaders has created numerous local conflicts.[301] The unquestioning recognition of traditional leaders in programmes to extend democracy or rule of law as representatives of their communities "actually reproduces rural populations as dependent subjects rather than as citizens capable of articulating political demands".[302] As a result, state recognition of traditional authority can "limit, rather than foster, the emergence of liberal civil society in the sense of groups of active citizens participating in politics and development".[303]

---

298   Kyed and Buur, 2007, p. 20.

299   Kimathi, 2005, p. 9.

300   Kyed and Buur, 2007, p. 14.

301   Tshehla in Kyed and Buur, 2007.

302   Kyed and Buur, 2007, p. 20.

303   Ibid., p. 12. For instance, President Museveni has used Uganda's decentralisation programme to dispense patronage and thereby splinter challenges to central government control (Oloka-Onyango, 2007, p. 6), while in Zimbabwe decentralisation has been exploited to bolster the monopoly of the ruling party, and in Mozambique to justify a decision not to expand locally democracy to the rural areas (Kyed and Buur, 2007, p. 9).

SUMMARY

Plural legal orders based on ethnic, religious or other identities establish different standards with regard to the same issues or disputes. A major consequence of the subordination of rights to an identity regime can be discrimination and inequality before the law, both among and between those subject to the various laws.

An identity-based regime can limit freedom of religion or belief, and often discriminates against those who do not fall within the neat categories it recognises (such as atheists, mixed marriages or the adopted). They also bestow substantial power on those who determine identity.

Plural legal orders provide wide scope for confusion over personal and subject matter jurisdiction and the application of law. This is aggravated when mechanisms for addressing such uncertainties, never easy to design, remain unclear. In such cases, even constitutional protections may be inaccessible. Through such confusion, plural legal orders can increase litigants' costs, lead to abuse of power, weak law enforcement, and impunity.

The jurisdictional and procedural complexity underlying plural legal orders can greatly disadvantage those who are poor and otherwise marginalised, and reinforce socio-economic inequality.

While the weaknesses of the formal system are indeed real, non-state legal orders that gain some form of recognition by the state or ADR mechanisms raise particular concerns regarding dilution of due process and procedural aspects that in effect limit access to justice and violate human rights.

Separate civil law regimes for minorities can render substantive and institutional problems within these regimes invisible or so 'politically sensitive' that reform eventually becomes very difficult.

State recognition of non-state legal orders can undermine democratic processes by conferring greater power on unelected leaders and reinforcing hegemonic or majoritarian interpretations of custom. Identity-based laws can segregate society in ways that may strengthen ethnic and religious fundamentalisms, and thereby undermine plurality.

PART THREE

POLICY CHALLENGES POSED BY PLURAL LEGAL ORDERS

VII. PLURALITY AND THE ROLE OF THE STATE – RECOGNITION, INCORPORATION AND DECENTRALISATION

This chapter examines some of the conceptual and practical challenges involved in policy-making and human rights analysis that arise when a non-state legal order becomes, or seeks to become, part of a state legal order. Such a situation can occur as a result of decentralisation;[304] incorporation of a non-state legal order; or recognition of a claim for the law to reflect cultural diversity.

Though decentralisation and recognition of claims to cultural diversity are indeed distinct and are therefore analysed separately, this project finds that a set of issues are shared by both – and that highlighting these commonalities can strengthen human rights analysis of plural legal orders. Shared issues include: the use of multiple terms with diverse meanings; the dilemma as to whether entering the state order facilitates the survival and healthy development of a non-state order or ossifies it; the political questions, of who 'speaks for' any given community, and how the boundaries of any cultural group (ethnic, indigenous, religious) are defined; and the need to examine the state's motivations behind its relationship with non-state orders. For both, finally, questions arise concerning the degree to which a non-state legal order is granted sovereignty and authority. In many ways, the debate about plural orders is "really a debate about the state of the state today, one that asks where power actually resides".[305] This chapter discusses these issues and in several instances draws upon local case law for illustrations.

Despite the commonalities, identity-based claims to recognition of cultural diversity are given particular attention in the final section of the chapter, because they are a major force driving the development of plural legal orders. Points raised include questioning exactly what 'culture' is in the context of recognition of diversity.

RECOGNITION, INCORPORATION AND DECENTRALISATION: TERMS AND MEANINGS

In developing a human rights analysis of the relationship between the state and non-state legal orders, a major challenge is that the lines between them are

---

304 Decentralisation is used here to refer to contexts in which governance-administrative decentralisation is accompanied by devolution of certain judicial powers. Typically this would mean the coupling of administrative and judicial functions at the level of local self-government bodies.

305 Moore, 2001, p. 11.

blurred and power flows both ways between them (see Chapter IV). Another is that a wide variety of terms are used and analysts differ on how they should be understood. Several studies suggest, some usefully, how various forms of recognition and incorporation can be categorised and named.[306] Overall, however, the task of categorising can divert attention from human rights advocacy concerns. Moreover, as with most categorisation, actual recognition or incorporation arrangements, when examined in detail, rarely fit the categories neatly. Exceptions rather than matches tend to be the rule.

There is no consensus about what 'recognition of customary or religious laws' means in practical terms. The Australian Legal Reform Commission provides a good example of the daunting range of recognition options available to states when they are confronted by specific issues of legal pluralism. On the question of recognising traditional marriage, the Commission outlines the following possible policy options:

- To enforce Aboriginal customary marriage rules under the general law;

- To equate Aboriginal customary marriage to *de facto* relationships;

- To recognise traditional marriage as 'marriage' for all purposes of Australian law;

- To equate traditional marriages with 'marriage' under the general law for particular purposes only.[307]

At one level, a normative order does not need to enjoy state recognition as 'law' if it exists as a *social fact* for the people whose lives it regulates. In other cases, the state may acknowledge that a body of norms is 'law' as a matter of fact, but may not enforce the norms in question. Examples include rules in the private spheres of a church or association, or the reference in Australian native title jurisprudence to 'traditional law', which exists as a determination of fact but is not subject to common law recognition.[308]

Alternatively, states may incorporate some or all of their norms into the state legal system. Examples of formally-enacted state law that incorporates normative plurality may be found in all regions. At a minimum, incorporation entails acknowledgement of, and giving effect to, a non-state legal order's *outputs* – i.e., its 'laws';[309] it may extend to acknowledging the non-state legal order's *processes* of generating laws (discussed later).

---

306   See for example the far-reaching study of the Australian Law Reform Commission, 1986. See also Michaels, 2005; Sezgin, 2004, 2008.

307   ALRC, para. 254, vol. 1.

308   McLaughlin, 1996.

309   Gover, 2008a, p. 6.

Incorporation is operationalised in various ways, as some of the examples below illustrate:

- The state occasionally incorporates selected substantive principles or normative practices of a non-state legal order into the state's legal system. For instance, British courts have recognised Sikh traditions regarding the naming of children.[310] South African courts appear to have taken a similar position with respect to witchcraft. Though witchcraft is illegal, they have accepted that genuine fear of witchcraft is an extenuating circumstance, and on these grounds may mitigate murder to culpable homicide.[311]

- The state may incorporate the substantive principles or normative practices of a non-state legal order in specific subject areas (usually family and property laws). In India, judges in the unified state court system can hear personal status issues under various religious and personal codes (some officially codified and some not), depending upon the law governing the parties involved. In Britain, marriage laws combine elements of Christian canon and secularised law as well as formally recognising aspects of Jewish and Quaker marriage laws.

- The state may grant social groups or communities a private legal space, a process sometimes referred to as 'deference'. Examples include religion-based arbitration in family matters, or *lex mercatoria* used to arbitrate banking disputes. Such private ordering enters the substantive law of the state – or is incorporated – at the time of enforcement (i.e., when a state court upholds a privately arbitrated agreement). The private legal space is subordinate to state law in that it can only fill the space that the state legal system leaves open to it. The decision to grant such a space does not derive from the community's sovereignty but from the state's decision that such recognition is appropriate.

- In another variation of incorporation, the state not only accepts plural norms (again, usually in family and related property matters) but also the adjudicative forums that are associated with them. Recognition of a non-state order's adjudicative forums may appear to entail delegation by the state of legal self-regulation to a social group or community. But the extent to which states actually permit or require a group to self-regulate can vary enormously. For example, states may intervene to outlaw a specific practice, as in Israel's ban on *talaq* (unilateral divorce initiated by a Muslim husband), or may control judicial appointments and the functioning of a community's adjudicative forums through state budgets. African Chieftaincy courts may be restricted in the types of cases they are allowed to handle (only traditional and social cases in Mozambique), the amount of damages/compensation they are allowed to enforce (Zimbabwe), or the severity of the cases they are allowed to handle (only petty crimes in Zambia).

---

310   *Re S. (change of names: cultural factors)* 15 May 2001, [2001] 2 FLR 1005.

311   Ludsin, 2003, pp. 92-93.

- On the other hand, the Constitutional and legal reforms that established Special Indigenous Jurisdiction in Colombia, and to varying extents in other Latin American countries, translate into a high degree of normative and institutional integration of indigenous justice into the formal legal system. In essence, Colombian law recognises indigenous communities and their law as *sui generis*. In Tanzania and Kenya for example, customary law is exempt from having to conform to the standards set out in the Constitution.

Like 'incorporation', the term 'decentralisation' covers a wide range of possibilities. Oloka-Onyango distinguishes between decentralisation as *deconcentration* (some power is given over but remains under tight central control); *delegation* (power is handed over but can be recalled at any moment); and *devolution* (involving a greater and more permanent relinquishment of power).[312] Although largely an administrative measure or a governance arrangement, decentralisation, when presumed to be a metaphor for normative plurality, can become the basis for legal plurality. An example of decentralisation entails the dovetailing of non-state legal orders into lower levels of the formal judicial system, as in the case of Uganda's Local Council Courts. Here, traditional or customary chiefs' courts have been incorporated into the formal legal system and given limited powers to address certain kinds of cases.

From the human rights perspective, each variation of incorporation, recognition and decentralisation in the examples mentioned above would need to be evaluated for its impact on human rights. This is clearly an enormously complex task, especially because human rights policy recommendations to states need to consider the specific manner in which legal plurality is recognised, in its context.

National constitutions are central to understanding the relationship between human rights, recognition and plural legal orders for two reasons: first, because they often outline how far a recognised legal order is subject to fundamental rights provisions; and second, because they indicate how far the state has recognised the 'laws' or *outputs* of a non-state legal order, as well as the authority and autonomy of the *processes* by which the non-state legal order produces its laws.

Where any substantive part of a constitution provides for the right of members of an ethnic or religious community to order their lives in accordance with their customary or religious laws, it recognises the fact of legal plurality. The question then is what conditions, if any, are attached to its operation. Is the entity autonomous, or subject to the constitution and the constitution's fundamental rights provisions (to a 'repugnancy clause' for example)? Sierra Leone exempts matters relating to adoption, marriage, divorce, burial, devolution of property on death, and other interests of personal and customary law, from the purview

---

312   Oloka-Onyango, 2007, pp. 6-7.

of its non-discrimination provisions.[313] In the United States, through the Indian Civil Rights Act (1968), "Congress selectively has derived essential civil rights protections from the Bill of Rights and applied them to Indian tribes",[314] and rendered Native American authorities immune from suits in federal courts with the exception of cases involving illegal detention.[315] In contrast, South Africa's 1996 Constitution recognises customary law, but only in so far as it is not contrary to statutory law, constitutional standards or any legislation that specifically deals with customary law.[316]

Apart from the variable extent to which the state theoretically acknowledges the autonomy of non-state legal orders in generating legal norms, the extent to which it accepts in practice that non-state legal orders are beyond the scope of the state order also varies. In Sudan since 1983, as well as in Malaysia and Indonesia in the past decade, the powers of the civil system to influence decisions by religious courts has been considerably reduced in practice. This has resulted from changes in the legal system, but is also because superior court civil judges have been increasingly unwilling to preside over appeals against decisions of religious courts when the civil judge is from a religious background different to the religion in question.

It is important to note that, abstracted from its operational detail, incorporation *per se* does not necessarily have positive or negative human rights outcomes. A few points illustrate this. First, if the recognition of the non-state legal order may initially be seen to imply that the state has incorporated non-state norms into state law, in some instances the state in question may in fact be reaffirming its monopoly on the production of legal norms and taming non-state law by co-opting it. As a result, ironically, both progressive human rights advocates and the most extreme advocates of identity politics may find themselves opposing state recognition – one because recognition accords too much weight to non-state norms, the other because it entails too much state control. Second, recognition may have paradoxical outcomes. In Mexico, "expert anthropological testimony – originally conceived as a tool for the defence of groups especially vulnerable to the blindness of national law to cultural differences – has become a weapon wielded by powerful elites to protect their wider interests". In one case, such

---

313   Chapter III, Section 27(4)(d) and (e). Similar provisions in the Zambian and Zimbabwean Constitutions exempt customary law from conformity with constitutional standards, including non-discrimination clauses.

314   Executive Memorandum, Department of Justice Policy on Indian Sovereignty, and Government-to-Government Relations with Indian Tribes, Office of The Attorney General, Washington, D.C. 20530, 1st June 2005.

315   *Santa Clara Pueblo vs. Martinez*, 436 U.S. 49 (1978), pp. 65-6.

316   1996 Constitution of the Republic of South Africa Chapter 12 on Traditional Leaders, Section 211; the Bill of Rights has a similar provision requiring consistency with its provisions (Section 39(3)). Uganda has a stringent repugnancy clause that subordinates customary law to common law principles and statutory law.

testimony was used to assert that brutal paramilitary suppression of the Zapatista movement in Chiapas, Mexico, was simply 'customary interfamilial fighting' among the local indigenous population.[317]

THE DILEMMAS AND CONCEPTUAL CHALLENGES OF RECOGNISING NON-STATE LEGAL ORDERS

At the outset, some presumptions need to be addressed. First, recognition is invariably understood to concern minorities and to be a matter of making special accommodations for such groups and their members in order to allow them to preserve and maintain their culture and unique way of life.[318] However, demand for recognition should not been seen as uniquely an issue for minorities. The indigenous people of Bolivia, who have led demands for legal pluralism, represent some 70% of the population. Second, claims based on religious, minority ethnic or indigenous identities have distinct legal foundations as well as different socio-political and historical origins. Their claims are ontologically different and the recognition of a claim in one category should not be presumed to apply automatically to claims under another. Third, the impetus to recognise the customary does not always imply a retreat into the past: it may be used to legitimate present and future political claims.[319] These are often justified by assertions of 'cultural insensitivity' or 'threats to cultural survival'. It is important in such cases, building on this report's earlier discussion of the sources and scope of cultural difference (see Chapter II), to ask how truly different is the difference that is claimed, and to remain mindful that culture and law are mobilised in support of political interests (see Chapter II).

An unintended outcome of recognition is that it can erode the popular legitimacy of non-state authorities. This was the case in Somalia, where recognised traditional authorities became part of a state order considered unacceptable and problematic. A similar situation occurred in Afghanistan where the lack of the legitimacy of the state caused NSLOs that were incorporated into the state order to lose legitimacy.[320] For similar reasons, decentralisation can paradoxically lead to greater dependence on the centre, as ever-smaller units become less viable. In Uganda this has led to a reversal of decentralisation, to what Oloka-Onyango terms *re-centralisation*.[321]

Questions of recognition, incorporation and decentralisation involve: normative content; jurisdiction (over territory, issues and persons); authority (who has it,

---

317   Hernandez Castillo, 2002, p. 8 (pagination as in manuscript).

318   Kymlicka in Stopler, 2007.

319   Franz von Benda-Beckmann, comments at ICHRP Meeting.

320   Höhne, 2007, p. 24; Barfield *et al.*, 2006.

321   Oloka-Onyango, 2007, p. 35.

but also how and by whom authority is bestowed); the adjudicatory process (the procedural dimension); and enforcement of decisions. If a plural legal order is to operate smoothly, all these elements need to be defined clearly – yet this is rarely achieved. International standards (as discussed in Chapter III) may establish certain principles but cannot elaborate the kind of operational detail needed to resolve the contextual dilemmas of implementation. Practical and conceptual challenges arise at every step which the state initiates in relation to a plural legal order.

Any recognition, incorporation or decentralisation must also take into account the politics of culture and cultural production, rather than merely the externally observed practices of culture.[322] This means that colonial-style state enumeration of customary practices is not the solution. Applying this reasoning in the legal sphere, Gover argues that the recognition of non-state legal orders such as those of ethno-cultural groups should include recognition of "practices of normative deliberation and decision-making – the processes by which normative claims are discussed, disagreement adjudicated (in the largest sense of 'adjudicate', including all means of settling disputed norms), and the resultant norms interpreted and elaborated".[323]

Discussions about the legal and political consequences of recognition of non-state legal orders are premised on a broader uncertainty. When we talk about recognition, what exactly is being recognised? Is it a 'thing', a claim, a process or a combination of these three?[324] In a 1998 report, the New Zealand Law Commission identified two distinct usages of the term "Maori custom law", recognition of which would entail quite different outcomes.[325] Similarly, does recognition of 'Shari'ah' imply recognition of an on-going jurisgenerative process among Muslims, recognition of the interpretation of certain classical Islamic scholars (in specific texts) or recognition of the codified laws of certain Muslim countries?

Once culture is seen as a dynamic human endeavour that does not exist as an independent entity, it becomes clear that the question of recognition is not just a technical matter but deeply political in character. This applies not only to the incorporation of non-state orders into the state order but also to decentralisation. As Davidheiser argues with respect to decentralisation in Africa, any law reform project that extends beyond reform of ineffective institutions and aims at re-shaping governance necessarily enters political terrain.[326] Both the political Left and Right may have reasons to elevate non-state law to the level of law or to

---

322   Gover, 2008a.

323   Webber in Gover, 2008b, p. 8.

324   Gover, 2008a, p. 21.

325   Law Commission Report, para. 4, p. 1. See also Webber in Gover, 2008a, p. 18.

326   Davidheiser, 2007, p. 23.

resist doing so. Hernandez Castillo warns that "discourses which emphasise the right to equality and discourses which emphasize the right to difference can *both* be used to hide, reproduce, or deepen the marginalization and exclusion...".[327] Thus, monist ahistorical assertions that 'everyone is equal before the law' increased discrimination against indigenous people in Latin America by rendering them invisible. On the other hand, recognition can also serve as a discriminatory instrument by establishing rigid communal boundaries. In Israel, for example, Orthodox and conservative forces from both the Jewish and Muslim communities support the recognition of religious family laws as a means to enforce communal boundaries.

Acknowledging that recognition has political aspects brings a new dimension to examination of state responsibilities with respect to recognition and plural legal orders. It means that motivations and power dynamics must be considered. When a state introduces alternative dispute resolution, for example, it may claim to incorporate non-state norms or 'traditional' non-adversarial approaches to justice. Such claims were made when *lok adalats* were introduced in India. However, analysis of the way in which *lok adalats* were actually structured, and function, indicates that recognition of 'tradition' was by no means the real motivation. Similarly, decentralisation is not always about recognition of normative plurality, even though this claim may have been made by advocates of reform or the authorities who were being 'recognised'. Instead, the project may be a political one to *extend* and consolidate state power,[328] or may be motivated by a desire to reduce expenditure on the state justice system.

The problems of translation (finding equivalent rules or institutions) present some of the most significant challenges to the incorporation or recognition of customary law.[329] Alternatively, the state may recognise customary laws "without stating their content specifically".[330] In this case, the ALRC correctly notes that the resulting degree of "uncertainty as to the exact content of the law" may make it necessary to qualify "the incorporated rule in a way which does not correspond with customary law".[331] So, for example, the same legislation that protects Aboriginal sacred sites from intrusion provides a defence where intrusion was 'innocent' (where the accused person did not know the location was sacred, etc.); aboriginal customary law would not accept such a defence. In other cases, the nature of some non-state legal orders can make a policy

---

327 Hernandez Castillo, 2002, p. 14 (pagination as in manuscript).

328 As discussed in Chapter IV, 'traditional' authorities may be (re)invented by the state to consolidate specific political interests. For more on the link between human rights and decentralisation, see ICHRP, 2002, 2005 – both reports are available at www.ichrp.org.

329 Australian Law Reform Commission, para. 204, vol. 1.

330 Ibid., para. 200, vol. 1.

331 Ibid.

decision to recognise that order difficult to implement in practice. For instance, Ahrén details the challenges that Scandinavian countries face in recognising the diverse customs and laws across the Sápmi of the Saami peoples, many of which have not survived unbroken as result of assimilationist policies.[332] In addition, it is inherently difficult for an oral culture, that aims to live in harmony with the land and to leave no traces upon it, to prove its presence in a particular area.[333]

A final important issue in relation to recognition of a non-state legal order is that there is often an emphasis on 'purity' and 'authenticity'. The "rush to *finding* and *recognizing* the 'authentic'",[334] a process which characterised colonialism in much of Africa and Asia, has human rights as well as policy implications. For instance, it is common for governments and even courts today to consult 'experts' (such as religious scholars, community 'leaders', elders or academics) to ascertain the 'true' interpretation of certain customary or religious codes, or the precise nature and meaning of certain practises. Several questions arise here. First, *who* is recognised as an expert and *by whom*? Then, on *what basis* are they able to speak for a community or a culture and *why*? In Mozambique, the power to bestow such recognition often lies in the hands of "the politico-legal complex of institutions related to the state, the FRELIMO party, and international donor aid organisations and NGOs" who all need a single 'community leader' to talk to.[335] In the same vein, a report by Nigeria's National Centre for Women Development asks pertinent questions about intragroup rights and chieftaincy councils (customary forums recognised by Nigerian law).[336] How do these forums perpetuate gender roles, stereotypes and division of labour? What privileges are conferred through chieftaincy titles? To whom are titleholders accountable? Has resistance to change been shrouded under the guise of cultural preservation? It is particularly relevant, for example, to ask who is in a position to negotiate confusing and arbitrary parallel family laws to their advantage?

---

332   Ahrén, 2004.The *Svartskog* case (Supreme Court judgement 5B/2001, no. 240/1999, Oct. 5, 2001) is the first example of a Fennoscandinavian court finding that the Saami people have acquired ownership to a land area by *traditional use*; but its approach does not help all indigenous land rights claims (p. 102).

333   Ibid.

334   Karima Bennoune, comments at ICHRP Meeting.

335   Buur and Kyed, 2006, p. 19.

336   NCWD, 2005, p. 42.

SUMMARY

A non-state legal order may become part of a state legal order as a result of decentralisation, incorporation, or recognition of a claim for the law to reflect cultural diversity. Each of these are understood and operationalised in a wide variety of ways in different contexts and have the potential to advance or obstruct human rights. In consequence, their impact on human rights needs to be taken into account.

Questions of recognition, incorporation and decentralisation involve normative content; jurisdiction (over territory, issues and persons); authority (who has it, but also how and by whom authority is bestowed); the adjudicatory process (the procedural dimension); and enforcement of decisions. If a plural legal order is to operate smoothly, all these elements need to be defined clearly – yet this is rare.

From a rights perspective, any recognition, incorporation or decentralisation must also take into account the politics of culture and cultural production, rather than merely the externally observed practices of culture.

National constitutions are important tools for human rights analysis as they outline how far legal orders are subject to fundamental rights guarantees; and, indicate how far the state has recognised both the *outputs* of a non-state legal order, as well as the authority and autonomy of its *processes*.

However, there is also variation in the extent to which the state in practice acknowledges the autonomy of non-state legal orders in generating and applying legal norms.

Recognition of non-state or customary law presents numerous conceptual challenges and policy dilemmas. Firstly, what exactly is being recognised? Is it a 'thing', a claim, a process, or a combination of these?

Once culture is seen as a dynamic human endeavour, it becomes clear that recognition is not just a technical matter but deeply political in character.

Claims to recognition that are based on religious, or minority ethnic or indigenous identities each have distinct legal and socio-historical foundations. Their claims are ontologically different and the recognition of a claim in one category should not be presumed to apply automatically to claims under another.

The incorporation or recognition of customary law presents particular challenges. One approach is to 'translate' – find equivalent rules or institutions that can be recognised or incorporated, which may not always be possible because they may be based on profoundly different worldviews and procedures; another, is to recognise customary laws without elaborating their specific content, which also raises questions of adherence to rights standards.

The impetus to recognise the 'customary' does not always imply a retreat into the past: it may be used to legitimate present and future political claims. The demand for recognition should not be seen as uniquely an issue for minorities.

Additionally, recognition often entails a "rush to finding and recognizing the 'authentic'". Characteristic of colonialism, this tendency has policy implications (e.g., what is the process for acknowledging someone as an 'expert') as well as human rights impacts (e.g., the knowledge and power of some is privileged).

Both progressive human rights advocates and the most extreme advocates of identity politics may find themselves opposing state recognition – one because recognition accords too much weight to non-state norms, the other because it entails too much state control.

VIII. CULTURAL DIVERSITY, PLURAL LEGAL ORDERS AND JUSTICE – POLICY OPTIONS AND PRINCIPLES

One of the major debates this project considers is the demand by ethno-cultural groups (especially indigenous peoples, and ethnic and religious minorities and majorities) that the law should reflect their distinct cultural identity, practices and customs, or provide outright juridical autonomy. These demands usually go far beyond programmes to cultivate cultural awareness or appoint more persons from minorities to judicial positions, steps that are usually perceived to be inadequate.[337] How are such demands to be understood? Who speaks for these groups and for their culture, tradition, religion or way of life? What do such demands tell us about how group membership is defined? What are the pitfalls of recognising such demands in practice – in terms of *who* makes the demand and its *substance*?

This chapter analyses some proposed approaches to recognising cultural diversity within the legal system. It first examines the dilemmas and challenges that confront the legal system in the context of multiculturalism, particularly the processes by which people are recognised as communities. It also looks at how recognition of cultural diversity in the legal sphere affects inter and intragroup rights; an important aspect here is the right of individuals to exit the community. The chapter emphasises the need to adopt a wider understanding of justice in the context of multiculturalism, that takes political and economic dimensions into account.

The chapter concludes with a discussion of religious arbitration in family law matters, an issue that is especially current in Northern multicultural contexts. This case study illustrates many of the issues raised in the chapter and also has implications for wider processes of state regulation of non-state legal orders in general.

MULTICULTURALISM AND THE CHALLENGES OF CULTURAL DIVERSITY

"Is the legal system sensitive to cultural diversity? Should it be? Should the law *reflect* cultural diversity? Does it? Should the law expressly protect distinctive and differentiated cultural rights?"[338] In a case involving an Aboriginal offender, J. McHugh of the High Court of Australia argued that "real equality before the law cannot exist when ethnic or cultural minorities are convicted or acquitted of murder according to a standard that reflects the values of the dominant class

---

337   Ahrén, 2004, pp. 108-110; McNamara, 2006, p. 9; Bhandar, 2005, p. 9.

338   McNamara, 2006, p. 2.

but does not reflect the values of these minorities".[339] However, the remaining six judges rejected the idea that an accused person's identity (in this case, his ethnicity) should (re)shape the "objective standard which is at the heart of the criminal law defence of provocation".[340] With regard to indigenous peoples, the case for state recognition of legal plurality has been most clearly articulated when non-recognition has been perceived as discriminatory and a denial of effective access to justice.[341] More broadly, Taylor eloquently makes the case for recognition of cultural diversity: "The grant of equal respect to one's culture along with its survival is a prerequisite for the successful formation of a person's identity as well as for their self realization."[342] Recognition addresses cultural domination, non-recognition (being rendered invisible) and disrespect (being routinely maligned or disparaged).[343]

Yet the entire notion of recognition of cultural diversity is constructed on a paradox. Underlying the demand for recognition of diversity is a principle of universal equality; but by definition this requires acknowledging and giving status to something that is not universally shared. "[T]he universal demand powers an acknowledgement of specificity."[344]

'Mainstream' or 'core values' are often seen as "outside the reach of multiculturalism", while it is also often assumed that the location of laws "*within* culture, mean that 'mainstream' legal standards and norms will incrementally, but inevitably be transformed in response to the influences of cultural difference".[345] How this contradiction is to be resolved in practice remains unanswered. An example illustrates the dilemma. If the British state recognised the status of wives in illegal/unrecognised polygamous marriages, would this bring such women within the ambit and protection of the law, or would the effect be to encourage a rise in polygamy (and associated rights violations), because polygamy would be 'recognised'? Accepting that the liberal state cannot impose religious or indigenous jurisdiction without the clear consent of citizens,[346] the way questions are shaped in consent-seeking exercises is crucial to determining the answers, and can produce very different rights outcomes.

---

339   *Masciantonio vs. R* (1995) 183 CLR 58 at 74 in McNamara, 2006, p. 5.

340   McNamara, 2006, p. 6. He also notes that in *Walker vs. NSW,* the Court held that: "[A] construction which results in different criminal sanctions applying to different persons for the same conduct offends" the principle of equality before the law.

341   This is especially true in the case of indigenous people – see Chapter III on human rights standards.

342   Taylor in Stopler, 2007.

343   Fraser in Stopler, 2007, p. 348.

344   Ghai, 2008.

345   McNamara, 2006, p. 4.

346   Sezgin, 2003, p. 35.

In the case of indigenous rights advocacy, the problem is even more complex. Some advocates argue that when recognition occurs within the framework of state law, it can perpetuate discrimination because all state law is inherently alien and tainted by inequitable power relationships. For example, in some settler states this would entail "reserving for 'white' decision-makers the authority to define the 'Other' – whether favourably or unfavourably".[347] The ALRC notes that certain forms of incorporation of customary law would not only confer on courts substantial discretion in determining the 'underlying law' but that the colonial 'ideal type' codification underlying it may eventually result in loss of Aboriginal ownership, erasure of diversity and distortions.[348] This is echoed in criticisms of the Canadian Supreme Court that claim the Court has treated 'Aboriginal' as a term that is entirely retrospective and therefore relegated Aboriginal peoples to the backwaters of social development. (The Court had demanded that custom be established by proving that the activity or practice was "integral to the distinctive culture" of the community prior to contact with Europeans.[349]) Across different regions, there is widespread concern that, because recognition often requires custom to pass the stringent test of being "readily ascertainable and sufficiently certain", often the end result is the ossification of customary and indigenous laws, blocking their dynamic and internally contested development.

A demand to recognise a 'community's' legal autonomy begins with defining the community, what has been called the 'dirty work of boundary maintenance'.[350] Who draws these boundaries – individuals, communities, the culture, the Executive, the Judiciary or a combination of them all? Deciding who belongs and who does not is a political process communities engage in internally and states engage in *vis-à-vis* communities they recognise. Both state and non-state law give substance to boundary maintenance by (a) constructing legal identities (i.e. classifying the population in different categories, according for example to class, caste, ethnicity, gender, citizenship, alien status, etc.); (b) prescribing the norms for, and structure of, relationships between these categories; and (c) stipulating the rights and duties of those falling into the categories in question.[351] "Different legal orders construct the identity of the population differently and thus the same group of people may be categorised differently by different legal orders and have different statuses, rights and obligations."[352]

---

347 Bhandar, 2005, pp. 12-14; McNamara, 2006, p. 22.

348 The example given by the ALRC is what it terms 'general incorporation' whereby customary law rules are codified in statutory form "with the courts required to apply the customary law as set out in the code". See paras 200 and 202, vol. 1.

349 *R. vs. Van der Peet* (1996) 2 S.C.R.507 at p. 549, per Lamer CJC quoted in John Borrows, 1996, Report of the Royal Commission for Aboriginal Peoples, p. 60.

350 Crowley in Yuval-Davis, 2006.

351 Pradhan, 2007.

352 Ibid., p. 2.

The question of identity, belonging and the role of law, frequently arises in national case law, for example in the context of membership status (especially of adopted children) of indigenous peoples in Canada and the United States, and the religious identity of the children of convert parents in Malaysia and Indonesia.

Is there a danger that when the state recognises a community's identity, it only does so in its own image? The *Lovelace* case, relating to the disputed membership of a Maliseet Indian woman who had married outside the tribe,[353] showed how Canada's Indian Act had reduced a complex process of determining kinship to patriarchal descent; and how indigenous culture had been appropriated and manipulated to fit the dominant group's patriarchal reconstruction of a minority in its own image.[354] Alternatively, the desire to fulfil international obligations by recognising indigenous identity presents particular problems in the case of those indigenous populations who, by virtue of suffering centuries of discrimination, have lost much of their continuous and cohesive 'difference' – what Yrigoyen Fajardo refers to as the "pulverising [of] many peoples into communities".[355]

States have taken different approaches to the practical difficulties of identifying a group in order to grant it recognition. In the United States the government has taken a largely 'hands-off' approach to tribe membership and the issue of adoption. Most tribes (74% according to Gover[356]), while emphasising blood descent, have resolved the matter by allowing for the special incorporation of persons who are not blood descendants at the discretion of the tribe. Canada, on the other hand, insists that adopted children be included in membership rolls which means they are included in the community of persons who will formulate subsequent membership rules. In other words, the state establishes certain ground rules. For example, the Canadian Human Rights Act applies to decisions of a band regarding Band Membership; any decision to treat adopted children differently would be subject to a human rights challenge under that Act.

A link is often made between 'purity' and survival which raises further policy dilemmas (and human rights concerns) in terms of inclusion and exclusion. In *Grismer vs. Squamish Indian Band*, it was held that "[r]estricting membership to persons who have a bloodline connection to the Squamish Nation is a rational way of preserving and protecting" Squamish identity.[357] The judgement noted that the Nation had "sought to balance the potential rights of persons with no

---

353 See Chapter III for a discussion of the *Lovelace* case.

354 Banda and Chinkin, 2004, p. 25.

355 Yrigoyen Fajardo, 2004, p. 36. See also Ahrén, 2004, on the Saami in Scandinavia; and McNamara, 2006, on indigenous peoples in Settler States.

356 Gover, 2008b, p. 23.

357 2006 fc 1088, 146 c.r.r. (2ND) 68 (2007).

Squamish blood against the Squamish tradition and the need to preserve the unique Squamish culture and identity". However, even numerically large groups can raise the flag of 'threat to survival'. In Malaysia, conversion into and out of Islam has been a historical practice. Today, however, the 'threat to survival' claim has led to increasing instances of religious conversion being disputed in court. It has also increased pressure on the courts to decide that the person's disputed identity is Muslim. This 'threat to survival' is despite the fact that Muslims compose the majority (54%) of Malaysians.

People have multiple identities which can include simultaneous ones as citizens (membership of a political community) and as members of an ethno-religious cultural community. When state law is based on ethno-religious identity or when the state recognises an identity-based non-state legal order this multiplicity of identities is formalised, and problems can arise because "we are expected to act as undifferentiated citizens in the public sphere, but remain free to express our distinct cultural or religious identities in the private domain of family and communal life. Yet multiple tensions have exposed cracks in this privatizing identities formula: for instance, where precisely does the 'private' end and the 'public' begin"?[358]

One way around this difficult question is to adopt an approach that does not validate rights claims on the basis that claimants have a shared *culture* or belong to a *community*, but in terms of the "legitimate interests of the members of the group".[359] As Jones maintains, "cultures are not moral entities to which we can owe obligations of fairness. Insisting that we should be fair to cultures merely as cultures is like insisting that we should be fair to paintings or to languages or to musical compositions.... So, if we seek to deal fairly with cultural diversity, it is not cultures who will be the ultimate objects of our concern but the people who bear them". [360]

Cultural diversity, group rights and individual rights

Will Kymlicka[361] raises the key issue of intra and intergroup rights in assessing claims to recognition designed to reflect cultural diversity. The first are rights which groups may claim against their own members ('internal restrictions'); the second ('external protections') are rights that groups may claim against the state or society to protect their identity and ways of life. Kymlicka's formula maintains that special minority rights should only be granted if they promote relations of equality (non-dominance) between groups and as long as they

---

358   Shachar, 2008, p. 574.

359   Barry, 2001, p. 67.

360   Jones in Barry, 2001.

361   Kymlicka, 1999.

protect the freedom of individuals within the group,[362] including their rights to person, agency and expression.[363]

However, this framework does not provide criteria to measure when the critical intra/intergroup balance has been reached, or the specific content of 'adequate safeguards'. In addition, it has been criticised for promoting an "uncontextualized discussion of multicultural claims" that "threatens to turn the right to culture (or to recognition) into a meta-right that supersedes all other rights".[364] In other words, prescriptions calling for 'recognition-with-protection' can be tantamount to offering no protection at all, especially if state monitoring is weak – a very common problem for human rights advocates everywhere.[365]

Mechanisms of intercultural dialogue are a possible solution to resolving intergroup differences.[366] International human rights law has called for the establishment of procedures for 'resolving conflicts', for example, in Article 8(2) of ILO Convention 169. However, as Yrigoyen Fajardo points out, countries with Special Indigenous Jurisdiction have failed to implement this. Her more concrete proposal for 'intercultural interpretation' mechanisms include the creation of mixed courts composed of state judges and indigenous or community authorities which will employ negotiated rules to resolve apparent conflicts between the special jurisdiction and human rights.[367] Though far-reaching, this proposed fusion of state and non-state legal orders does not escape many of the problems identified with other approaches to addressing cultural diversity in the legal sphere.

Granting rights to a cultural collective forces it to define a "uniform set of interests", which can not only freeze culture but, by endorsing *one* representation or interpretation of culture among the many in circulation, can create conditions which allow dominant sub-groups within the culture to repress marginalised or dissenting voices.[368] For example, recognising private religious arbitration in family law matters will result in the authority of such arbitrators being legitimised by the state and also enhance the resources to which they have access and their power to draw and police ethno-cultural boundaries.[369]

---

362 Kymlicka in Stopler, 2007, p. 16.

363 Kymlicka, 1992. Taylor takes a similar view, see Taylor in Stopler, 2007, p. 18. See also Sarat and Berkowitz, 1994.

364 Stopler, 2007, p. 326.

365 The challenges of monitoring is discussed in Chapter IX.

366 See for example An-Na'im and Deng, 1992; Raz, 1998; Gover, 2008a; and the discussion in Chapter II.

367 Yrigoyen Fajardo, 2004, p. 44.

368 Tamir, 2003, p. 200; see also Gover, 2008a, p. 27.

369 Rights and Democracy, 2005a, p. 5.

If the state facilitates dialogue *within* the community regarding its legal order, this is still fraught with questions. Will the state provide the environment and sufficient resources to ensure a qualitatively meaningful dialogue? Is such a process merely re-centring the state? Who will be recognised as a legitimate recipient of state support for such a dialogue and will this state-sponsored process itself be legitimate in the eyes of the community? A narrowing of the representatives of 'community' often occurs in multiculturalist states, which tend to see secular commitment as equivalent to religious or cultural inauthenticity. One result is that progressive voices are systematically marginalised.[370] Those marginalised include believers who do not support the privileging of religion in public policy or who support the strict separation of state and religion. This emphasis on authenticity is also used by 'community leaders', especially religious fundamentalists, to deflect criticism and conceal political interests.[371]

Thus, certain kinds of recognition of difference can exacerbate rather than resolve social conflict.[372] Ultimately, when policy-makers or other actors assess the human rights impact of measures to recognise cultural diversity, they need to ask: how tolerant of diversity are those who seek recognition in the name of equality in diversity?[373] According to Benhabib: "[T]he goal of any public policy for the preservation of cultures must be the empowerment of members of cultural groups to appropriate, enrich, and even subvert the terms of their own cultures as they may decide."[374]

Additionally, some argue that the availability of an 'exit option' – the right to exit from the jurisdiction of a legal order – is an essential guarantee of individual rights in the context of state recognition of cultural diversity.[375] India's Special Marriages Act (1954), for example, allows couples an exit option from the

---

370   Bhatt, 2006, p. 114. See also Vaggione, 2005, p. 251. For example, contestation within Muslim societies over the production of laws (*fiqh*) and elaboration of the Shari'ah is a battle that has raged for centuries (see El-Fadl, 2001; Masud, 2009) yet even the existence of this battle is contested.

371   Bhatt, 2006, pp. 102 and 108.

372   Tully, 2004.

373   Bhatt, 2006.

374   Benhabib in Gover, 2008a, p. 30.

375   Kymlicka, 2002; Benhabib, 2002. Benhabib in Sezgin, 2003 argues that as long as pluralist systems do not violate three normative conditions they can be quite compatible with a universalist democracy model. She identifies these conditions as egalitarian reciprocity, voluntary self-ascription, and freedom of exit and association.

jurisdiction of family laws framed with reference to their religions.[376] Countries such as Malaysia, which do not even recognise certain interreligious marriages conducted as civil marriages abroad, clearly fail the exit option test. Although an exit option may be a necessary condition, it is clearly an insufficient guarantee against the violation of rights in a plural legal order. In addition, many question how far the option is a real one. First, it requires the presence of a welcoming community outside. Second, having and exercising choice presumes autonomy (in several areas), and access to other resources, which many individuals lack. Third, pressure to conform to 'tradition' is usually strong and may also block exit.[377] Ultimately, assessing the extent of 'free choice' in such cases can be next to impossible. As a result, the greater the margin of appreciation granted, *de facto* or *de jure*, to community authorities to govern the 'private' lives of individual members, the narrower the possibility for individuals to invoke a broader set of citizenship rights.

Moreover, the exit option can become a falsely dichotomised choice for individuals who wish to exercise their rights and also to remain within their community (or are unable to exit) – for people who want simultaneously to be culture- and rights-bearers.[378] Choices, even where they exist, are invariably not defined by those supposed to exercise them and may involve an 'all or nothing' situation. For instance, in some indigenous communities, marrying outside the tribe may imply losing access to land and other community resources.

Finally, some critique the exit option for undermining the entire goal of recognition. For example, the Andean Special Indigenous Jurisdiction provisions do not offer an exit option, "otherwise the very validity of the system itself would be at stake".[379]

---

376   Exit options come in two slightly different forms. The first offers a secular alternative, while the second simply allows people to move between jurisdictions framed with reference to various religions and/or customs. For example, the plural systems prevailing in much of Anglophone Africa – where religious, customary and 'civil' family laws operate side by side – fall more in the latter category since the 'civil' laws are invariably carry-overs of conservatively constructed colonial-era Christian family laws. This in itself can limit access to the exit option.

377   Sezgin, 2003; Lynn Welchman, comments at ICHRP Meeting; Rights and Democracy, 2005a, illustrated the last in detail in the case of Canadian women whom the Canadian Council of Muslim Women feared would be pressurised into accepting religious arbitration to prove they are 'good Muslims'.

378   Shachar, 2008, p. 593.

379   Yrigoyen Fajardo, 2004, p. 42. Cases before the Colombian Constitutional Court illustrate the point that the apparently rights protective exit option has a flipside that facilitates the violation of rights by the powerful. The Court has consistently held (generally in cases where people seek to evade punishment) that members cannot escape from the jurisdiction of indigenous legal orders when it is convenient.

Multicultural Justice: Looking Beyond Culture

Suggestions have been made about how to approach demands for state recognition of cultural diversity, especially from religious or ethnic minorities or indigenous people in the context of multiculturalism. Gila Stopler[380] suggests a useful framework in her comparative analysis of the Israeli state's policy towards Jewish ultra-Orthodox and Arab Muslim minorities. She begins from the position that "the obligation of a polity to accommodate and support a minority culture cannot and should not be absolute, just as the preference of a polity to advance its majority culture cannot and should not be unlimited".[381] Any demand for recognition and accommodation, and relevant state obligations, must be contextualised "in relation to all other ethnic and cultural groups… as well as in reference to the relations and power disparities within the group"[382] and in light of the political, economic and cultural conditions of the minority and within the polity in which it resides. The appropriateness of accepting a demand would then depend upon its impact, in context, on inter and intragroup dynamics, what she terms "participatory parity". Stopler also rightly sets the human rights bar high on the grounds that it is not sufficient to say that recognition must not damage rights. "[T]he requested remedy for discrimination or demand for accommodation must be shown to advance the parity of participation" within and between groups.[383]

Participatory parity is to be assessed "across the three dimensions of justice": recognition, redistribution and political participation, which Stopler derives from the work of Nancy Fraser.[384] 'Recognition' relates to cultural dimensions, while 'redistribution' is the socio-economic dimension. Often, discourse on recognition and redistribution is framed in such a way that it creates the need to choose between them, for example where class claims for justice have been replaced by claims framed as race equality.[385] Instead, she argues that these dimensions are to be seen as co-fundamental and mutually irreducible, and neither should be overlooked.[386]

---

380 Stopler, 2007.

381 Ibid., p. 327. Other steps in Stopler's framework would likely lead to recognition of indigenous peoples' legal orders. However, it is not clear whether she regards indigenous peoples' claims as ontologically different and therefore not subject to her framework's starting declaration of conditionality, or whether her framework would not regard indigenous peoples' rights to their own legal orders as absolute.

382 Ibid., p. 327.

383 Ibid., p. 319 (emphasis added).

384 See Fraser, 1997, 2000, 2001, 2003.

385 See Fraser in Stopler, 2007, p. 310.

386 Ibid.

Regulating religious arbitration in family law matters

How can state responsibility be invoked in relation to private religious arbitration and where, apparently, the parties consent to the terms of the arbitration? The Canadian Council of Muslim Women in its campaign against official recognition of religious arbitration argued that although arbitration tribunals or 'Shari'ah courts' constituted under the 1991 Arbitration Act were not public bodies as such, governmental authority makes Arbitration Act decisions legally binding, and "surely decisions enforceable by public courts must be Charter [Canadian Charter of Rights and Freedoms]-compliant".[387]

Focusing on private religious arbitration, particularly in the context of Jewish and Muslim minorities in Canada, Shachar offers a detailed model setting out how the state can regulate religious arbitration. Although this is a very specific case, the general issues raised have potentially wider application and therefore merit analysis here.

In brief, Shachar proposes permitting "regulated interaction between religious and secular sources of law, so long as the baseline of citizenship guaranteed rights remains firmly in place".[388] This proposal includes both 'ex post judicial review' of decisions by arbitrators that are considered to violate rights; and 'ex ante oversight'. The latter includes several elements: mandatory training and a licensing programme for arbitrators; mandatory counselling by an independent legal adviser before arbitration starts; an obligation on the arbitrator to maintain systematic documentation of evidence and notes taken during hearings; and separate screening of parties to detect signs of domestic violence or coercion (evidence of which immediately exclude use of arbitration). Finally, "any solution reached through a dispute resolution process that was the result of duress, coercion, or violence will automatically be invalidated as a matter of law".[389]

This approach demands, first, state investment in training, licensing and monitoring processes. In other words, the net outcome of privatised religious arbitration could ironically be more state regulation rather than less.

Second, it must be asked: who will conduct such training, licensing and monitoring? Apart from the fact that state or public authorities may lack understanding of the processes and content of different religious legal orders, questions arise as to whose voices and which interpretations will be given

---

387   Rights and Democracy, 2005a, p. 7.

388   Shachar, 2008, p. 575.

389   Ibid.

priority.[390] In the context of Canada, those who campaigned against private religious arbitration criticised the Boyd Report's recommendations (which were similar to those made by Shachar): "Not only do arbitrators lack guidelines and expertise to 'screen,' they also have a financial or political interest in conducting arbitrations…. Effective 'regulation' of arbitration to provide full and adequate protection to women in family law disputes would defeat its purpose to deliver speedy, private, and less costly results."[391]

Third, the invalidation of an arbitrated agreement on account of duress would still require duress to be proved. Experience of court practice in most jurisdictions, and the difficulty of proving psychological duress, indicate that protection on these grounds may not be effective. Moreover, if the victim has to raise the alarm, how can the mechanism be 'automatic'? Some suggest, as an alternative, that privately arbitrated agreements should be referred for review to the formal system.[392] However, this would defeat the purpose, if done thoroughly, or would entail pointless rubber-stamping, if the mechanism is merely designed to filter out only the most rights-abhorrent decisions.

Fourth, Shachar suggests that, for their decisions to become publicly enforceable, "tribunals should voluntarily agree to abide by the basic floor of rights offered by the existing family legislation". Even in Canada, which has a relatively clearly expressed set of rights in the Charter, this might generate considerable litigation concerning the precise content of that 'basic floor'. In addition, the concept of 'basic' implies a minimal rather than maximal position.

Fifth, Shachar hopes that state recognition and regulation of religious arbitration would promote moderate interpretations of religious laws. Yet in the estimate of some Muslim women's organisations in Canada: "Making religious tribunals readily available and their decisions enforceable under Ontario law will only

---

390   Policy research for example in Britain, indicates that in contexts with migrant Muslim populations, state authorities lack even basic understandings of the content and process of Muslim laws, or Shari'ah (Warraich and Balchin, 2006). Further, there is a tendency among public service providers to accept family violence within minority communities on the grounds of 'not wishing to offend cultural sensibilities'. (See for example, www.timesonline.co.uk/tol/news/uk/article3295487.ece.) Given this lack of in-house expertise, the presumption is that such training would be contracted out. In the multiculturalist context where, as already discussed, the state privileges conservative patriarchal interpretations of non-state legal orders, it is highly likely that the least progressive visions would predominate in contracted training provision. Thus, what many women's rights activists in migrant Muslim communities and in women's movements in Muslim countries would regard as human rights violative interpretations of Muslim laws would receive sanction from the British state. A similar problem may affect *ex post* judicial review, particularly given the powerful presence of cultural relativist and orientalist expert opinion in Muslim family law cases to date (Warraich and Balchin, 2006).

391   Rights and Democracy, 2005a, p. 6.

392   For example, Ludsin, 2008.

legitimize women's lack of real choices"[393] rather than lead to the emergence of progressive interpretations.

Lastly, state recognition can exacerbate existing confusion regarding the status of non-state legal orders. As already discussed, plural legal orders are a highly politicised field, and state-backed recognition processes that declare themselves to be human rights-compliant are liable to be rejected as 'inauthentic' by a portion of the community. Further, if regulation is as extensive as suggested, few religious organisations would have the capacity, resources or will to submit to such stringent regulation. This raises the possibility of a three-tier system, consisting of formal state courts, a recognised non-state order and an unrecognised non-state order. What would be the human rights impact of precipitating such complexity?

The above discussion illustrates several issues. First, serious practical challenges will arise from regulation of religious arbitration in family law matters. Second, no matter how carefully they are crafted, regulatory measures cannot compensate for power imbalances within the community. This reminds us again of the limitations of law and that state and NGOs need to act in ways that will increase economic and political equality between and within groups. Finally, national policy-makers will need to decide where best to invest limited resources.

---

393   Rights and Democracy, 2005a, p. 3.

SUMMARY

It is common today for indigenous peoples, and ethnic and religious minorities and majorities to demand that the law should reflect their distinct cultural identity, practices and customs, or provide outright juridical autonomy. Yet the entire notion of recognition of cultural diversity is constructed on a paradox. Underlying the demand is a principle of universal equality; but by definition this requires acknowledging and giving status to something that is not universally shared.

Also paradoxically, some reject recognition within the framework of state law as likely to perpetuate discrimination because all state law is inherently alien and tainted by inequitable power relationships, while an unintended outcome of recognition can be the erosion of the popular legitimacy of non-state authorities.

When recognition is interpreted to mean that custom must pass the stringent test of being 'readily ascertainable and sufficiently certain', this could result in the ossification of customary and indigenous laws, blocking their dynamic and internally contested development.

Those who demand recognition of their cultural diversity may prove intolerant of other pluralities, notably of sexual and religious minorities and atheists.

Recognising a 'community's' legal autonomy involves defining it as well as who is included and excluded. This is a political process that both communities and states engage in, and which has human rights implications that need to be examined.

When state law is based on ethno-religious identity or when the state recognises an identity-based non-state legal order, people's multiple identities become formalised. This leads to the unrealistic expectation that people will act as "undifferentiated citizens in the public sphere", but "express distinct cultural or religious identities in the private domain of family and communal life". However where exactly does the *private* end and the *public* begin?

One solution to dealing fairly with cultural diversity is to validate rights claims in terms of the "legitimate interests of the members of the group" rather than on the basis that claimants have a shared *culture* or belong to a *community*. It can be argued that "[c]ultures are not moral entities to which we can owe obligations of fairness."

Additional helpful perspectives include assessing how recognition of cultural diversity in law affects both intra and intergroup rights in practice. Granting rights to a cultural collective can force a definition of "uniform set of interests", which can freeze culture and also create intragroup inequality by privileging certain voices and interpretations.

An option to exit from an identity-based regime is a necessary but insufficient guarantee against the violation of rights in a plural legal order; such an option may also not be accessible.

Overall, justice in a multicultural context, and any state facilitation of dialogue between and within communities, must take into account differences in social, economic and political power and how a plural legal order affects each of these.

A case study of religious arbitration in family law matters illustrates the serious practical challenges to human rights posed by the recognition and state regulation of cultural diversity.

It is arguable that the obligation to accommodate and support a minority culture cannot and should not be absolute, just as the preference to advance a majority culture cannot and should not be unlimited.

IX. AN ASSESSMENT OF JUSTICE SECTOR REFORM IN THE CONTEXT OF PLURAL LEGAL ORDERS

A 2001 ICHRP study demonstrated that, while foreign aid programmes have facilitated constitutional development and helped transform the justice system, they have also suffered from several weaknesses.[394] These included inconsistency in focus; export of inappropriate models; political influence over programmes; distortion of domestic institutions; shifting priorities; and inadequate local participation. However, the study did not touch on the relationships between justice sector reform programmes and the expansion and consolidation of plural legal orders, the focus of this chapter.

The chapter examines some of the debates and concerns around programmes supported or initiated by intergovernmental institutions and donor agencies. It focuses on the motives and goals of such programmes and how they are designed, researched, planned, implemented and monitored.

INTERESTS UNDERLYING THE PROMOTION OF NON-STATE LEGAL ORDERS

For some time, it has been perceived that justice outcomes are inextricably tied to the extent to which the legal system is socio-legally rooted, given that "the successful provision of justice services requires serious engagement with the social and legal particularities of a given context. Indeed, an earlier generation of efforts to provide justice services in the 'third world' failed because of an unwillingness to heed sociolegal specificity".[395] This understanding appears to influence the programming of intergovernmental agencies and donors (and in many cases states) when they support legal reforms that promote legal plurality – notably programmes that involve recognising, strengthening or developing non-state legal orders, community-based justice systems, or alternative dispute resolution mechanisms. Plural legal orders are certainly an element of socio-legal specificity, and are undeniably present in the lives of many people. Yet it is important not to confuse "the empirical question of the current state of legal pluralism and the political question of how far non-state law should officially be 'recognized'".[396] Harmonising pluralities to create a coherent justice system involves "technical considerations and inputs" but is essentially a political process.[397] While recognition of non-state law in the name of community participation and empowerment does have potential for "producing consequences that are desirable for all, in present policies, community is

---

394   See ICHRP, 2000.

395   Maru, 2006, p. 429.

396   Weilenmann, 2007, p. 4.

397   Le Sage, 2005, p. 8.

predominantly used as a technical means of producing entities (communities) that can engage in government projects and be administered".[398]

The goals behind the focus on legal plurality also reflect ideological orientations. For example, Tripp describes two very different lines of reasoning that underpin support for community-based land titling in Uganda: "The World Bank, for example, sees the reliance on customary arrangements as a simpler and less conflictual route to the eventual titling, registration, and privatization of land ownership, whereas Oxfam sees the reliance on customary systems as a way to strengthen and democratise local communities, and promote bottom-up grassroots initiatives."[399] Some donors acknowledge that reform involves political choices and impacts and "is not a neutral, technical activity, but one that raises broader governance issues", and that "intervention may ... have an impact on existing power relations at both local and national levels".[400]

Interest in non-state legal orders or ADR stems in large measure from the failings of over-burdened state justice systems and the desire to promote a more efficient justice system. The aim has been to free up the ability of formal courts to take on more 'serious' cases, by resolving 'minor' ones in other forums. Examples include the *barangay* justice system in the Philippines, introduced in 1978 in part to reduce the volume of court litigation; the partial incorporation of indigenous systems as a form of ADR in post-conflict Guatemala; and *lok adalats* in India.[401] In general, it is considered that efficient justice requires deregulation and a reduction in state inputs, the achievement of which is linked to options such as ADR and a greater focus on non-state legal orders. For example, the 2008 report of the Commission on Legal Empowerment of the Poor[402] suggests that one way to achieve access to justice "is gradually liberalising the market for legal services by reducing regulatory entry barriers – such as 'unauthorised practice of law' restrictions – for service providers, including non-lawyers, who are interested in offering legal services to the poor.... Reforms in pluralistic legal systems might include combining formal or tacit recognition of the non-state justice system with education and awareness campaigns that promote evolution of the informal legal system. These systems may also be strengthened with

---

398   Kyed and Burr, 2006, p. 19. There are similar concerns that World Bank and UNDP-sponsored decentralisation programmes in the Gambia "appear designed to increase state control over rural areas rather than transfer power to the periphery" (Davidheiser, 2007, p. 4).

399   Tripp, 2004, p. 1.

400   DFID, 2004, p. 3.

401   Tachibana, 2006, p. 8; Sieder, 2008, p. 13 (page number as in manuscript on file); the *lok adalats* were discussed in Chapter VII.

402   The Commission was a high-powered international initiative that ran from 2005 to 2008. The UNDP has now taken on some of its work www.undp.org/legalempowerment.

the support of civil society and community-based organisations".[403] However, if state regulation of legal services is reduced, who will ensure that human rights standards are observed? It is unrealistic to expect civil society to bear the burden of monitoring the legal services market, fill gaps in legal services and address the shortcomings of non-state legal orders, when the support that community organisations receive "is often insufficient, and almost always manipulative".[404]

Numerous studies in Africa, Asia and Latin America underline the limitations of a market-driven approach to rule of law and justice sector reform.[405] Efficiency may be a necessary condition for human rights compliance but, as Macaulay's discussion of the handling of domestic violence by newly-introduced ADR mechanisms in Latin America shows, a policy driven by 'efficiency' can entail significant human rights costs. In some Latin American countries, many domestic violence offences were decriminalised, downgraded to civil disputes or misdemeanours and processed through new, non-adversarial and 'consensual' forms of conflict resolution which aim "to unburden an overstretched and inefficient criminal justice system" and reduce public expenses by reducing custodial sentences and processing cases more quickly. However, research has found that the new process achieved the opposite of rapid, effective resolution.[406] Elsewhere, the most unlikely forces have taken advantage of the current emphasis on 'efficiency' and ADR to justify rights-violating non-state legal orders.[407] In other words, if efficiency rather than improved human rights outcomes is prioritised as an end goal of justice sector reform, access to justice is most definitely not enhanced.

INADEQUATE RESEARCH AND ANALYSIS

Dezalay and Garth refer to the "burgeoning global industry dedicated to the import and export of the 'rule of law'".[408] In this field, access to justice and

---

403 Commission on Legal Empowerment of the Poor, 2008, pp. 63-64. The language of 'supply' and 'demand' or 'service providers' and 'service demanders' often features in development agency materials on justice. See, for example Byrne *et al.*, 2007, pp. 10-11.

404 Faundez, 2003, p. 49.

405 Davidheiser, 2007; Galanter and Krishnan, 2004; Sieder, 2008; Benda-Beckmann *et al.*, 2002-2003.

406 Macaulay, 2005, pp. 105, 111.

407 An example are the right-wing Hindu Shivsena's 'courts' in Mumbai, India, run by what Eckert calls the Shivsena's 'criminal gangs' (Eckert, 2002, p. 4).

408 Dezalay and Garth in Sieder 2008, p. 3 (page number as in manuscript on file). Sieder also cites Domingo and Sieder, 2001; Carothers, 1999. Others who critique the self-serving nature of donor policies include Benda-Beckmann and Benda-Beckmann, 2006 and Menzies, 2007.

promotion of non-state legal orders are among the more recently fashionable areas. Yet work on these subjects is replete with examples of poor scholarship (by academic consultant-researchers, or development agency staff), with the result that policies are often inconsistent, incoherent or unrealistic. Criticism of 'experts', especially their lack of willingness to take responsibility for the outcomes of their work, is not uncommon.[409]

The inadequate research base is a basic issue. An internal Inter-American Development Bank (IDB) review notes: "Early Bank justice projects tended to be based on rather general diagnoses of the justice sector."[410] More recently, DFID acknowledged that the evidence base for work on NSLOs is generally weak, partly because such research can be difficult and time-consuming.[411] Researchers have noted the scarcity of studies that examine the content and implications of indigenous peoples' world views on justice, and that debate about non-state law tends to be conceptual rather than empirical and is therefore dominated more by ideology than a real understanding of the ways in which remote and marginalised communities deal with governance and resolve their disputes.[412] A study of the problems of legal plurality in the Solomon Islands, where no baseline of local justice systems existed, quotes a local lawyer who pointed out that "it is hard to recommend that something be supported without knowing exactly what it is".[413]

Research into plural legal orders in the context of development projects faces several challenges. Firstly, there are concerns regarding the short project cycles and limited resources available for researching the policy context, even though sound research is critical to achieving meaningful outcomes.[414] Some believe that the 'project approach' is designed to circumvent difficult political questions. Mednicoff, for example, claims that "most U.S.-based rule-of-law programs are conceived in technical terms that avoid political sensitivity".[415] Such approaches avoid in-depth analysis of socio-economic and political contexts, which can lead to simplistic conclusions and recommendations. On the other hand, longer-term academic research to fill gaps in knowledge is not always policy oriented and the results may also not be available very quickly. In addition, there are often questions over the independence of commissioned research. Given the resources involved, and the human rights implications of these investments, the absence of empirical information about plural legal

---

409   See Kennedy, 2006, for example.

410   Biebesheimer and Payne, 2001, p. 25.

411   DFID, 2004, p. 7.

412   Faundez, 2003, pp. 18, 61.

413   Menzies, 2007, p. 15.

414   Anne Griffiths, comments at ICHRP Meeting.

415   Mednicoff, 2005, p. 12.

orders ought to worry governments, judicial institutions and organisations that finance or support such programmes.

Analysis of justice reform in post-conflict Guatemala suggests that reforms may fail or be counterproductive when there is insufficient research or understanding of the reform context. While the basic steps taken to re-establish the rule of law could not be faulted,[416] "the 'rule of law' meant significantly different things to different sectors". For international donors it included strengthening national economic performance; for the indigenous Mayan widows' association, it meant an end to impunity, and material and symbolic restitution for victims of human rights abuses; and for people in general, it promised tough policies on law and order.[417] Much of the literature displays a tendency to presume that providing the necessary conditions for access to justice are sufficient to guarantee realisation. In the context of Uganda's decentralisation programme, Oloka-Onyango rightly criticises the "running presumption that because local councillors are able to exercise judicial power, access to justice has improved".[418] Expertise in law, in a country's legal system or even in legal pluralism does not guarantee the presence of a human rights perspective, or vice versa, and both are clearly needed in order to develop a sound basis for policy.

Some have pointed to the swings of fashion in the field of justice sector reform between denigration and idealisation of tradition.[419] Due to lack of information, policies characteristically fall back on generalisations. So, one USAID (United States Agency for International Development) report on improving access to justice in Afghanistan recommended that "research should be conducted to determine what 'rules' and 'principles' utilised or applied by some within the informal justice sector are inconsistent with correctly interpreted Sharia or Islamic principles",[420] disregarding the fact that interpretations of Shari'ah are diverse and highly contested. Such approaches have a pedigree: 1990s studies funded by USAID and the Ford Foundation distinguished between 'true' and 'untrue' traditional authorities; portraying custom in a reified and timeless way, they provided a highly romanticised view of communal authorities.[421] The

---

416 These included collaboration between the international community (World Bank, the UN mission in Guatemala, UNDP, IDB, USAID and bilateral government assistance) and Guatemalan authorities; increased resourcing; reform of the text of law; consultation with various civic and professional groups; measures to increase judicial independence and tackle corruption; guarantees for basic rights; and efforts to make access to justice more multicultural (Sieder, 2008).

417 Sieder, 2008, p. 9 (page number as in manuscript on file).

418 Oloka-Onyango, 2007, p. 4.

419 Benda-Beckmann et al., 2002-2003, p. 301.

420 USAID, 2005a, p. 15.

421 Buur and Kyed, 2006, p. 5.

romanticisation of non-state legal systems also affected reform programmes for Latin America.[422]

Both donors and local institutions construct stereotypical models of traditional law for their own purposes[423] and can paradoxically subvert the organic development of community leadership. In Mozambique, for fear of losing aid, a sub-chief was registered as a chief in order to match the official governance structure, while in one of the war zones eight chiefs were reinstated as 'rightful' chiefs under the government's decentralisation programme, even though six of them had been absent during the war.[424] Such essentialisation is therefore not just an international malady.

With regard to non-state legal orders, the tendency to romanticise and essentialise 'tradition' causes some studies to recommend the establishment of hybrid systems, because they recognise that NSLOs sometimes violate rights. Yet the recommendation is rarely accompanied by discussion of how to harmonise two legal systems (the state and non-state order) acknowledged as being so different. A similar vagueness is found in other development analyses of legal reform. A UNDP conceptual framework on access to justice reappears in documents relating to non-state or plural legal orders.[425] It offers a 6-step process towards 'appropriate remedies'. Step 2 is "Legal awareness: claim holders are aware of the law and their rights under it and know what to do in case of a grievance"; step 3 is "Access to appropriate forum: claim holders seek remedies for grievances through appropriate mechanisms and grievances are received by duty bearer". Yet the disadvantaged confront a yawning chasm between steps 2 and 3 – between being familiar with content and procedure, and having their cases heard. The framework does not suggest how to bridge this gap, and it is unclear how so tidy an analysis would work on the ground.

Examples of inconsistent analysis, reflected in reform of plural legal orders, are numerous. For instance, one study affirms that "the complex set of changing realities ... makes it difficult to assess exactly what role traditional leadership can play in governance as a whole", but goes on in the next paragraph to say that "traditional leaders have an important role to play in narrowing the

---

422   Faundez, 2003, p. 55.

423   Benda-Beckmann *et al.*, 2002-2003, p. 301.

424   Buur and Kyed, 2006.

425   Wojkowska, 2006, p. 30, which reappears in, for example, World Bank, 2007.

gap between policy and its practice".[426] Programmes that support 'traditional' peace-building in post-conflict contexts often note that "many of the traditional ways of living have been disrupted or lost altogether", and are in need of some modernisation in order to be "better able to meet the contemporary needs of the communities".[427] One is tempted to ask what, then, is 'traditional' about the forums being promoted. Buur and Kyed point out a contradiction in Mozambique's decentralisation process, which had been supported by many international donors.[428] While the operational Decree recognising traditional authorities was supposed to affirm a "recognition of what already exists", it was accompanied by an elaborate state process of chieftaincy approval because so many chieftaincies (i.e. 'what already existed') were disputed.

Finally, across the literature, it is claimed that non-state systems and ADR offer the best options for increasing access to justice, from which the poor and dispossessed are invariably assumed to have been excluded. Yet the same documents betray fundamental doubts regarding such systems. For instance, a UNDP study suggests that "informal justice systems generally do not work in the resolution of disputes between parties who possess very different levels of power or authority" and that "the goal of harmony can be used to force weaker parties to accept agreements and local norms, which in turn can result in discrimination against minorities and women".[429] Another study, supported by the Swiss Agency for Development and Cooperation, suggests: "[I]t is far from clear that a direct link can be made between decentralisation and poverty reduction, particularly where the most vulnerable are concerned."[430] For this project, ICHRP conducted a broad survey of related literature, but found few examples where there was an adequate and transparent discussion of the development and other policy priorities leading to the continuing interest in non-

---

426   Malzbender *et al.*, 2005, p. 11. This report is by the Natural Resources Institute, whose website makes the academic-development consultancy link very clear: "NRI is an internationally recognised multi-disciplinary centre for research, consultancy and education for the management of natural and human resources. Our mission is to provide distinctive, high quality and relevant research, consultancy, learning and advice in support of sustainable development, economic growth and poverty reduction."

427   ActionAid, 2008, www.actionaid.org.uk/index.asp?page_id=1338. The ActionAid programme relates to Burundi. Barfield *et al.*, 2006, contains similar statements regarding Afghanistan.

428   Kyed and Buur, 2006, p. 20.

429   Wojkowska, 2006, p. 20. Other examples include Barfield *et al.*, 2006 and World Bank, 2007, p. 7.

430   Byrne *et al.*, 2007, p. 8.

state or plural legal orders despite the weak research base and the concerns regarding the impact of non-state legal orders.[431]

INCONSISTENT ADHERENCE TO HUMAN RIGHTS PRINCIPLES AND STANDARDS

The titles of prominent legal reform policies and programmes (Justice for the Poor (World Bank), Access to Justice for All (UNDP), The Commission on Legal Empowerment of the Poor) raise the hope of greater human rights compliance than past legal reform policy.[432] One report notes: "The poor are not the objects of legal empowerment, but its co-designers and facilitators. They must participate and provide feedback in all phases of the reform, including the close monitoring of the results."[433] A UNDP study lists criteria which "all informal justice systems should meet". It suggests they should be participatory, accountable, non-discriminatory and linked to human rights standards.[434] A DFID Briefing suggests that working with non-state legal systems "is not applicable to situations where [they] violate basic human rights such that donor engagement is both inappropriate and unlikely to achieve reform".[435] Unfortunately, practice often fails to reflect such thinking.

Policies that recommend mediation, arbitration and other ADR mechanisms for 'minor' matters, reserving the state court system for 'serious' matters,[436] in effect help prolong discrimination if they do not acknowledge that such a division can reinforce socio-economic power imbalances or fail to develop effective ways to redress them. Though Uganda's decentralisation policy has been hailed as a 'flagship programme' and has been supported by major donors including USAID, DANIDA, the World Bank, DFID and SIDA, no document produced

---

431 It was suggested to ICHRP that a good study in this respect was undertaken by the OHCHR Office in Guatemala which examined the effectiveness or justiciability of human rights guarantees in state and non-state justice systems in Guatemala: *Asociación de Investigación y Estudios Sociales* (ASIES), *Oficina del Alto Comisionado de las Naciones Unidas para los Derechos Humanos en Guatemala* (OACNUDH), *Acceso de los pueblos indígenas a la justicia desde el enfoque de derechos humanos: Perspectivas en el derecho indígena y en el sistema de justicia oficial*, Guatemala, 2008.

432 Some are more cynical about the language of current legal reform programmes: referring to Gambia's decentralisation, Davidheiser writes that "discussing community empowerment provides a nice contrast to the bitter effects of currency devaluation and other SAP-related policies that have negatively impacted the living standards of rural populations in the global peripheries" (Davidheiser, 2007, pp. 4-7).

433 Commission on Legal Empowerment of the Poor, 2008, p. 9. See also Gruss, 2000.

434 Wojkowska, 2006, p. 16.

435 DFID, 2004, p, 4.

436 See for example Byrne *et al.*, 2007, p. 17; Wojkowska, 2006, p. 17; Barfield *et al.*, 2006.

between the early 1990s and 2006 outlined the policy framework coherently, or linked it to human rights standards or outcomes. Uganda's 1995 Constitution reserves one-third of Local Council membership for women (A.180), but the observation, protection and promotion of human rights is not one of the seven principles applied by the Constitution (A.176(2)) to local government, and the 2006 Local Council Courts Act (which was designed to streamline their operation) does not expressly mention human rights principles. "None of them linked the support given to decentralization – at either the national or local level – to the support that they have extended to human rights."[437]

On one hand, UNDP rightly recommends that "any oversight mechanisms need to forward to the formal system those cases which are against natural justice, corrupt, politically motivated or breach international standards of human rights".[438] Yet UNDP supported Pakistan's 2001 Local Government Ordinance (Articles 102-106), which established the framework for *musalihat anjumans*. This ADR mechanism for "amicable settlement of disputes" includes no provision for appeal, while lawyers are explicitly prohibited from representing parties, and court endorsement is only required where a matter is already pending before a court. Extraordinarily, these forums are presented as vehicles for gender justice, in a context of severe gender inequality and systemic violence against women.[439]

Gendered aspects of reforms relating to plural legal orders appear to be particularly overlooked. Suggestions that elements of Shari'ah should be incorporated in civil cases in the lower courts fail to take account of the gendered impact of such changes to civil law.[440] In Canada, the Native Women's Association of Canada was invited to provide a culturally relevant, gender-based analysis in policy dialogues but did not receive funding equivalent to other national Aboriginal organisations, while Aboriginal women were referred to in just one paragraph of the background document to the Canada Aboriginal Peoples Roundtable Discussion on Negotiations in 2005.[441]

Despite assertions to the contrary, therefore, there appears certain tentativeness in commitment to human rights standards. For example "any interventions or

---

437   Oloka-Onyango, 2007, p. 30.

438   Wojkowska, 2006, p. 42.

439   www.undp.org.pk/gender-justice-through-musalihat-anjuman.html.

440   See for example Le Sage, 2005, p. 8, who argues that such incorporation is possibly "the best means of tempting moderates and traditionalists from the *Sharia'h* courts to join the [transitional government], and undercut support for militants".

441   Native Women's Association of Canada, Report in Response to Canada's Fourth and Fifth Reports on the International Covenant on Economic, Social and Cultural Rights covering the period September 1999 to December 2004, p. 12: www.nwac-hq.org/en/documents/NWACResponsetoCanadaReportonIntlCovenant onEconomicSocialandCulturalRights.pdf.

initiatives undertaken should work towards gradually enhancing the quality of dispute resolution and getting the informal justice systems to adhere to [these] human rights based principles" and a 'principle for action' in reforms recognising NSLOs is to "work together with a truly representative section of the national community to as great an extent as possible".[442] It is almost as if they have adopted a 'progressive realisation' approach to non-state legal systems, different from the standard human rights benchmarking applied to the formal state system. In a critique of the Indian *lok adalats*, Galanter and Krishnan note the extraordinarily low expectations underlying the reforms, aimed not at the delivery of a superior form of justice but merely "deliverance from the agony of litigation in a system conceded to be terrible".[443]

LACK OF CONSULTATION AND MEANINGFUL LOCAL PARTICIPATION

As law is transnationalised, 'local' lawyers can tend to be sidelined, even though many are "more skilled and experienced than the emerging elite", because they lack the language skills (specifically English) needed to communicate with foreigners.[444] The use of foreign experts unfamiliar with local contexts is criticised elsewhere. In some Arab contexts, for example, if Western specialists are "unprepared for the extent to which and the diversity in which indigenous Arab language of legal change is saturated with Islamic terminology, even within the reform trend, their ability to see nuances and connect with actual legal change will be hobbled".[445]

Failure to consult is another issue. Many of the policy claims and practice in projects that promote alternatives to the state system lack coherence for this reason. Ironically, this was one of the major criticisms of earlier state sector reforms.[446] An internal review of the IDB's justice sector reform policies in Latin America hints at such problems, for example, when it suggests that an increased emphasis on civic education regarding justice "might be a logical next step" in order "to help form or consolidate consensus regarding the need for reforms in the system".[447]

The UN Special Rapporteur on indigenous peoples reports frequent claims that public institutions, established to review indigenous legislation and its implementation, were not representative of their communities and peoples, and (as in the Philippines and Australia) were often composed entirely of government

---

442   Wojkowska, 2006, pp. 16 and 31.

443   Galanter and Krishnan, 2004, p. 808.

444   Mattei, 2003, p. 58.

445   Mednicoff, 2005, p. 10.

446   See for example, Davidheiser, 2007; Malzbender *et al.*, 2005; Wojkowska, 2006.

447   Biebesheimer and Payne, 2001, p. 22.

officials.[448] In Kyrgyzstan, campaigns of local self-governance have always been initiated from the top by state authorities, mostly with the help of international consultants and donors.[449] Similarly, the *Casas de Justicia* legal service centres in Colombia are sometimes perceived by shantytown dwellers as a device for smuggling the repressive arm of the state into their communities.[450] This was the case in Ciudad Bolívar, barrio Jerusalén, where a *Casa de Justicia* was established with no proper analysis, and without consulting the community. Reflecting the main objective of its promoters – to control outbreaks of violence – the two most prominent officials of the 'non-state' mechanism were the local Police Inspector and Public Prosecutor.[451]

Mozambique's decentralisation Decree No 15/2000 provides no formal guidelines concerning the consultative and representational role of 'community authorities'. It seems to presume that traditional leaders represent the rural populations' interests. As revealed during field visits, most disputes over leadership took place within, and were resolved by, small and exclusive circles of people, composed mainly of members of the chief's family, the council of elders (men), the traditional police and local NGO workers – reflecting a rather narrow understanding of 'community consultation'.[452] Moreover, it became difficult to get rid of community authorities who performed badly.[453] The implication is that consultation and accountability in forums with adjudicative responsibilities diminished with state recognition. Oloka-Onyango notes that the introduction of more local justice mechanisms does not translate into improved access to justice in the absence of mechanisms that enable people to challenge decision-makers who fail to follow rules about how the public should be consulted.[454] Others are concerned that funding for legal reform involving non-state legal orders may cause local decision-makers to regard themselves as accountable to the funder rather than the community they are supposed to serve.[455] Clearly, accountability mechanisms make a vital contribution to the effectiveness of non-state legal orders that the state order incorporates or recognises. One way to ensure that such accountability works in practice is to empower users. Unfortunately, legal empowerment is often seen as "something done *for* the poor rather than *by* them".[456]

---

448   UNSRIP, 2006, p. 25.

449   Beyer, 2007, p. 9.

450   Faundez, 2003, p. 46.

451   Ibid.

452   Burr and Kyed, 2006, pp. 2 and 6.

453   Ibid., p. 20.

454   Oloka-Onyango, 2007, p. 4.

455   Kimathi, 2005, p. 14.

456   USAID, 2007.

Ultimately, formulaic demands for participatory approaches (often required by donors) can curtail broad-based community participation. For example, water users' associations in South Africa are subject to highly formalised procedures, and are therefore not compatible with traditional systems whose processes are more fluid.[457]

A DFID 2004 Briefing Note on Non-state Justice and Security (NSJS) systems affirms the importance of commitment to a "pro-poor approach". It emphasises the importance of evidence-based research into the outcomes from reforms of non-state legal orders[458] and presents a useful "checklist for appraisal" of non-state legal orders – which, nevertheless, makes no reference to human rights standards.[459]

- *Is an intervention needed?* What measures will enhance safety, security and access to justice? Have alternative options, such as improving state institutions, been considered?

- *Will the measures taken contribute to poverty reduction?* Will they help improve the living standards or well-being of disadvantaged populations? Will they strengthen the position of people who rely on NSJS systems for security and justice?

- *How to intervene?* Should the intervention support state policy towards NSJS systems, and/or work with civil society organisations? Can non-justice entry points be used? Does the approach taken build on the NSJS system's positive features?

- *Efficiency and fairness:* Will the action help the system perform better? Have principles of fairness and respect for fundamental rights been taken into account?

- *Accountability:* Will the initiative help to make the system more accountable to its users and to other state or non-state institutions?

- *Inclusiveness:* Will the measures taken enhance inclusiveness and enable women and marginalised groups to participate in, and benefit from, NSJS systems?

- *Linkages:* Will the intervention help to clarify and improve linkages with state, other NSJS systems and civil society organisations?

---

457   Malzbender *et al.*, 2005, p. 6.

458   The Note also indicates what research should cover: the historical context; the role of the non-state legal order; its linkages to the state; the non-state legal order's features (values, users, authority, standards, human rights compliance, funding and enforcement processes); key stakeholders; incentives and disincentives for reform; and myths held about non-state legal orders.

459   DFID, 2004, pp. 5-8.

- *Approach:* Is there a sufficiently extended time line to allow social and political change to take place? Is the process flexible enough to adjust to changing local contexts and national politics?

- *Research:* How will new research findings be incorporated into the strategy?

- *Change strategy:* How is the intervention likely to affect the local or national political context? How will likely resistance to change be managed (such as from local elites, judiciary, legal profession)?

PLANNING, IMPLEMENTATION, MONITORING AND EVALUATING LEGAL REFORM PROJECTS

Donor agendas often mutually conflict.[460] A study on decentralisation and access to justice extensively critiques poor donor coordination, noting that "donor coordination is essential to successful judicial reform in order to avoid duplication of efforts, but also to make sure that all relevant parts of the legal system are addressed during reform so as to avoid unintended side effects of particular reform efforts".[461] The Office of the UN High Commissioner for Human Rights (OHCHR) similarly calls for greater donor coordination in the context of post-conflict justice sector reform.[462] Both reports were prepared after the 2005 Paris Declaration, an international agreement which had been designed to improve the efficacy of international aid, one of whose five principles is donor harmonisation to avoid duplication.[463]

Another significant challenge in planning is the promotion of a holistic approach. One study notes "a consensus is emerging in development cooperation that pushes for a more 'holistic' view of co-operation in the field of justice".[464] Le Sage introduces six strategic recommendations for the rule of law in Somalia and argues they are best viewed as a package, "not a menu of options".[465] A national framework document for access to justice in Indonesia similarly

460   Carothers, 2001, discusses this problem.

461   Byrne *et al.*, 2007, pp. 24-25.

462   OHCHR, 2006, p. 39.

463   www.oecd.org/document/18/0,3343,en_2649_3236398_35401554_1_1_1_1,00.html.

464   Byrne *et al.*, 2007, p. 10.

465   Le Sage, 2005, pp. 9-11. They are roughly summarised as a need for dialogue to reach consensus; structural reform of the judicial system; building judicial capacity; legal empowerment of the Somali public; establishment of a stable political environment; requisite international political and financial support.

emphasises that the five proposed components cannot be addressed in isolation and are mutually reinforcing.[466]

However, there are dangers in recommending a 'do everything' approach that fails to recognise resource and capacity constraints.[467] It is particularly problematic where international agencies have high expectations but limit funding and adopt a cost-cutting approach.[468] In Somalia, inadequate funding means that international community interventions each address isolated aspects of access to justice and that "few of these projects are being implemented together with a single group of Somalis in a single location".[469] Despite recommending a holistic approach, Le Sage quickly notes that insecurity and the political context may mean that selectivity is necessary.[470] This returns us to the question of the criteria policy-makers use to identify priorities. Given the pressure to produce demonstrable results, are the more complex aspects of legal reform likely to be sidelined in favour of goals that are easily achievable?

Some studies do make detailed suggestions regarding "ways for mitigating social justice concerns" regarding non-state systems – for example judicial review of all cases, training and education, making decisions by non-state mechanisms subject to appeal before the state courts, and allowing choice of forum and law.[471] However, such recommendations are often made without regard to national resource constraints or external policy pressures. Moreover, they rely heavily on intervention by the same state system whose shortcomings were the original justification for promoting non-state legal orders.

Meanwhile, the question of resourcing legal reforms must be placed in a broader national political context. For example, even though fairly effective, the reinvented *shalishes* in Bangladesh are currently not financially self-sustaining, and continued reliance on donor funding could affect their political legitimacy and outcomes in the long-run.[472] Similarly, competition over the national budget and foreign aid can lead judiciaries and ministries to view proposed support to non-state legal orders as a threat to their own funding.[473]

---

466   World Bank, 2007. They are: normative legal framework; legal awareness; access to appropriate forums; effective administration of justice; monitoring and oversight.

467   Menzies, 2007, p. 14.

468   Ibid.; Le Sage, 2005.

469   Le Sage, 2005, pp. 11-12.

470   Ibid., p. 11.

471   Davidheiser, 2007, p. 22.

472   Wojkowska, 2006, p. 39.

473   DFID, 2004, p. 6.

Resourcing non-state legal orders presents serious challenges; their financial sustainability needs far more attention than it has received. For instance, it is not helpful to presume that non-state arbiters will work for free or even minimal remuneration. At the same time, investing a large amount of resources raises questions of credibility and sustainability. For example, some community courts and community policing forums in Mozambique disappeared because they were financially unsustainable.[474]

Despite the volume of literature on non-state and plural legal orders, and on their outcomes and human rights impacts, reforms that promote pluralism have seldom been monitored effectively. Several studies – on Asia, the Middle East, the Pacific region – have commented on this gap.[475] An interesting example is the *Casas de Justicia* in Colombia: "USAID officials acknowledge that such an evaluation is necessary, but claim that they have no time to do it if they are to meet the target of 40 *Casas* by the year 2005."[476] It is an extraordinary situation if donors are too busy implementing projects to evaluate their value.

Where attempts have been made to assess the outcomes of reform projects promoting plural legal orders, they often conflate outputs with impact. Counting the number of workshops on non-state legal orders that an organisation holds with rural communities, or the number of cases handled by an ADR mechanism, does not tell us about the *effect* of those activities, or the quality of justice outcomes.

Indeed, DFID's 2004 Briefing Note warns against "the danger of 'perverse incentives', where measurement of activities and outputs is emphasised at the expense of quality and substantive outcomes". The emphasis on quantitative listing of activities is all the more questionable in the absence of empirical data, because it means that projects are often designed on the basis of perceptions and anecdote but results are reported in numbers, shorn of perceptions. For example, "USAID experimented with the use of quantitative indicators in its justice projects, but abandoned it when project managers began emphasizing activities that could easily be measured rather than those that might be most important in terms of improving the quality and effectiveness of the justice system".[477]

Admittedly, it is notoriously difficult to collect meaningful impact indicators without heavy investment of resources; even so, it is unclear that sufficient efforts are being made. Obliquely critiquing reliance on Log-Frame-style project tools, a review of IDB legal assistance projects in Latin America noted that "not

---

474   Comment by Helene Maria Kyed.

475   See Beyer, 2007, p. 9; Mednicoff, 2005, p. 11; Menzies, 2007.

476   Faundez, 2003, p. 45.

477   Biebesheimer and Payne, 2001, p. 33.

many of the means of verifying indicators (MoVs) include means of measuring accountability to the public (through polls or surveys, for example) and not many are geared toward measuring improved public service".[478] Galanter and Krishnan note that the campaign to institutionalise *lok adalats* in India "comes in spite of (and perhaps because of) the fact that little is known about their performance".[479]

Although state and non-state systems clearly need different forms of monitoring and evaluation, it should not be the case that less stringent monitoring standards are applied to non-state systems. At the same time, to the degree that non-state forums are less formal, it will be more difficult to assess whether they are accountable to those they serve,[480] whether state oversight is effective,[481] and whether human rights are being respected or violated. In this respect, the same qualities that make non-state systems attractive – fluidity, informality, accessibility, their operation in isolated communities – make them difficult to monitor and evaluate effectively. Even DFID's 2004 Briefing Note appears to offer no solution to this question. It outlines some interesting indicators, designed to "vary with the specific context", which are both quantitative and qualitative, but the collection of such data and its evaluation can itself become a project, requiring special visits and expert or public surveys disaggregated by gender, age, social status, etc.[482] This implies a perhaps complex relationship between justice sector reform and academic research – but highlights again the pressing need for careful research to provide a baseline against which processes and outcomes of reform can be assessed. In most contexts, such a baseline does not exist.

The evaluation and monitoring of plural legal orders that operate in the context of measures like the Special Indigenous Jurisdictions in some Latin American countries present additional complications. Because such measures recognise claims to autonomy or self-determination, human rights monitoring in such systems should not undermine (or be seen to undermine) the principle of autonomy, and the monitoring obligations (if any) of states and donors involved should also be clarified.

The difficulties of monitoring and evaluating plural legal order reforms are often compounded by donor impatience, which in turn can undermine the possibility

---

478   Biebesheimer and Payne, 2001.

479   Galanter and Krishnan, 2004, p. 825, note: "[I]t is unclear whether this seemingly continuous drop in the number [of cases] settled per *Lok Adalat* is due to the increasing number of *Lok Adalats*, less success in achieving resolution, fewer cases, smaller numbers of mediators, or more difficult and complex cases."

480   Musembi in Kimathi, 2005, p. 14.

481   Galanter and Krishnan, 2004, p. 822.

482   DFID, 2004, p. 16.

of more effective interventions though some donor analyses recognise the long-time span required to achieve successful justice sector reforms.[483] The UNDP study referred to earlier notes as a downside that it took over two years to successfullly train 25-30 competent paralegals – it is not obvious that this is an extraordinarily lengthy period given the competencies involved.[484]

Donors and states can obviously adopt more nuanced approaches and some donor publications that promote engagement with non-state legal orders are measured and thoughtful.[485] The IDB's internal review of its justice sector assistance, while couched in diplomatic language, is forthright.[486] A survey conducted for the Swiss Agency for Development and Cooperation notes that "methodological difficulties alone do not explain why few lessons so far seem to have been learned. It is also a matter of political priority and willingness of each donor agency. It seems to us that this political will has been weak, and that far too few efforts have been made at all to promote evaluation-based better practices".[487] Yet even where good donor policy is developed, it does not necessarily percolate into all aspects of programming. Clearly, donors, states, international human rights NGOs – indeed all those involved in policy and advocacy that bear on the development of plural legal orders – still have much they can learn from past experience. That the recommendations of ICHRP's 2001 study on foreign aid to the justice sector, referred to at the start of this chapter still need reiterating indicates the scale of this problem – and perhaps the difficulty of improving practice in this area.

---

483   Biebesheimer and Payne, 2001, p. 1.

484   Wojowska, 2006, p. 35.

485   For example, DFID, 2004.

486   Ibid.

487   Skaar in Byrne *et al.*, 2007, p. 25.

SUMMARY

Interest in promoting non-state legal orders or ADR stems in large measure from the failings of over-burdened state justice systems and the desire to promote a more socio-culturally rooted justice system.

Where improving efficiency, rather than expanding access to justice for all, is an end in itself, reforms may have undesirable human rights consequences.

While accounting for local socio-legal specificity is important for effective justice sector reform, the concept of 'community' is often used as a technical means of producing entities that can be engaged in government projects and be administered.

While justice sector aid has facilitated constitutional development and helped transform the justice system, it has also suffered from several weaknesses.

Justice sector reform often lacks a sound research base and may be underpinned by poor scholarship with the result that policies are often inconsistent, incoherent or unrealistic. This also results in swings of fashion in the field of justice sector reform between denigration and idealisation of tradition and non-state legal orders.

The design of plural legal order projects on the ground, especially those involving decentralisation and ADR mechanisms often involves an inconsistent adherence to human rights standards on the part of donors.

The lack of consultation and meaningful local participation as well as effective monitoring and evaluation also pose serious threats to the effectiveness of justice sector reform programmes.

Donor agendas often mutually conflict and can lead to unintended side effects of particular reform efforts. Such lack of coordination also prevents learning from positive experiences and successful initiatives.

PART FOUR

WAYS FORWARD

X. DEVELOPING A HUMAN RIGHTS APPROACH TO PLURAL LEGAL ORDERS

While plural legal orders present several challenges to human rights protection, existing human rights standards and principles nevertheless offer advocates and policy-makers ways of responding to them. This chapter outlines some of these, and points to areas where standards need to be developed or clarified. It also highlights other areas of law and policy relevant to plural legal orders to which a range of actors concerned with access to justice and protection of human rights need to give attention. The chapter concludes by summarising broader human rights-based approaches to plural legal orders that offer a way ahead and inform the framework presented in the chapter that follows.

THE SCOPE FOR USING EXISTING HUMAN RIGHTS STANDARDS

Human rights standards are clear on a range of matters, including that the prohibition of discrimination (for example on grounds of gender) cannot be derogated from; and that no cultural defence is admissible with regard to violence.[488] Also, some of the standards and their interpretation contain nuanced language on culture. Although this is not always apparent from comments by the Treaty Bodies and other official commentaries, international human rights standards permit distinctions to be made between aspects of culture that are discriminatory (and therefore need reform or removal) and those that are not (and should be retained or strengthened). For example, HRC General Comment No. 28 (paragraph 5) and CEDAW General Recommendation No. 19 both state clearly that discrimination is often a result of specific *attitudes* or *values* rather than culture or religion as a whole. The Protocol to the African Charter on Human and Peoples' Rights on the Rights of Women in Africa is particularly clear on this point: rather than treat culture as a homogenous object, it uses the term 'harmful practices' when it examines gendered discrimination. The UN Special Rapporteur on violence against women has also clarified that "human rights such as the equal dignity of human beings resonate in all the cultural traditions of the world. In that sense, there is sufficient basis in every cultural tradition to foster and promote the value of human rights".[489] Similarly, it is not the practice of the CEDAW Committee simply to ask state parties to end plurality in legal

---

488　This is explicitly included in the new Ecuadorian Constitution; the insertion of the relevant Articles was the result of a very effective campaign by indigenous women's organisations to ensure that the new Constitution recognised indigenous culture, but also recognised that culture could not be invoked to the detriment of gender equality. The 1995 Ugandan Constitution recognises that people have a right to cultural expression but also confronts the issue of potential conflicts between the right to culture and the right to be free from sex discrimination; Article 33(6) states: "Laws, cultures, customs or traditions which are against the dignity, welfare or interest of women or which undermine their status, are prohibited by this Constitution."

489　Report to the Commission on Human Rights, E/CN.4/2003/75, para. 62.

systems; instead, as illustrated in the case of Sri Lanka, the Committee has urged the government to take into account recommendations from the 1991 Muslim Personal Law Reform Committee and seek out best practice from other jurisdictions where law interprets Muslim laws in line with the Convention.[490]

The standards also help to frame the notion of intersectionality.[491] This idea must underpin responses to a demand frequently advanced in the context of plural legal orders – that rights need to be 'balanced'.[492] Affirmation of the indivisibility of human rights (their 'enjoyment in totality') implicitly acknowledges intersectionality and guards against fragmentation of identity. In general, this has been recognised by human rights bodies. For example, in General Comment No. 28 (paragraph 30) the HRC notes that "discrimination against women is often intertwined with discrimination on other grounds such as race, colour, language, religion, political or other opinion, national or social origin, property, birth or other status" and calls on states to "address the ways in which any instances of discrimination on other grounds affect women in a particular way". In a similar vein, the CERD (International Convention on the Elimination of All Forms of Racial Discrimination) Committee's General Recommendation No. 25 on Gender Related Dimensions of Racial Discrimination provides a methodology for analysing intersectionality. This requires "[a] comprehensive gender analysis … of the effects of gender, the effects of race and the effects of gender and race combined". CERD now routinely requires states to report on the impact of racial discrimination on women. Positive trends are also visible at national level. The South African Constitution, widely regarded as the most responsive to international standards and human rights theory, explicitly recognises intersectionality, rather than requiring rights violations to be established on a single ground which often pits religion or ethnicity against gender.[493] However, a

---

490   Sri Lanka 07/05/2002 A/57/38 (Part I), paras 256-302.

491   Examples include the Maastricht Guideline No. 4, and HRC General Comment No. 28 on Equality of Rights between Men and Women (para. 2). Maastricht Guideline No. 4: "It is now undisputed that all human rights are indivisible, interdependent, interrelated and of equal importance for human dignity." HRC General Comment No. 28, para. 2: "The full effect of this provision [right to gender equality] is impaired whenever any person is denied the full and equal enjoyment of any right. Consequently, States should ensure to men and women equally the enjoyment of all rights provided for in the Covenant."

492   We understand intersectionality to mean that the various aspects of a person's being (their race, ethnicity, gender, age, class, religion, ability, sexual orientation, etc.) do not just occasionally cross over or add to each other but are mutually constitutive. Thus, one cannot understand a person's experience of ethnic or racial discrimination without noting how this is gendered or influenced by class.

493   The Bill of Rights, Article 9(3) prohibits state discrimination "on one or more grounds". Its enabling legislation, the Promotion of Equality and Prevention of Unfair Discrimination Act of 2000 "is especially important for women and particularly those women who suffer from intersecting forms of discrimination". (Jagwanth and Murray, 2005, p. 238.)

more nuanced understanding of culture in the development and enforcement of international human rights standards will require a more consistent application of the concept of intersectionality.

Regional human rights standards also offer ways forward. Legal plurality was one of the issues at the heart of the European Court of Human Rights Grand Chamber decision in *Refah Partisi (The Welfare Party) and Others vs. Turkey*.[494] The case involved the forcible dissolution of the Welfare Party in Turkey on several grounds, including the charge that the Welfare Party's advocacy of a plurality of legal systems violated Turkey's Constitution. In appeal, the Court upheld the conclusion that a plurality of legal systems, as proposed by Refah (which entailed categorising all individuals on the basis of religion with "rights and freedoms not as an individual but according to his allegiance to a religious movement"), could not be considered compatible with the European Convention on Human Rights. It is important to note that the Court's ruling did not address plural legal systems *per se* but Refah's proposed model of plurality;[495] the single dissenting judge in fact maintained that the Court had "missed the opportunity to analyse in more detail the concept of a plurality of legal systems".[496]

The Court cited two reasons for its position. First, it concluded that Refah's societal model would oblige individuals to obey rules laid down by a religious order and would undermine the state's role as the guarantor of individual rights and freedoms, and that as a result it could not "ensure that everyone within its jurisdiction enjoys in full, and without being able to waive them, the rights and freedoms guaranteed by the Convention". Second, it concluded that "such a system would undeniably infringe the principle of non-discrimination between individuals" and that "a difference in treatment between individuals in all fields of public and private law according to their religion or beliefs manifestly cannot be justified under the Convention". As Moe notes, the Chamber rejected Refah's argument that "prohibiting a plurality of private-law systems ... amounted to establishing discrimination against Muslims who wished to live their private lives in accordance with the precepts of their religion".[497] Instead, the Court "reiterates that freedom of religion, including the freedom to manifest one's religion by worship and observance, is primarily a matter of individual conscience, and stresses that the sphere of individual conscience is quite different from the field of private law, which concerns the organization and functioning of society as a whole.... Any Contracting Party, may legitimately prevent the application within its jurisdiction of private-law rules of religious inspiration prejudicial to public

---

494 European Court of Human Rights, Grand Chamber, *Case of Refah Partisi (The Welfare Party) and Others vs. Turkey*, Judgement, Strasbourg, 13 February 2003.

495 Cahn, forthcoming.

496 Moe, 2003, p. 48.

497 Moe, 2003.

order and the values of democracy for Convention purposes (such as rules permitting discrimination based on the gender of the parties concerned…".[498]

National courts across the world have grappled with the same questions. Their case law provides additional perspectives on human rights standards and legal plurality, often in the course of addressing customary or personal laws based on religion. For example, in *Bhewa vs. Govt. of Mauritius*,[499] the Supreme Court of Mauritius took a position similar to that of the European Court of Human Rights in the *Refah* case. It held that repeal of provisions of a Muslim personal law code did not infringe the religious freedom of the Muslim community guaranteed in the Constitution, because Articles 23(4), along with Articles 2 and 3, of the ICCPR, did not permit Mauritius to allow plaintiffs to apply their own religious law when this would result in denying women equal rights within marriage. Elsewhere, the South African Constitutional Court has upheld the right of communities to develop customary law, subject to constitutional values of equality and non-discrimination.[500] In this case, the eldest son of a deceased chief challenged the community's decision to confer the Chieftainship on the daughter of the deceased's brother. Ruling out the challenge, the Constitutional Court not only recognised that customary law evolves over time but also that constitutional values of gender equality and non-discrimination provide the appropriate direction for its development. This judgement is consistent with South Africa's Promotion of Equality and Prevention of Unfair Discrimination Act (2000), that places obligations on non-state as well as state actors and specifically prohibits traditional, customary or religious practices that undermine the dignity of women or gender equality.[501]

Bennoune suggests how claims to recognition of cultural difference that are articulated as human rights claims might be assessed. Though developed in the context of rights to freedom of religion and from gender discrimination, the same principles could be applied to other areas relating to plural legal orders and discrimination. She calls for a contextual and inter or intragroup focus and emphasises the need to assess "the actual result our approach is likely to produce".[502]

---

498   Ibid.

499   *Bhewa vs. Govt. of Mauritius* (1991) LRC const.

500   *Shilubana and Others vs. Nwamitwa* (Case CCT 3/07).

501   Jagwanth and Murray, 2005, p. 239.

502   Bennoune, 2007, pp. 393 and 396. In the specific context of veiling, Bennoune suggests the following factors should be considered: the impact of the veil on other women (or girls) in the same environment; coercion, including by religious extremist organisations; gender discrimination; violence against women, in context and related to the question at hand; the motivation of those imposing the restriction; religious discrimination and Islamophobia; alternatives to restrictions; the human rights consequences of restriction and non-restriction; the extent of consultation with impacted communities and their views.

This is somewhat similar to a framework developed by Sullivan,[503] which contained two other interesting elements, also with potential for wider application. Sullivan argues that, when considering gender equality and religious freedom, it is necessary to assess the proportionality of any restriction, and whether the proposed measure would have a cumulative effect (on either gender or religious rights) such that it would result in a qualitatively new dimension of discrimination.[504]

In terms of adopting a more nuanced approach to resolving apparent conflicts of rights, there is merit in the suggestion that human rights bodies "focus less on which rights trump other rights according to either the cultural relativist or universalist position, but instead on an outcome that minimizes the extent to which each conflicting right must be compromised".[505] The ALRC's report on recognition of indigenous customary law advances the same principle through what it calls a functional approach to recognition, which it contrasts with other forms that it considers categorical. It argues that the "form of recognition [of customary law] may vary with the context and with the problems being addressed.... The approach to be adopted must be flexible rather than categorical [sic] and must pay particular regard to the practicalities of the situation".[506] It underlines the importance of meeting at least four key concerns:

- Avoid the categorical and "one all purpose definition of 'customary laws and practices'";

- Aim to secure all the basic human rights for every member of the community;

- Deal with internal stresses and difficulties within the community that are due to external forces;

---

503   Sullivan, 1992.

504   With regard to gender equality and religious freedom, Sullivan proposes (until gender equality falls within the group of peremptory rights) "a balancing approach that takes into account particularized facts concerning the impact of the rights involved on one another, and on the underlying principles of gender equality and religious freedom". She argues that such an approach must take into account: (1) the relationship between the specific equality right at issue and the overarching goal of gender equality; (2) the importance of the religious law or practice to the right of religious freedom on which it is premised (i.e. how significant is that practice for the religion); (3) the degree to which each practice infringes the other or the underlying rights and interests (i.e. does the conflict result in only a slight degree of interference or is either of the practices totally barred and the exercise of the underlying right extensively restricted or foreclosed); (4) whether other human rights are implicated; (5) the cumulative effect of the restriction of women's status, and the effect of multiple restrictions on religious practice (i.e. the final straw argument); (6) the proportionality of the restriction, (1991, pp. 822-823).

505   Charters, 2003, p. 21, in the context of Maori women's exclusion from speaking rights on customary forums.

506   Ibid.

- Avoid establishing distinct and possibly conflicting systems of law that generate inequities and inefficiencies.[507]

THE SCOPE FOR FURTHER DEVELOPMENT OF HUMAN RIGHTS STANDARDS[508]

Due Diligence: The meaning and practical application of due diligence in the context of plural legal orders needs to be explored.[509] While due diligence might possibly be invoked to impose an obligation on a state (requiring it to act, for instance, to prevent human rights abuses by non-state legal authorities or customary law bodies), it is not clear how the obligation translates into clear and practical responsibilities in the context of a plural legal order. Though the notion has been elaborated recently in other areas, such as the right to health,[510] it has not been explored in the context of family laws. Where non-state legal orders are unrecognised, yet are operational and result in violations, could the notion of due diligence be expanded to include situations "where the state condones a pattern of pervasive non-action".[511] For example, would due diligence require a state to provide legal awareness training or to ensure, by provision of resources and other support, that disadvantaged minorities are properly represented in inter and intracommunity dialogues about the development of laws relevant to them?

Family law: The area of family law demands far greater attention from human rights bodies at all levels. Standards in this area have not been elaborated in any detail, despite their evident impact on the rights of women and children. Advocacy in this field is led by the women's movement, while mainstream human rights organisations are largely absent: a dialogue between the two is vital if standard-setting is to progress.

Different avenues are available for developing and strengthening standards relevant to family laws and plural legal orders. They include:

- Develop language similar to that in Article 4 of the UN Declaration of Basic Principles of Justice for Victims of Crime and Abuse of Power, which could address the manipulation of parallel legal orders in family law that result in discriminatory outcomes;

---

507 Para. 209, vol. 1.

508 For information on standard-setting processes see ICHRP, 2006.

509 For example, under the Maastricht Guidelines 15(d), a state commits a violation through omission in the event of any "failure to regulate activities of individuals or groups so as to prevent them from violating economic, social and cultural rights".

510 See for example the Maastricht Guidelines.

511 UNSR VAW UNDOC/E/CN.4/1996/53, 6 February 1996, para. 33.

- Use the right not "to be prevented from having access to the conditions that guarantee a dignified existence"[512] to discuss rights violations stemming from parallel family law systems;

- Examine how far the emphasis on 'best interests of the child' in Article 3(1) of the CRC can be used to discuss discrimination in family laws that affects mothers and thereby the interests of children in their care;

- Examine the links between discriminatory family laws and violence against women, and expand human rights responses to violence against women to include reform of family law.

Development of standards on intercountry family law issues: Although some existing standards govern disputes regarding recognition of intercountry marriage, divorce, adoption and related matters, this area of international law needs significant attention. Many of the developments in international private law have occurred in parallel to developments in the global human rights arena. Governments, intergovernmental organisations, and non-state actors such as NGOs should therefore give attention to the application of law in this area as well as to standard-setting and the need for research. The rapid increase in the number of intercountry marriages and relationships, as well as migration and the multiplication of minority rights discourses related to immigrant populations, all underscore the need for this.

Perhaps the clearest statement on plural legal orders in relation to this issue is a Council of Europe Resolution that called on states to refuse "to recognise foreign family codes and personal status laws based on religious principles which violate women's rights, and ceasing to apply them on their own soil, renegotiating bilateral treaties if necessary".[513] The resolution became necessary because some representatives of immigrant populations increasingly sought to restrict a range of women's rights (notably their freedom of movement and access to contraception) on grounds of freedom of religion and respect for culture and tradition.[514]

Address human rights implications of 'minor'-'major' subject matter classification: While the allocation to different jurisdictions of 'minor' and 'major' disputes or offences is an old practice, it raises problems. As underlined in Chapters III and IV, when this classification is used to define the jurisdiction of non-state forums, significant human rights issues may be relegated to the 'minor' sphere (family disputes, domestic violence or even customary offences that may attract significant punishments) and may consequently be subject to lower or unacceptable standards of legal process.

---

512   *Villagran Morales vs. Guatemala*, Series C no 63, 19 November 1999, para. 144.

513   Resolution No. 1464 (2005), Women and religion in Europe, Council of Europe.

514   Ibid.

Due process standards: Reasonably clear fair trial standards have been developed for "courts based on customary law or religious courts" in international human rights law (see Chapter III). However, it is essential to further elaborate due process standards in the context of civil disputes governed by non-state legal orders, including those that have a measure of state recognition. It is important to assess such mechanisms not only in terms of their economic and institutional efficiency (i.e. cost and rapidity) but also by the quality of the justice they provide, both in substantive and procedural terms. It may be useful to elaborate a set of guiding principles for arbitration and quasi-judicial mechanisms, on the model of those developed for non-judicial mechanisms such as truth and reconciliation commissions.

Recognition of non-state legal orders, especially indigenous people's legal orders: If recognition of any non-state legal order is to be meaningful, it is necessary to have a thorough understanding of the contemporary context and justice needs of the community whose laws are being recognised, and of changes which are occurring to their customary practices. Overall, more national research is required to make known the extent to which recognition of indigenous people's legal orders (and indeed all non-state legal orders) contributes to or obstructs progress in human rights. Research of this kind would help to strengthen best practice at national level. It would also permit experiences of plural legal orders to be shared internationally, which could ultimately inform the further development of international standards. As highlighted in Chapter III, international human rights law provides little guidance about what recognition of indigenous peoples' legal orders entails in practice, or how conflicts of law or underlying principles are to be resolved. Further insight into these issues can be gained from studying the experience of indigenous legal autonomy in a range of national contexts, including the United States, Canada, Colombia and Mexico, as well as the work of law reform commissions in Australia, New Zealand and South Africa.

The need for a comprehensive human rights response: Understanding that plural legal orders relate to a wide variety of human rights instruments and mechanisms is the key to addressing many of these issues. To develop a comprehensive human rights response, and to address the issue of fragmentation of standards, international and national human rights bodies and human rights organisations will need to work together to develop standards that are congruent across the different areas in question – including women's rights, minority ethnic and religious rights, indigenous peoples' rights, sexual orientation, etc.

SUMMARY

Notwithstanding their limitations, existing human rights standards offer some scope for an effective engagement with plural legal orders. For example, that the prohibition on discrimination cannot be derogated from, and no cultural defence is admissible with regard to violence against women.

Human rights instruments also contain scope for understanding the complexities of identity and for seeing culture as internally diverse, both of which rise above a 'balancing' approach. There is a great deal to be learned from the way human rights principles have been used by regional and national courts to address the issues of rights conflicts and violations associated with plural legal orders.

Effective approaches to recognise claims to cultural difference through plural legal orders must assess: a) actual human rights outcomes for inter and intragroup equality; b) the proportionality of any restriction on rights that such recognition may cause; and, c) whether the cumulative effect of the proposed measure would be such that it would result in a qualitatively new dimension of discrimination.

A functional rather than a categorical approach to the recognition of indigenous peoples' customary law or justice mechanisms is more likely to produce positive human rights outcomes. According to the ALRC, the key to such recognition is to: a) avoid the categorical and "one all purpose definition of 'customary laws and practices'"; b) secure all the basic human rights for every member of the community; c) deal with internal stresses and difficulties within the community that are due to external forces; and, d) avoid establishing distinct and possibly conflicting systems of law that generate inequities and inefficiencies.

Nevertheless, there is considerable scope for the further development of human rights standards relevant to plural legal orders.

The meaning and practical application of due diligence in the context of plural legal orders needs to be explored. Where non-state legal orders are unrecognised yet exist and result in violations, could the notion of due diligence be expanded to include situations "where the state condones a pattern of pervasive non-action"?

The area of family law demands far greater attention from human rights bodies at all levels. Dialogue between the women's movement and human rights organisations is vital if standard-setting is to progress in this area.

The significant human rights consequences of the allocation of disputes or offences to 'minor' or 'major' jurisdictions need to be examined and addressed creatively.

While fair trial standards are clear, it is essential to further elaborate due process standards in the context of civil disputes governed by non-state legal orders, including those that have a measure of state recognition.[515] It may be useful to elaborate a set of guiding principles for arbitration and quasi-judicial mechanisms, on the model of those developed for non-judicial mechanisms such as truth and reconciliation commissions.[516]

The extent and processes by which recognition of indigenous people's legal orders (and indeed all non-state legal orders) contributes to or obstructs human rights protection needs more national research and transnational sharing of experiences.

Understanding that plural legal orders relate to a wide variety of human rights instruments and mechanisms is key to addressing many of the human rights concerns.

To develop a comprehensive human rights response, and to address the issue of fragmentation of standards, international and national human rights bodies and human rights organisations will need to work together to develop standards that are congruent across the different areas in question – including women's rights, minority ethnic and religious rights, indigenous peoples' rights, sexual orientation, etc.

---

515   Due process, while vital, provides insufficient protection in the case of parallel family laws (see Chapter V).

516   See Mungoven, 2001, pp. 25-26, regarding the Joinet Principles and Van Boven–Bassiouni Principles.

XI. PLURAL LEGAL ORDERS: A FRAMEWORK FOR HUMAN RIGHTS POLICY AND ADVOCACY

As highlighted in an earlier chapter, how we think about human rights changes the way we 'do' them.[517] How then do the discussions, analyses and evidence in this report (and elsewhere) help human rights advocates to protect human rights in plural legal contexts? This chapter proposes a set of principles and a framework that is designed to enable human rights advocates to engage more effectively with plural legal orders.

It is not enough to say that advocacy positions or policy options 'can be decided only on the basis of local specificities'; or simply recommend that plural legal orders 'must comply with international human rights standards'. Such positions will leave human rights advocates holding a handful of uncontextualised platitudes; without tools that allow them to apply lessons from other contexts, and with unanswered questions about who defines 'local specificities' or 'compliance with human rights'.

What is needed is a framework that can guide human rights advocates as they analyse and grapple with the complex challenges to human rights advocacy and policy generated by plural legal orders *both* existing and proposed. No simple solutions to these challenges exist. Their absence is felt the more when it is remembered that virtually every criticism levelled at non-state orders for failing to match the characteristics of an 'ideal' justice system has also been levelled against formal state legal systems, often in the same national context.[518] Many have therefore questioned whether a single set of policy recommendations can offer helpful guidance at all, given the diversity of non-state legal orders,[519] the variety of issues they deal with (family law, criminal law, land, water, etc.), and the complexity of their relationships with the state legal order. It is often recommended, as a result, that case-by-case recognition of informal or traditional systems is the best approach.[520] A similar approach is often recommended too in situations in which state law is plural (see categories of plural legal orders in Chapter I).

Despite the complexities, human rights advocates engage with plural legal orders in many ways. They promote and monitor them; they challenge their

---

517   Nyamu-Musembi, 2002, p. 8.

518   "The central characteristics of a justice system that is able to perform its functions effectively are fairness and impartiality, sound decisions, accessibility, efficiency, independence and accountability, and credibility" (Biebesheimer and Payne, 2001, p. 4).

519   Faundez, 2003, p. 57.

520   Malzbender *et al.*, 2005, p. 11. Griffiths, 1998, p. 133 also warns against generalisations.

performance; they question relevant national and international policies; they empower individuals and communities who use them; they train arbiters, judges, chiefs, and national and international policy-makers; they provide legal services.

The kind of detailed assessment put forward in the framework below requires considerable expertise and resources. Human rights advocates and policy-makers who operate from outside the context will also need to coordinate with local human rights advocates when they apply it. We believe the potential benefits of applying a more carefully framed, multifaceted analysis justifies the additional investment of resources. Human rights advocates and others who use such frameworks, will still need to exercise judgement in deciding how to apply the information their analysis generates. In the framework proposed below, for example, the 'what to do?' question is frequently resolved implicitly, but rarely with ease. For example, it invites organisations to ask who determines the normative content of the legal order and to consider who may be excluded from such a process. It implies that, if further inquiry shows that the non-state legal order in question cannot be reformed internally because dissident voices within the community are silenced, then advocates should act to protect those voices and enlarge the spaces in which alternative opinions can be expressed.[521] Given the richness and complexity of the many environments in which human rights advocates may seek to intervene, the framework positively discourages a mechanical application of policy.

Though the framework presumes that multiple human rights interventions need to be considered, it would still represent a significant forward step if human rights advocates and policy-makers routinely took account of plural legal orders, and the impacts they have on human rights, in their monitoring work. This would require holding states to account under national and international standards for violations of rights that arise from plural legal structures, not just from the discriminatory content of laws: such monitoring would examine parallel family laws, the outcomes of state recognition of non-state legal orders, decentralisation of powers to customary chiefs' courts, state-established ADR mechanisms, Special Jurisdictions, and other issues that have been identified in this report. As discussed in the previous chapter, human rights advocates need also to engage in the further development and elaboration of standards that are relevant to plural legal orders.

---

521 Charters, 2003, p. 22 recommends this in the case of the Maori, and Sezgin, 2008, in the case of hermeneutic communities in Egypt, India and Israel. In her presentation at an ICHRP workshop in October 2008, Slyvia Chirawu, National Coordinator for WLSA Zimbabwe, similarly suggested the "reinforcement of positive cultural contexts".

Some Guiding Principles for Human Rights Advocates

These principles represent the most important points that human rights advocates need to bear in mind when they engage with plural legal orders. They are also at the core of the framework for advocacy and policy presented later in the chapter.

- Start from the perspective of those who experience inter and intragroup discrimination, and the need to redress this and analyse the role of state and non-state actors at the level of family and community, as well as at national, regional and international levels.

- Plural legal orders are neither intrinsically good nor bad for human rights – use a power lens to examine the processes behind their development, content and structure, and human rights implications.

- Adopt a comprehensive contextual approach to analysis taking into account historical as well as current social, economic and political factors.

- The benefits and disadvantages of state and non-state legal orders need to be questioned and supported by quantitative and qualitative empirical evidence.

- Discussion of, and decisions about, how best to promote and protect rights in relation to plural legal orders involves moral and political preferences. All those involved – including human rights advocates – must be reflexive and transparent about these preferences.

- Despite limitations, international human rights standards offer useful tools for policy and advocacy, especially when advocates can apply universal standards meaningfully to their local contexts.

- People are bearers of both rights and culture – transcend the apparent problem of 'balancing' rights by: a) adopting an intersectional approach to identity; b) seeing culture, custom, tradition and religion as changing, internally diverse and contested; and, c) using a situated analysis that regards rights-holders as simultaneously individuals and members of multiple collectives.

How to use the framework

The framework can be used in a variety of situations: to evaluate the impact of an *existing* plural system; to assess a *proposal* to establish or recognise plurality; or to assess a *claim for recognition* of non-state legal orders. Clearly, some of its questions may be more applicable to one or the other of the above situations, or will need to be understood differently according to context. Take the example of deciding whether evidence admissible in a forum will advance human rights (amongst the first questions proposed in the framework below). If a state official is hearing an indigenous land rights claim in a court that incorporates indigenous understandings of 'ownership', admitting *oral* evidence is a prerequisite for advancing human rights. On the other hand, women's rights advocates in Muslim contexts have struggled to ensure that all cases of divorce are subject to a formal *written* procedure. As emphasised, a mechanical diagnosis cannot be made. It is nevertheless useful to present a unified framework, because this highlights human rights concerns that are shared across all forms of legal plurality.

The framework generally helps analyse a plural legal order as it is at the moment of analysis; it provides a static snapshot. Some of the steps proposed nevertheless provide a window on the future because they require advocates to assess forms of internal and external intervention that will address potential human rights violations or prevent the future occurrence of violations.

The framework recommends a holistic analysis of plural legal orders, and their potential and human rights impact. Each of the proposed analytical steps is equally important. However, it is not necessary that every organisation should complete all the analysis proposed by the framework. On the contrary, a coordinated division of labour might have advantages, and might also strengthen human rights movement building.

The framework poses a series of questions, about policy and about demands for the introduction, preservation or reform of a plural legal order. Most of the questions can be answered 'yes', 'no' or 'partly'. To the extent that answers are negative, it implies that the plural legal order in question is likely to have negative human rights impacts. The objective is not to generate two simple categories of 'good' and 'bad' plural legal orders, but a broad spectrum of responses describing situations in which legal orders violate rights to a greater or lesser extent. The further a particular legal order falls towards the negative pole of the spectrum, the more serious are the human rights concerns it raises.

The answers given to questions in the framework therefore indicate a direction, whereas responses – specific steps to remedy or repair problems – are shaped by the political considerations, as well as the strategic or tactical options and alternatives that are available to human rights advocates in the given context.

THE FRAMEWORK

STAGE ONE: ASSESSING POLICIES AND DEMANDS FOR THE PRESERVATION, REFORM OR INTRODUCTION OF PLURAL LEGAL ORDERS

Policies and demands for the preservation, reform or introduction of a plural legal order should be assessed along six dimensions:

1. Clarity about the basis of the policy or demand;

2. Information about the advocates and their motivations;

3. The internal coherence of the policy or demand;

4. The extent to which the policy advances human rights nationally;

5. The wider national context; and

6. The impact of the policy or demand on intra and intergroup rights.

1. Is the basis of the policy or demand clear?

- Is the policy or demand clear? Is it clear what problem the existing or proposed plural legal order addresses?[522]

- Have those supporting the plural legal order clarified whether: a) the problem it is supposed to address is substantive (content), procedural (structural) or both; and, b) the issue is about choice of law or choice of forum or both?

- Is there sufficient qualitative and quantitative empirical evidence to support the policy or demand?

2. Is the range of actors advocating the policy or demand inclusive? What are the actors' motivations?

- Who proposes or promotes the plurality? Is the policy or demand supported by economically or politically disadvantaged members of a community (taking into account discrimination on the basis of gender, ethnicity, minority, religion, sexuality, etc.) or on the contrary by state or other powerful and privileged actors?

---

522 It is not always possible to match a rights issue neatly with a standard. For example, it was many years before standards recognised levirate marriage – 'widow inheritance' – as slavery.

- What motives and concerns underlie the policy or demand made by each actor?

3. Is the policy or demand internally coherent?

- Does the policy or demand match:

    - The identified rights issue;

    - The substantive or procedural problem identified; and

    - The empirical evidence?

- Does the analysis advanced by those who support the policy or demand align with the empirically-identified needs of users of the plural legal order?

- Where the policy or demand relates to the recognition or introduction of a non-state legal order, have popular generalisations about non-state legal orders been questioned sufficiently?

- Has the possibility of unintended outcomes been considered? (Might official recognition delegitimise a non-state order, or freeze custom, cancelling the presumed benefits of recognition?)

- Has the introduction, preservation or reform of a plural legal order elsewhere, in similar contexts, improved human rights and access to justice?

4. Is the policy or demand in line with rights-protecting national laws and policies? Does it advance human rights nationally?

- Is the policy or demand in line with national law and policy that promotes human rights (e.g., local government or decentralisation laws, case law, gender policies, policies on indigenous people or minorities, etc)?

- Is the plural legal order subject to fundamental rights guarantees and open to constitutional scrutiny on human rights grounds?

- Where the existing or proposed plural legal order is based on religion, does the policy or demand contribute to strengthening inclusive citizenship (or does it privilege religion in public policy and with what implications)? What is the relationship between religion and the state?

- Where a country has assumed international and regional human rights obligations, is the policy or demand in line with them?

- Where national law and policy do not contain adequate human rights protections and where national commitment to international and regional human rights standards remains weak or non-existent, does the policy or demand help improve this situation?

- Does the policy or demand match current and emerging international human rights standards (for example does it protect the rights of indigenous peoples, ethnic and religious minorities, and women)?

- Is the introduction or preservation of a plural legal order the only or best legal solution? (Or would the rights violation be addressed better by strengthening or introducing a unitary state system?)

- If the existing state legal order is not plural but unitary, would introducing plurality advance human rights more than institutional, procedural or substantive reforms to the unitary state order?[523] (Or do better legal alternatives to introducing plurality exist?)

- Do legal solutions suffice to address the problem? (Or, would it be more effective to address the problem's socio-economic or political roots – instead, or in addition?) What are the views on this of existing and potential users of the legal order?

5. Does the policy or demand take into account the wider national context?

- Does the policy or demand take into account and, where effects are negative, help to redress:

  - "The ways in which law has historically been configured, exercised, engaged with and understood by different groups",[524] including past experiences of failed legal reform efforts?

  - Contemporary and historical national social inequalities and structural discrimination (e.g. racism, patriarchy, class inequalities, etc.)?

---

523 Such as language training for judges or enabling religious authorities to conduct civil marriages.

524 Sieder, 2008, p. 22 (page number as in manuscript on file).

- The quality of democracy and governance in the country; the quality and independence of rule of law institutions; and the state's commitment to human rights and legal accountability?

- The role and influence of powerful private and public actors such as business and the military, and of organised crime?

- The quality of administrative and judicial institutions; the availability of financial, human and other resources that are required to ensure the proposal is implemented in a manner that will advance rights, especially of the marginalised?

- The impact of conflicts (on the social fabric; on the rule of law; on stability and security?

- Varying population densities (especially rural-urban differences)?

- Environmental implications (especially when plurality affects land rights)?

- Continuity and changes in social relations and cohesion that are transforming (or may have transformed) traditions, customs and communities?

6. Does the plural legal order have a negative impact on inter and intragroup equality?

- Does the existing or proposed plurality affect intragroup equality and relations, including political and economic power imbalances?

- Does the existing or proposed plurality affect intergroup equality and relations, including political and economic power imbalances and social harmony? How does the existing or proposed plurality affect relations between the state and ethno-cultural groups? Are there any transnational implications of such impacts?

- If the demand is backed by claims to recognise difference and diversity, are claimants themselves committed to accommodating intra and intergroup diversity, in practice and theory? Was the policy or demand developed in an inclusive way?

STAGE TWO: ASSESSING A PLURAL LEGAL ORDER IN OPERATION

A plural legal order may be made operational by interventions that are substantive, procedural or institutional. A current plural legal order, or one that is proposed, should be assessed along six dimensions:

1. The process for developing the content and structure of the plural legal order;

2. Resourcing issues;

3. Substantive content;

4. Procedural functioning;

5. Rights safeguards within the plural legal order; and

6. The broader space for rights protection in relation to the existing/ proposed plural legal order.

1. Is the process for developing the content and structure of the plural legal order inclusive and participatory?

- Are all social groups who are, or will be, affected by the plural legal order involved in developing the content and structure of the plural legal order? Are they equipped to participate in its development?

- Have inclusive and participatory mechanisms been established to review and assess the content and structure of the plural legal order, especially regarding human rights outcomes?

- Are sufficient opportunities available to feed findings on human rights outcomes into future possible reform?

2. Have resource issues been considered carefully?

- Has planning ensured that sufficient financial, human, technological and other resources are available for the effective, properly monitored, and sustainable operation of the plural legal order? How will these resources be mobilised?

- What wider implications (social, economic, political) of such resourcing need to be considered?

- Are conditionalities attached to the (local, national, international) provision of resources for the plural legal order? Will these weaken or undermine its adherence to human rights or protection of human rights in the wider national context?

3. **Does the substantive content of the existing or proposed plural legal order advance human rights?**

   - Are the applicable laws and rules clear and coherent?

   - Are the laws non-discriminatory? Do they safeguard the rights of user groups and individuals who are most likely to suffer discrimination from other users, and the rights of non-members?

   - What penalties and punishments are envisaged? How do they relate to principles such as proportionality and prohibition of torture and cruel and inhuman treatment?

4. **Does the procedural functioning of the plural legal order advance human rights?**

   - Regarding jurisdiction:

     □ Is jurisdiction clear (with regard to issues, territory, who is covered, and appellate processes)? Is jurisdiction determined in ways that maximise positive human rights outcomes for all users, especially the disadvantaged or discriminated and people with hybrid identities (such as individuals who married outside the group, or who are of mixed ethnicity or religion, etc.)?

     □ Has attention been paid to the human rights implications of separate jurisdiction for 'minor' and 'major' issues?

     □ Have exit options been formulated? Do they protect the rights of marginalised users, and restrict 'forum shopping' that advantages powerful users?

     □ Do mechanisms exist to resolve potential conflicts of law and to settle jurisdictional confusions with other legal orders in the system? Where mechanisms exist, are they accessible in practice?

   - Regarding procedural matters:

- Are the rules of procedure clear and coherent? Are legal practitioners allowed to participate? If not, what mechanisms exist to render the forum accessible to everyone?

- Are decisions by all forums recorded? If so, how and by whom? How is recording resourced? If only selected decisions are recorded, how is the decision to select taken and by whom?

- Are the rules on admissible evidence and the standing of witnesses clear and explicit? Do they protect the human rights of users, especially the marginalised?

- Regarding enforcement:

  - What are the mechanisms by which decisions are enforced? What biases or weaknesses of enforcement can be identified (including resource deficiencies)? What are their likely human rights impacts?

5. Do adequate rights safeguards exist within the existing or proposed plural legal order?

- Do adequate *ex ante* rights safeguards exist?

  - Are adjudicators chosen by a transparent and inclusive process? Have measures been taken to ensure that adjudicators have an appropriate profile and the qualifications required to ensure positive human rights outcomes?

  - Has provision been made to provide human rights training to adjudicators, both in the plural legal order and in any relevant state appeal or review mechanisms? Does the content of such training take into account the needs and perspectives of marginalised users?

- Is adequate provision made for appeals and review (*post facto* safeguards)?

  - In the event that decisions or procedures of a plural legal order violate rights, do appeal and review procedures exist? Are these accessible, especially to the marginalised?

  - Is provision made for monitoring the practice of the plural legal order? Does it rely on victims to raise the alarm?

    □   If legislation allows for review of a non-state forum's decisions within the formal court system, how willing and able are courts to hear appeals? Do higher courts emphasise human rights and act to protect them?

6.   Is the broader context conducive to rights protection in relation to the existing/proposed plural legal order?

- Are users aware of the substantive content and procedural provisions of the existing or proposed plurality? Are they aware of human rights implications? Are there adequately resourced state and/or non-governmental mechanisms or initiatives to empower users?

- Are there adequately resourced state and/or non-governmental legal awareness initiatives to build users' capacity to understand and shape the content and procedures of the existing or proposed plural legal order?

- Are national civil society groups engaged in human rights monitoring and advocacy in areas relating to the existing or proposed plurality?

- Do governance mechanisms exist within the community of users or nationally that enable those who advocate for a plural legal order or its reform to be held accountable for the outcomes of policies they support?

- What is the relative strength of forces within the community of users, or proponents of the plural legal order (taking account of knowledge, legitimacy, resources, membership, relationships with the state etc.)?

The number of areas covered and the level of detailed attention the questions in the framework demand are really a re-affirmation of a point made several times in this report – plural legal orders are not only diverse but also cut across and influence a number of human rights concerns. As such, there are no straight forward prescriptions but as this report demonstrates there is a lot to be learned from the experience and analysis of human rights advocates, policy-makers and scholars across the world

BIBLIOGRAPHY

Abiad, Nisrine. *Sharia, Muslim States and International Human Rights Treaty Obligations: A Comparative Study.* London: British Institute of International and Comparative Law, 2008.

Addario, Lise. *Six Degrees from Liberation: Legal Needs of Women in Criminal and Other Matters.* Department of Justice, Canada, 2002.

Ahrén, Mattias. "Indigenous Peoples' Culture, Customs, and Traditions and Customary Law – the Saami People's Perspective." *Arizona Journal of International and Comparative Law* 21, no. 1 (2004): 63-112.

Akan, Murat. "Contextualizing Multiculturalism." *Studies in Comparative International Development* 38, no. 2 (2003): 57-75.

Ali, S. S., and K. Arif. "Parallel Judicial Systems in Pakistan and Consequences for Human Rights." In *Shaping Women's Lives: Laws, Practices and Strategies in Pakistan*, edited by F. Shaheed *et al.* Lahore: Shirkat Gah, 1998.

Amien, Waheeda. "Overcoming the Conflict between the Right to Freedom of Religion and Women's Rights to Equality: A South African Case Study of Muslim Marriages." *Human Rights Quarterly* 28 (2006): 729-754.

Amnesty International. *Gulf Cooperation Council (GCC) Countries: Women deserve dignity and respect.* MDE 04/004/2005. AI, 2005a.

—. *Making Rights a Reality: Building your campaign.* ACT 77/051/2004. AI, 2004a.

—. *Making Rights a Reality: The duty of states to address violence against women.* ACT 77/049/2004. AI, 2004b.

—. *Maze of Injustice: The failure to protect Indigenous women from sexual violence in the USA.* AMR 51/035/2007. AI, 2007.

—. *Nigeria – Unheard Voices – violence against women in the family.* AFR 44/004/2005. AI, 2005b.

—. *Prevent the legalisation of the jirga system.* Action circular, ASA 33/009/2005. AI, 2005c.

—. *Sierra Leone Briefing Paper: No one to turn to: Women's lack of access to justice in rural Sierra Leone.* AFR 51/011/2005. AI, 2005d.

—. *Sierra Leone: Women face human rights abuses in the informal legal sector.* AFR 51/002/2006. AI, 2006.

—. *The Tribal Justice System*. ASA 33/024/2002. AI, 2002.

An-Na'im, Abdullahi. "Promises We Should All Keep in Common Cause." In *Is Multiculturalism Bad For Women?* edited by J. Cohen, M. Howard and M. Nussbaum. Princeton: Princeton University Press, 1999.

An-Na'im, Abdullahi, and Francis Deng, eds. *Human Rights in Cross-cultural Perspectives: Quest for Consensus*. Philadelphia: Pennsylvania University Press, 1992.

Antons, Christoph, and Volkmar Gressner. *Globalisation and Resistance: Law Reform in Asia since the Crisis*. Oxford: Hart Publisher, 2007.

Assies, Willem. "Indian Justice in the Andes: Re-rooting or Re-routing?" In *Imaging the Andes: Shifting Margins of a Marginal World*, edited by Ton Salman and Annelies Zoomers. Amsterdam: CEDLA (forthcoming). www.geocities.com/alertanet2/F2b-WAssies-en.htm#_ednref1.

Australian Law Reform Commission. *Multiculturalism and the Law*. ALRC Report no. 57, 1992.

—. *The Recognition of Aboriginal Customary Laws*. ALRC Report no. 31, 1986.

AWID. *Exposed: Ten Myths about Religious Fundamentalisms*. Toronto: Association for Women's Rights in Development, 2008a. www.awid.org/eng/About-AWID/AWID-News/Ten-myths-about-religious-fundamentalisms.

—. *Religious Fundamentalisms on the Rise: A Case for Action*. Toronto: AWID, 2008b. www.awid.org/eng/About-AWID/AWID-News/Religious-Fundamentalisms-on-the-Rise-A-case-for-action.

Balchin, Cassandra. "Muslim Women and Moderate Muslims: British Policy and the Strengthening of Religious Absolutist Control over Gender Development." In *The Power of Labelling: How and Why People's Categories Matter*, edited by Rosalind Eyben and Joy Moncrieffe. London: Earthscan, 2007.

—. "With Her Feet on the Ground: Women, religion and development in Muslim communities." Society for International Development. *Development* 46, no. 4 (December 2003): 40-47.

—. *Women, Law and Society: An action manual for NGOs*. Lahore: Shirkat Gah Women's Resource Centre, 1996.

Banda, Fareda, and Chinkin Christine. *Gender, Minorities and Indigenous Peoples*. UK: Minority Rights Group International, 2004. www.minorityrights.org/?lid=987.

Banerjee, Vikramjit. *Out of Asia: The Universalisation of Western Human Rights Values and the Critiques Emanating Out of Asia*. Paper presented at the Commission on Folk Law and Legal Pluralism, 15th International Congress, "Law, Power and Culture: Transnational, National and Local Processes in the Context of Legal Pluralism", 2006.

Barfield, Thomas. *Afghan Customary Law and Its Relationship to Formal Judicial Institutions*. Washington DC: United States Institute for Peace, 2003.

—. *Informal Dispute Resolution and the Formal Legal System in Contemporary Northern Afghanistan*. Washington DC: United States Institute for Peace, 2006.

Barfield, Thomas, Neamat Nojumi, and J. Alexander Their. *The Clash of Two Goods: State and Non-State Dispute Resolution in Afghanistan*. Washington DC: United States Institute for Peace, 2006.

Barry, Brian. *Culture and Equality*. Cambridge: Polity Press, 2000.

Basu, Srimati. *Playing off Courts: The Negotiation of Divorce and Violence in a Plurality of Legal Settings*. Paper presented at the Commission on Folk Law and Legal Pluralism, 15th International Congress, "Law, Power and Culture: Transnational, National and Local Processes in the Context of Legal Pluralism", 2006.

Benda-Beckmann, Franz von, and Keebet von Benda-Beckmann. "How communal is communal and whose communal is it? Lessons from Minangkabau." In *The Changing Properties of Property*, edited by Franz von Benda-Beckmann, Keebet von Benda-Beckmann, and Melanie Wiber. London: Berghahn, 2006.

Benda-Beckmann, Franz von, Keebet von Benda-Beckmann, and Anne Griffiths, eds. *The Power of Law in a Transnational World*. New York-Oxford: Berghahn, 2009.

Benda-Beckmann, Franz von, Keebet von Benda-Beckmann, J. Eckert, F. Pirie, and B. Turner. *Vitality and Revitalisation of Tradition in Law: Going Back into the Past or Future-Oriented Development?* Max Planck Institute for Social Anthropology, Report 2002-2003: 296-306.

Bennoune, Karima. "Secularism and Human Rights: A Contextual Analysis of Headscarves, Religious Expression, and Women's Equality Under International Law." *Columbia Journal of Transnational Law* 45, no. 2 (2007).

Beyer, Judith. *Imagining the State in Rural Kyrgyzstan: How Perceptions of the State Create Customary Law in the Kyrgyz Aksakal Courts*. Max Planck Institute for Social Anthropology, Working Paper no. 95, 2007.

—. "Making Politics before and after the March Revolution in Kyrgyzstan." *Danish Society for Central Asia Journal* 1 (2005a): 79.

—. "Revitalisation, Invention and Continued Existence of the Kyrgyz Aksakal Courts: Listening to Pluralistic Accounts of History." *Journal of Legal Pluralism and Unofficial Law* 53/54 (2006): 141-176.

—. "Rhetoric of 'Transformation: The Case of the Kyrgyz Constitutional Reform." In *Realities of Transformation: Democratisation Policies in Central Asia Revisited*, edited by Andrea Berg and Anna Kreikemeyer. Baden-Baden: Nomos, 2005b.

Bhandar, Brenna. *Recovering the Limits of Recognition: The Politics of Difference and Decolonisation in John Borrows' Recovering Canada: The Resurgence of Indigenous Law.* Colombia Law School: Law and Humanities Workshop, 2005. www.law.columbia.edu/center_program/law_culture/lh_workshop/ Workshop2005.

Bhatt, Chetan. "The Fetish of the Margins: Religious Absolutism, Anti-racism and Postcolonial Silence." *New Formations* 59 (2006): 98-115.

Biebesheimer, Christina, and Mark J. Payne. *IDB Experience in Justice Reform: Lessons Learned and Elements for Policy Formulation.* Washington, DC: Inter-American Development Bank, 2001.

Biebesheimer, Christina, and Mejfa Francisco. *Justice Beyond our Borders: Judicial Reforms for Latin America and the Caribbean.* Washington, DC: Inter-American Development Bank, 2000.

Binawan, Al Andang L. *The Battle of Human Rights in the Field of Religious Freedom in Indonesia during the New Order Era.* Paper presented at the Commission on Folk Law and Legal Pluralism, 15th International Congress, "Law, Power and Culture: Transnational, National and Local Processes in the Context of Legal Pluralism", 2006.

Boast, Richard. "The Waitangi Tribunal and Transitional Justice." *Human Rights Research Journal* 4 (2006): 1-13.

Bosniak, L. "Citizenship Denationalised." *Indiana Journal of Global Legal Studies* 7 (2000): 447–509.

Boyd, Marion. *Dispute Resolution in Family Law: Protecting Choice, Promoting Inclusion.* Ontario: Ministry of the Attorney General, 2004.

Boyle, Kevin. "Human Rights, Religion and Democracy: The Refah Party Case." *Essex Human Rights Review* 1, no. 1 (2004): 1-16.

Buur, Lars, and Helene Maria Kyed. *State Recognition of Traditional Authority in Mozambique: The Legible Space between State and Community.* DIIS Working Paper 36 (2006): 1-24.

Byrne, S., Mirescu G., and Müller S. *Decentralisation and Access to Justice.* Fribourg: International Research and Consulting Centre Series, 2007.

Cahn, Claude. *Autonomous Lawmaking and the Implementation of International Human Rights Law and Norms: Case Study of the Real and Potential Role of the Romani Kris.* European Yearbook on Minority Issues, forthcoming.

Calma, Tom. *Human Rights Perspective on Family Violence and Child Sexual Assault in Indigenous Communities.* Queensland Centre for Domestic and Family Violence Research Conference, 2007.

Chanock, Martin. *Law, Custom and Social Order: The Colonial Experience in Malawi and Zambia.* Cambridge: Cambridge University Press, 1985.

Charters, Claire. "Universalism and Cultural Relativism in the Context of Indigenous Women's Rights." In *Human Rights Research*, edited by P. Morris and H. Greatrex. Victoria University of Wellington. Wellington: Milne Printers Limited, 2003.

Chr. Michelson Institute, and Makerere University. *The Institutional and Legal Context of the 2006 Elections in Uganda.* Research Report: Lessons from the Referendum for the 2006 Elections.

Clarke, Jennifer. "Abolishing Customary Law Will Do Little to Reduce Violent Aboriginal Crime." *Canberra Times*, 3 July 2006.

Coates, Richard. *'Towards Mutual Benefit' – The Inquiry into Customary Law in the Northern Territory of Australia and other Initiatives.* Paper presented at the Australasian Law Reform Agencies Conference, 2004.

Commission on Legal Empowerment of the Poor. *Making the Law Work for Everyone.* Report, vol. 1 (2008).

Cook, Rebecca, and Lisa Kelly. *Polygyny and Canada's Obligations under International Human Rights Law.* Family, Children and Youth Section Research Report, Department of Justice, Canada, September 2006.

Cornish, Mary, Faraday Fay and Verma Veena. "Securing Gender Justice: The Challenges Facing International Labour Law." In *Globalisation and the Future of Labour Law*, edited by John D. R. Craig and S. Michael Lynk. Cambridge: Cambridge University Press, 2006.

Cowan, J., M. Dembour, and Richard Wilson. *Culture and Rights Anthropological Perspectives.* Cambridge: Cambridge University Press, 2001.

Danardono, Donny. *Imagining a Fair Trial: Feminist Legal Spaces as a Strategy in Deconstructing the Dominant Legal System in Semarang.* Paper presented at the Commission on Folk Law and Legal Pluralism, 15th International Congress, "Law, Power and Culture: Transnational, National and Local Processes in the Context of Legal Pluralism", 2006.

Davidheiser, Mark. *Governance and Legal Reform in the Gambia and Beyond: An Anthropological Critique of Current Development Strategies.* Max Planck Institute for Social Anthropology, Working Paper no. 93, 2007.

Department of Justice – Canada. *Aboriginal Justice Strategy Summative Evaluation: Final Report.* Government of Canada, 2007.

DFID. *Non-state Justice and Security Systems.* UK: DFID, 2004.

Domingo, Pilar, and Rachel Sieder, eds. *Promoting the Rule of Law: Perspectives on Latin America.* London: Institute of Latin American Studies, 2001.

Drzewieniecki, Joanna. *Indigenous People, Law, and Politics in Peru.* Presented at the Meeting of the Latin American Studies Association, 1995.

Dupret, Baudouin. "Legal Pluralism, Plurality of Laws, and Legal Practices: Theories, Critiques, and Praxiological Re-Specification." *European Journal of Legal Studies* 1 (2007).

Eckert, Julia. *Governing Laws – On the Appropriation and Adaptation of Control in Mumbai.* Max Planck Institute for Social Anthropology, Working Paper no. 33, 2002.

—. *The Trimurti of the State: State Violence and the Promises of Order and Destruction.* Max Planck Institute for Social Anthropology, Working Paper no. 80, 2005.

Emon, Anver M. "Conceiving Islamic Law in a Pluralist Society: History, Politics and Multicultural Jurisprudence." *Singapore Journal of Legal Studies* (2006): 331–355.

El-Fadl, Khaled Abou. *Speaking in God's Name: Islamic Law, Authority and Women.* Oxford: Oneworld Publications, 2001.

Faundez, Julio. *Non-State Justice Systems in Latin America Case Studies: Peru and Colombia.* Paper prepared for the DFID Workshop on Working with Non State Justice Systems, 2003.

—. *The Rule of Law Enterprise –Towards a Dialogue between Practitioners and Academics.* CSGR Working Paper no. 164/05, 2005.

Fianza, Myrthena L. *Indigenous Land Rights and Law in Transition: Some Issues Affecting Rural Moro Women in the Southern Philippines.* Paper presented at the Commission on Folk Law and Legal Pluralism, 15th International Congress, "Law, Power and Culture: Transnational, National and Local Processes in the Context of Legal Pluralism", 2006.

Fontaine, Lorena, and Pinto Anna. *Rights of Indigenous Peoples.* Proceedings from the 25th Annual Session of the International Human Rights Training Program, 2004.

Foster, Nicholas H. D. "A Fresh Start for Comparative Legal Studies? A Collective Review of Patrick Glenn's Legal Traditions of the World, 2nd Edition." *Journal of Comparative Law* 1, no.1 (2006): 100-199.

Fournier, Pascale. *The reception of Muslim family laws in western liberal states.* Dossier 27, London: Women Living Under Muslim Laws, December 2005. www.wluml.org/english/pubsfulltxt.shtml?cmd[87]=i-87-531768.

Fraser, Nancy. "From Redistribution to Recognition? Dilemmas of Justice in a "Post Socialist" Age." *New Left Review* 212 (1997): 11-39.

—. "Recognition without Ethics?" *Theory, Culture & Society* 18, no. 2-3 (2001): 21-42.

—. "Rethinking Recognition." *New Left Review* 3 (May-June 2000): 107-120.

—. "Social Justice in the Age of Identity Politics: Redistribution, Recognition and Participation." In *Redistribution or Recognition? A Political Philosophical Exchange*, edited by Nancy Fraser and Axel Honneth. London: Verso, 2003.

Fuest, Veronika. *Policies, Practices and Outcomes of Demand-oriented Community Water Supply in Ghana: The National Community Water and Sanitation Programme 1994 – 2004.* Center for Development Research, ZEF Working Paper no. 5, 2005.

Galanter, Marc, and Krishnan Jayanth K. "Bread for the Poor: Access to Justice and the Rights of the Needy in India." *Hastings Law Journal* 55, no. 4 (2004): 789-834.

—. "Personal Law Systems and Religious Conflict: A Comparison of India and Israel." In *Religion and Personal Law in Secular India: A Call to Judgment*, edited by Gerald James Larson. Bloomington: Indiana University Press, 2002.

Gellar, Sheldon. *Religion and Democratization in Colonial and Post-Colonial Africa: Parallels in the Evolution of Religious and Political Governance Structures.* Prepared for Working Conference: Designing Constitutional Arrangements for Democratic Governance in Africa: Challenges and Possibilities, March 30-31, 2006, Bloomington, Indiana. www.indiana.edu/~workshop/papers/gellar_wrkconf.pdf.

Genn, Hazel, and Alan Paterson. *Paths to Justice Scotland: What People in Scotland Do and Think about Going to Law.* Portland and Oregon: Hart Publishing, 2001.

Ghai, Yash. *Constitutionalism and the Challenge of Ethnic Diversity.* Draft presented at the American Bar Association Meeting in Vienna, 2008. Available on file.

Golub, Stephen. *Beyond Rule of Law Orthodoxy.* Rule of Law Series, Democracy and Rule of Law Project, no. 41, October 2003a.

—. *Non-state justice systems in Bangladesh and the Philippines.* Paper prepared for the United Kingdom Department for International Development, 2003b.

Gover, Kirsty. *Legal Pluralism and Legitimacy in Multicultural New Zealand: The Promise of Relational Approaches.* Strategic Policy Unit Working Paper Series, New Zealand Ministry of Justice, February, 2008a.

—. *Legal Pluralism and State-Indigenous Relations in Western Settler Societies.* Working Paper, International Council on Human Rights Policy, 2008b.

Gray, L., and M. Kevane. "Diminished Access, Diverted Exclusion: Women and Land Tenure in Sub-Saharan Africa". *African Studies Review* 42, no. 2. (September 1999): 15-39.

Gregg Benjamin. *State-Based Human Rights.* Paper Presented at the Annual Meeting of the Midwest Political Science Association, 2008.

Griffiths, Anne. "Legal Pluralism." In *An Introduction to Law and Social Theory,* edited by Reza Banakar and Max Travers. Oxford: Hart Publishing, 2002.

—. "Legal Pluralism in Botswana: Women's Access to Law." *Journal of Legal Pluralism and Unofficial Law* 42 (1998):123-138.

Griffiths, John. "The Social Working of Legal Rules." *Journal of Legal Pluralism and Unofficial Law* 48 (2003): 1-84.

—. "Village Justice in the Netherlands." *Journal of Legal Pluralism* 22 (1984): 17-42.

—. "What is Legal Pluralism?" *Journal of Legal Pluralism and Unofficial Law* 24 (1986): 1-56.

Gronfors, Martti. "Social Control and Law in the Finnish Gypsy Community: Blood Feuding as a System of Justice." *Journal of Legal Pluralism and Unofficial Law* 24 (1986): 101-125.

Gruss, Hans Jurgen. "The World Bank and Legal and Judicial Reform". Presentation at the International Symposium on Legal Assistance Projects, Nagoya University, Aichi, Japan, September 13-14, 2000.

Gundel, Joakim, and Omar Dharbaxo Ahmed A. *The Predicament of the Oday: The Role of Traditional Structures in Security, Rights, Law and Development in Somalia.* Danish Refugee Council and Novib/Oxfam, 2006.

Günther, Klaus. *Legal Pluralism and the Universal Code of Legality: Globalisation as a Problem of Legal Theory.* Available at www3.law.nyu.edu/clppt/program2003/readings/gunther.pdf.

Guzman, Mireya Martiza Pena. "Legal Pluralism as an Approach to Indigenous and Tribal Peoples' Rights." In *Human Rights in Development Yearbook (2003): Human Rights and Local/Living Law.* Leiden/Boston: Martinus Nijhoff, and Oslo: Nordic Human Rights Publications, (2003).

Hernández Castillo, R. Aída. "National Law and Indigenous Customary Law: The struggle for justice of indigenous women in Chiapas, Mexico." In *Gender Justice, Development, and Rights*, edited by Maxine Molyneux and Shahra Razavi. UNRISD, 2002.

—. "On Feminisms and Post Colonialisms: Reflections South of the Rio Grande." In *Coloniality at Large: Latin America and the Post – Colonial Debate*, edited by Mabel Morana, Enrique Dussel, and Carlos Jauregui. Durham: Duke University Press, 2008.

Hobsbawm, E., and Ranger, T., eds. *The Invention of Tradition.* Cambridge: Cambridge University Press, 1983.

Höhne, Markus V. "From Pastoral to State Politics: Traditional Authorities in Northern Somalia." In *State Recognition and Democratization in Sub-Saharan Africa: A New Dawn for Traditional Authorities?*, edited by Lars Buur and Helene Maria Kyed. New York: Palgrave MacMillan, 2007.

—. "Newspapers in Hargeysa: Freedom of Speech in Post-Conflict Somali Land." *Africa Spectrum* 43, no. 1 (2008): 91-114.

—. *Traditional Authorities in Northern Somalia: Transformation of Positions and Powers.* Max Planck Institute for Social Anthropology, Working Paper no. 82, 2006.

Honourable Justice Mildren, Dean RFD. *Aboriginal Sentencing.* Paper presented at the Seventh Colloquium of the Judicial Conference of Australia Inc., Darwin, 2003.

Hudson, Manley O. "One, Two, Three, Many Legal Orders: Legal Pluralism and the Cosmopolitan Dream." *New York University Review of Law and Social Change* 3, (2007): 641-659. (Delivered at the International Law Association, British Branch, University College London and School of Oriental and African Studies, 4 March 2006).

Hugh, Brian A. *Traditional Leadership in South Africa: A Critical Evaluation of the Constitutional Recognition of Customary Law and Traditional Leadership.* Dissertation: University of the Western Cape, 2004.

International Commission of Jurists. *Nepal: Justice in Transition.* Geneva: ICJ, 2008.

International Council on Human Rights Policy. *Human Rights Standards: Learning from Experience.* ICHRP, 2006.

—. *Local Government and Human Rights: Doing Good Service*. Geneva: ICHRP, 2005.

—. *Local Perspectives: Foreign Aid to the Justice Sector*. Geneva: ICHRP, 2000.

—. *Local Rule: Decentralisation and Human Rights*. Geneva: ICHRP, 2002.

International Legal Foundation. *The Customary Laws of Afghanistan*. New York: ILF, 2004.

Iturralde, Diego A. *Management of Multiculturalism and Multiethnicity in Latin America*. Management of Social Transformations Discussion Paper Series no. 5, UNESCO, 1995.

Jackson, Jean E. "Rights to Indigenous Culture in Colombia." In *The Practice of Human Rights: Tracking Law Between the Global and the Local*, edited by Mark Goodale and Sally Engle Mary. Cambridge: Cambridge University Press, 2007.

Jagwanth, Saras, and Christina Murray. "Constitutional Equality for Women in South Africa." In *The Gender of Constitutional Jurisprudence*, edited by Beverley Baines and Ruth Rubio-Marin. Cambridge: Cambridge University Press, 2005.

Jain, Pratibha. "Balancing Minority Rights and Gender Justice: The Impact of Protecting Multiculturalism on Women's Rights in India." *Berkeley Journal of International Law* 23 (2005): 201-22.

Joireman, Sandra Fullerton. "Inherited legal systems and effective rule of law: Africa and the colonial legacy." *Journal of Modern African Studies* 39 (2001): 571-596.

Jones-Pauly, Christina, and Neamat Nojumi. "Balancing Relations Between Society and State: Legal Steps Toward National Reconciliation and Reconstruction of Afghanistan." *American Journal of Comparative Law* 52 (2004): 852.

Jones, Richard. *Ethnic Minorities Net*. 17th BILETA Annual Conference, 2002.

Jones, Rochelle. *Why the UN Declaration on the Rights of Indigenous Peoples is so Important: The Case of Violence in Indigenous Australia*. AWID, 2006.

Kennedy, David. "One, Two, Three, Many Legal Orders: Legal Pluralism and the Cosmopolitan Dream." Speech at the International Law Association, British Branch, University College London and School of Oriental and African Studies, 4 March 2006.

—. *Remarks: Comparative Visions of Global Public Order Symposium Dinner Honoring Henry Steiner and Detlev Vagts*. Harvard Law School, 2005.

Kimathi, Leah W. *Non-State Institutions as a Basis of State Reconstruction: The Case of Justice Systems in Africa*. Codesria's 11th General Assembly, 2005.

Kiryabwire, Geoffrey W. M. *Alternative Dispute Resolution: A Ugandan Judicial Perspective*. Paper delivered at Continuation Seminar for Magistrates Grade One, 2005.

Kyed, Helene M. *State Recognition of Traditional Authority, Citizenship and State Formation in Rural Post-War Mozambique*. Dissertation: Roskilde University Centre, 2007.

Kyed, Helene M., and Lars Buur. *State Recognition and Democratization in Sub-Saharan Africa: A New Dawn for Traditional Authorities?* New York: Palgrave MacMillan, 2007.

Kymlicka, Will. *Contemporary Political Philosophy: An Introduction*. New York: Oxford University Press, 2002.

—. "Liberal Complacencies." In *Is Multiculturalism Bad For Women?*, edited by J. Cohen, M. Howard and M. Nussbaum. Princeton: Princeton University Press, 1999.

—. *Multicultural Citizenship*. New York: Oxford University Press, 1995.

—. "The Rights of Minority Cultures: Reply to Kukathas." *Political Theory* 20, no. 1 (February 1992): 140-146.

Lastarria-Cornhiel, Susana. *Gender and Property Rights within Postconflict Situations*. USAID, Issue Paper no. 12, April 2005.

Law Reform Commission of Western Australia. *Aboriginal Customary Laws: The Interaction of Western Australian Law with Aboriginal Law and Culture*. Project 94, 2006.

Leary, Virginia A. "Postliberal Strands in Western Human Rights Theory." In *Human Rights in Cross-Cultural Perspectives: A Quest for Consensus*, edited by Abduallahi Ahmed an-Na'im. University of Pennsylvania Press, 1992.

Le Sage, Andre. *Stateless Justice in Somalia Formal and Informal Rule of Law Initiatives*. Centre for Humanitarian Dialogue, 2005.

Likosky, Michael B. "Dual Legal Orders: from Colonialism to High Technology." *Global Jurist Topics* 3, issue 2, article 2 (2003).

Ludsin, Hallie. "Cultural Denial: What South Africa's Treatment of Witchcraft Says for the Future of its Customary Law." *Berkeley Journal of International Law* 21 (2003): 62-110.

—. "Relational Rights Masquerading as Individual Rights." *Duke Journal of Gender Law and Policy* 15 (2008): 195-221.

Lukito, Ratno. "The Enigma of National Law in Indonesia: The Supreme Court's Decisions on Gender-Neutral Inheritance." *Journal of Legal Pluralism and Unofficial Law* 52 (2006): 147-167.

Macaulay, Fiona. "Judicialising and (de) Criminalising Domestic Violence in Latin America." *Social Policy and Society* 5, no.1 (2005): 103–114.

MacDonald, Roderick A., and McMorrow Thomas. "Wedding a Critical Legal Pluralism to the Laws of Close Personal Adult Relationships." *European Journal of Legal Studies* 1 (2007): 1.

Macklem, Patrick. "Militant Democracy, Legal Pluralism, and the Paradox of Self-Determination." *International Journal of Constitutional Law* 4, no. 3 (2006): 488-516.

Malzbender, Daniel, Jaqui Goldin, Anthony Turton, and Anton Earle. *Traditional Water Governance and South Africa's "National Water Act" – Tension or Cooperation?* International Workshop on 'African Water Laws: Plural Legislative Frameworks for Rural Water Management in Africa, 2005. Gauteng, South Africa, 26-28 January 2005.

Mamdani, Mahmood. *Citizen and Subject: Contemporary Africa and the Legacy of Late Colonialism.* Princeton: Princeton University Press, 1996.

Maru, Vivek. "Between Law and Society: Paralegals and the Provision of Justice Services in Sierra Leone and Worldwide." *Yale Journal of International Law* 31 (2006): 428-468.

Masud, Muhammad Khalid. "Ikhtilaf al-Fuqaha: Diversity in Fiqh as a Social Construction." In *Wanted: Equality and Justice in the Muslim Family*, edited by Zainah Anwar. Malaysia: Sisters in Islam, 2009.

Mattei, Ugo. "A Theory of Imperial Law: A Study on U.S. Hegemony and the Latin Resistance." *Global Jurist Frontiers* 3, no. 2, article 1 (2003).

McLaughlin, Rob. "Some Problems and Issues in the Recognition of Indigenous Customary Law." *Aboriginal Law Bulletin* 3, 20 (1996).

McNamara, Luke. "Equality before the Law in Polyethnic Societies: The Construction of Normative Criminal Law Standards." *Electronic Journal of Law* 11, no. 2 (2004).

Mednicoff, David M. *Legalism Sans Frontières? U.S. Rule-Of-Law Aid in the Arab World.* Carnegie Papers no. 61, 2005.

—. "Think locally – act globally? Cultural framing and human rights movements in Tunisia and Morocco." *The International Journal of Human Rights* 7, no. 3 (October 2003): 72-102.

Menzies, Nicholas. *Legal Pluralism and the Post-Conflict Transition in the Solomon Islands: Kastom, Human Rights and International Interventions.* Berlin: Hertie School of Governance, 2007.

Merry, Sally E. *Human Rights and Gender Justice: Translating International Law into Local Justice.* Chicago: University of Chicago Press, 2006.

—. "Human Rights Law and the Demonization of Culture (And Anthropology Along the Way)." *Polar: Political and Legal Anthropology Review* 26, no.1 (2003): 55-77.

—. "Legal Pluralism." *Law and Society Review* 22, (1998): 872.

—. "Transnational Human Rights and Local Activism: Mapping the Middle." *American Anthropologist* 108, no.1 (March 2006a).

Michaels, Ralf. "The Re-State-Ment of Non-State Law: The State, Choice of Law, and the Challenge from Global Legal Pluralism." *Wayne Law Review* 51 (2005): 1209-1259.

Moe, Christian. "Refah Partisi (The Welfare Party) and Others v. Turkey." *The International Journal of Not-for-Profit Law* 6, issue 1 (September 2003). www.icnl.org/KNOWLEDGE/ijnl/vol6iss1/special_5.htm.

Moore, Sally Falk. "Certainties undone: fifty turbulent years of legal anthropology, 1949-1999." *The Journal of the Royal Anthropological Institute* 7 (2001): 95-116. www.dhdi.free.fr/recherches/theoriedroit/articles/sally.pdf.

Morel, Cynthia. "Defending Human Rights in Africa: The Case for Minority and Indigenous Rights." *Essex Human Rights Review* 1, no. 1 (2004): 54-65.

Mouffe, Chantal. "Artistic Activism and Agonistic Spaces." *Art & Research* 1, no. 2 (summer 2007).

Mulyani, Lilis. *The Dynamics of Inheritance Law and Legal Pluralism in Minangkabau: Choice of Laws or Conflicted Laws?* Paper presented at the Commission on Folk Law and Legal Pluralism, 15th International Congress, "Law, Power and Culture: Transnational, National and Local Processes in the Context of Legal Pluralism", 2006.

Mungoven, Rory. *Beyond the Courts: Developing Amnesty International's position on non-judicial mechanisms for accountability and redress.* AI Index POL 30/003/2001.

NCWD. *A compilation of the constitution, national and state statutes and regulations, local government bye-laws, customary laws and religious laws, policies and practices, and court decisions relating to the statuses of women and children, applicable in Nigeria.* Abuja, NCWD, October 2005.

New South Wales Law Reform Commission. *Sentencing: Aboriginal Offenders.* New South Wales Law Reform Commission Report 96, 2000.

Nina, Daniel, and Pamela J. Schwikkard. "The 'Soft Vengeance' of the People: Popular Justice, Community Justice and Legal Pluralism in South Africa." *Journal of Legal Pluralism and Unofficial Law* 36 (1996): 69-87.

Nkonya, Leticia K. "Customary Laws for Access to and Management of Drinking Water in Tanzania." *Law Environment and Development Journal* 2, no.1 (2006): 50.

Northern Territory Law Reform Committee. *Report of Committee of Inquiry into Aboriginal Customary Law.* Northern Territory Law Reform Committee Report no. 28, 2003.

Nyamu-Musembi, C. *Towards an Actor Oriented Perspective on Human Rights.* IDS Working Paper 169, 2002.

Odinkalu, Chidi Anselm. "Poor Justice or Justice for the Poor? A Policy Framework for Reform of Customary and Informal Justice Systems in Africa." In *The World Bank Legal Review, Volume 2: Law, Equity, and Development*, edited by Caroline Mary Sage and Michael Woolcock. The World Bank/Martinus Nijhoff, 2006.

OHCHR. *Rule-of-Law Tools for Post-Conflict States: Mapping the Justice Sector.* New York-Geneva: United Nations, 2006.

Oloka-Onyango, Joe. *Decentralisation without Human Rights? Local Governance and Access to Justice in Post-Movement Uganda.* HURIPEC Working Paper no.12, 2007.

OSCE. *Parallel Structures in Kosovo.* OSCE, 2007.

Parliamentary Assembly of the Council of Europe. *Women and Religion in Europe.* Resolution 1464 (2005).

Pirie, Fernanda. *Feuding, Mediation and the Negotiation of Authority among the Nomads of Eastern Tibet.* Max Planck Institute for Social Anthropology, Working Paper no. 72, 2005.

Pradhan, Rajendra. *Negotiating Multiculturalism in Nepal: Law, Hegemony, Contestation and Paradox.* 2007. www.uni-bielefeld.de/midea/pdf/Rajendra.pdf.

Prill-Brett, June. "Contested Domains: The Indigenous Peoples Rights Act (Ipra) and Legal Pluralism in the Northern Philippines." *Journal of Legal Pluralism and Unofficial Law* 55 (2007): 11-36.

Qiliang, Wang. *Religion, Legal Pluralism and Order in a Multiethnic (multiracial) Society: A Legal-anthropological Study in Contemporary China.* Paper presented at the Commission on Folk Law and Legal Pluralism, 15th International Congress, "Law, Power and Culture: Transnational, National and Local Processes in the Context of Legal Pluralism", 2006.

Rabo, Annika. "Family law in multicultural and multireligious Syria." In *Possibilities of Religious Pluralism*, edited by Göran Collste. Linköping Studies in Identity and Pluralism no. 3, Linköping University Electronic Press, 2005.

Raday, Frances. "Culture, Religion and Gender." *International Journal of Constitutional Law* 1, no. 4 (2003): 663-715.

Ragsag, Anabelle B. *Customary Justice System in Mindanao: Challenges and Opportunities for Philippine nation-making. Non-State Ordering: Rido, Clans and the State – Secessionist Dynamics in Southern Philippines*. Paper presented at the Commission on Folk Law and Legal Pluralism, 15th International Congress, "Law, Power and Culture: Transnational, National and Local Processes in the Context of Legal Pluralism", 2006.

Raz, Joseph. "Multiculturalism." *Ratio Juris* 11 (1998): 193-205.

Resnick, Judith. "Courts: In and Out of Sight, Site and Cite." The Norman Shachoy Lecture available at www.iapl2009.org/documents/3bJudithResnik.pdf.

Rights and Democracy. *Behind Closed Doors: How Faith-Based Arbitration Shuts Out Women's Rights in Canada and Abroad*. Quebec: Rights and Democracy, 2005a.

—. *Fundamentalisms and Human Rights*. Quebec: Rights and Democracy, 2005b.

Rogers, Ben, and Muir Rick. *The Power of Belonging: Identity Citizenship and Community Cohesion*. London: Institute for Public Policy Research, 2007.

Rouhana, Hoda. *Muslim family laws in Israel: The role of the state and the citizenship of Palestinian women*. London: Women Living under Muslim Laws. Dossier 27 (2006).

Rudy. *Decentralization in Indonesia: Reinventing Local Right*. Paper presented at the Commission on Folk Law and Legal Pluralism, 15th International Congress, "Law, Power and Culture: Transnational, National and Local Processes in the Context of Legal Pluralism", 2006.

Sage, Caroline Marym, and Michael Woolcock. *The World Bank Legal Review, Volume 2: Law, Equity, and Development*. The World Bank/Martinus Nijhoff, 2006.

Sahgal, Gita. "Legislating Utopia? Violence against Women: Identities and Interventions." In *The Situated Politics of Belonging*, edited by Nira Yuval-Davis, Kalpana Kannabiran and Ulrike Vieten. London: SAGE Publications Ltd, 2006.

—. *Purity or Danger? Human Rights and their Engagement with Fundamentalisms*. Proceedings of the Annual Meeting-American Society of International Law, 2006.

Sarwar, B. "Personal Political: Jirga injustice." *The News*, 14 November 2004, Karachi.

Sarat, A., and Berkowitz, R. "Disorderly Differences: Recognition, Accommodation, and American Law." *Yale Journal of Law and the Humanities* 6 (1994): 285.

Schärf, Wilfried. *Improving Access to Justice in Developing Countries*. www.ssrnetwork.net/documents/temp/Improving_Access_to_Justice_in_Developing_Countries.doc.

Schneiderman, David. "Pluralism, Disagreement, and Globalization: A Comment on Webber's 'Legal Pluralism and Human Agency'." *Osgoode Hall Law Journal* 44, no.1 (2006): 199.

Sezgin, Yüksel. *A Comparative Study of Personal Status Systems in Israel, Egypt and India*. Working Paper, International Council on Human Rights Policy, 2008.

—. *A New Theory of Legal Pluralism: The Case of Israeli Religious Courts*. Association for Israel Studies, 19th Annual Meeting, 2003. Available on file.

—. "Theorizing Formal Pluralism: Quantification of Legal Pluralism for Spatio-Temporal Analysis." *Journal of Legal Pluralism and Unoffical Law* 50 (2004): 101-118.

Shachar, Ayelet. "Privatizing Diversity: A Cautionary Tale from Religious Arbitration in Family Law." *Theoretical Inquiries in Law* 9, no. 2, article 11 (2008): 573-607.

Shah, N. "Faislo: The Informal Settlement System and Crimes Against Women." In *Shaping Women's Lives: Laws, Practices and Strategies in Pakistan*, edited by F. Shaheed *et al*. Lahore: Shirkat Gah, 1998.

Shah, Prakash. "Globalisation and the Challenge of Asian Legal Transplants in Europe." *Singapore Journal of Legal Studies* (2005): 348-361.

Siahaan, Bakti. *The Establishment of Islamic Law in Aceh vs National Law of Indonesia*. Paper presented at the Commission on Folk Law and Legal Pluralism, 15th International Congress, "Law, Power and Culture: Transnational, National and Local Processes in the Context of Legal Pluralism", 2006.

Sieder, Rachel. "Legal Globalization and Human Rights: Constructing the 'Rule of Law' in Post-Conflict Guatemala." In *Human Rights in the Maya Region: Global Politics, Moral Engagements, and Cultural Contentions*, edited by Pedro Pitarch, Shannon Speed and Xochitl Leyva. Duke University Press, 2008.

Skaar Elin, Samset Ingrid, and Gloppen Siri. *Aid to Judicial Reform: Norwegian and International Experiences*. Bergen, Norway: Chr. Michelsen Institute, 2004.

Smart, Carol. *Feminism and the Power of Law*. London: Routledge, 1989.

Solamo-Antonio, Isabelita. *The Shari'a Courts in the Philippines: Women, Men & Muslim Personal Laws*. Davao City: PILIPINA Legal Resources Centre, 2003.

Sona, Federica. *Polygamy in Britain*. Italy: OLIR, 2005.

South African Law Commission. *Alternative Dispute Resolution*. SALC, Issue Paper 8, Project 94, 1997.

—. *Customary Law of Succession*. SALC, Project 90, 2004.

—. *The Harmonisation of the Common Law and the Indigenous Law: Conflicts of Law*. SALC, Discussion Paper 76, Project 90, 1998.

—. *The Harmonisation of the Common Law and the Indigenous Law: The Application of Customary Law: Conflict of Personal Laws*. SALC, Issue Paper 4, Project 90, 1996.

—. *The Harmonisation of the Common Law and the Indigenous Law: Traditional Courts and the Judicial Function of Traditional Leaders*. SALC, Discussion Paper 82, Project 90, 1999.

Speed, Shannon. "Exercising rights and reconfiguring resistance in the Zapatista Juntas de Buen Gobierno." In *The Practice of Human Rights*, edited by Sally E. Merry and Mark Goodale. Cambridge: Cambridge University Press, 2007.

Stavenhagen, Rodolfo. *Conclusions and Recommendations of the Expert Seminar on Indigenous Peoples and the Administration of Justice*. United Nations Economic and Social Council, E/CN.4/2004/80/Add.4, 2004a.

—. *Human Rights and Indigenous Issues: Report of the Special Rapporteur on the Situation of Human Rights and Fundamental Freedoms of Indigenous Peoples*. United Nations Economic and Social Council, E/CN.4/2004/80, 2004b.

—. *Human Rights and Indigenous Issues: Report of the Special Rapporteur on the Situation of Human Rights and Fundamental Freedoms of Indigenous Peoples*. United Nations Economic and Social Council, E/CN.4/2006/78, 2006.

—. *Implementation of General Assembly Resolution 60/251 of 15 March 2006 Entitled "Human Rights Council"*. United Nations Economic and Social Council, A/HRC/4/32, 2007.

Steiner, Kerstin. *'Asian Values' and the 'War on Terror': A Re-Emergence of the Challenge for International Human Rights?* Paper presented at the Commission on Folk Law and Legal Pluralism, 15th International Congress, "Law, Power and Culture: Transnational, National and Local Processes in the Context of Legal Pluralism", 2006.

Stopler, Gila. "Contextualizing Multiculturalism: A Three Dimensional Examination of Multicultural Claims." *Law and Ethics of Human Rights* 1, issue 1, article 10 (2007): 310-353.

Sullivan, Donna J. "Gender Equality and Religious Freedom; Toward a Framework for Conflict Resolution." *New York University Journal of International Law* 23 (1992): 795.

Sunder, Madhavi. "Enlightened Constitutionalism." *Connecticut Law Review* 37 (2005). http://ssrn.com/abstract=744824.

Tachibana, Masami M. *Tensions and Compromises of Legal Pluralism: Case Study from a Philippine Migrant Community.* Paper presented at the Commission on Folk Law and Legal Pluralism, 15th International Congress, "Law, Power and Culture: Transnational, National and Local Processes in the Context of Legal Pluralism", 2006.

Tamanaha, Brian Z. *Understanding Legal Pluralism: Past to Present, Local to Global.* St. John's Legal Studies Research Paper no. 07-0080, May 2008. http://ssrn.com/paper=1010105.

Tamir, Yael. "Against Collective Rights." In *Rights, Culture and the Law: Themes from the Legal and Political Philosophy*, edited by Joseph Raz, Lukas Meyer, Stanley Paulson and Thomas Pogge. Oxford: Oxford Scholarship Online Monographs, 2003.

The International Symposium on "Legal Assistance Projects in Asia and International Cooperation". Nagoya University, 2001.

Tokhtakhodjaeva, Marfua. Between the Slogans of Communism and the Laws of Islam. Lahore: Shirkat Gah, 1995.

Tripp, Aili Mari. "Women's movements, customary law, and land rights in Africa: the case of Uganda." *African Studies Quarterly* 7, issue 4 (March 2004): 1-19.

Tubb, Daniel. "Statelessness and Colombia: Hannah Arendt and the Failure of Human Rights." *Undercurrent: Canadian Undergraduate Journal of Development Studies* 3, issue 2 (2006): 39-51.

Tully, James. "Recognition and Dialogue: the Emergence of a New Field." *Critical Review of International Social and Political Philosophy* 7, no. 3 (2004): 84-106.

Twining, William. *Law, Justice and Rights: Some Implications of a Global Perspective*. 2007. www.ucl.ac.uk/laws/academics/profiles/.../Law_Justice%20_Rights.pdf

Ubink, Janine. "Traditional Authority Revisited Popular Perceptions of Chiefs and Chieftaincy in Peri-urban Kumasi, Ghana." *Journal of Legal Pluralism* 55 (2007): 123-161.

UNCDF. *Investing in Least Developed Countries: Uganda Country Brief*. New York: UNCDF, 2006.

USAID. *Field Study of Informal and Customary Justice in Afghanistan and Recommendations on Improving Access to Justice and Relations between Formal Courts and Informal Bodies*. Washington, DC: USAID, 2005.

—. *Legal Empowerment of the Poor: From Concepts to Assessment*. Washington, DC: USAID, 2007.

Vaggione, Juan Marco. "Reactive Politicization and Religious Dissidence: The Political Mutations of the Religious." *Social Theory and Practice* 31, no. 2 (2005).

—. *Shared Insights: Women's rights activists define religious fundamentalisms*. Toronto: AWID, 2008.

Valenta, Lisa. "Disconnect: The 1988 Brazilian Constitution, Customary International Law, and Indigenous Land Rights in Northern Brazil." *Texas International Law Journal* 38 (2003): 643-662.

Vicenti, Carey N. "The Reemergence of Tribal Society and Traditional Justice Systems." *Journal of the American Judicature Society* 79, no. 3 (1995): 134-141.

Wardak, Ali. "Building a Post-War Justice System in Afghanistan." *Crime, Law and Social Change* 41, no. 4 (2004): 319-341.

Warman, Kurnia. *The Law of the Stronger Group: When State and Customary Law Do Not Apply*. Paper presented at the Commission on Folk Law and Legal Pluralism, 15th International Congress, "Law, Power and Culture: Transnational, National and Local Processes in the Context of Legal Pluralism", 2006.

Warraich, Sohail Akbar. "Text or Context? Islamization of the Pakistan Constitution." *Bayan: A Bi-Annual Sociolegal Journal*, Simorgh Women's Resource and Publication Centre, Lahore, vol. 2 (2004).

Warraich, Sohail A., and Cassandra Balchin. *Recognizing the Un-Recognised: Inter-Country Cases and Muslim Marriages and Divorces in Britain*. WLUML Publications, 2006.

Weilenmann Markus. "Legal Pluralism – A New Challenge for Development Agencies." In *Access to Justice in Africa and Beyond: Making the Rule of Law a Reality*, edited by Penal Reform International and Bluhm Legal Clinic, University of Chicago. South Bend: National Institute of Trial Advocacy, 2007.

Widlok, Thomas. *Equality, Group Rights, and Corporate Ownership of Land. A Comparative Perspective of Indigenous Dilemmas in Australia and Namibia.* Max Planck Institute for Social Anthropology, Working Paper no. 21, 2001.

WLUML. *Knowing Our Rights: women, family, laws and customs in the Muslim world.* 3rd edition. London: Women Living Under Muslim Laws, 2006.

Wojkowska, Ewa. *Doing Justice: How Informal Justice Systems Can Contribute.* UNDP, 2006.

World Bank. *A Framework for Strengthening Access to Justice in Indonesia.* World Bank, 2007. http://siteresources.worldbank.org/INTJUSFORPOOR/Resources/A2JFrameworkEnglish.pdf.

Yasuda, Nobuyuki. *Three Types of Legal Principle: A New Paradigm for the Law and Development Studies.* Graduate School of International Development, Nagoya University, 2000.

Yilmaz, Ihsan. "Muslim Alternative Dispute Resolution and Neo-Ijtihad in England." *Turkish Journal of International Relations* 2, no. 1 (2003): 117-139.

Yrigoyen Fajardo, Raquel Y. "Legal Pluralism, Indigenous Law and the Special Jurisdiction in the Andean Countries." *Beyond Law* 10, no. 27 (2004): 32-46.

Yuval-Davis, Nira. "Belonging and the politics of belonging." *Patterns of Prejudice* 40, no. 3 (2006): 197-214.

Zia, Shahla. *Violence Against Women and Their Quest for Justice.* Simorgh Women's Resource and Publication Centre, 2002.

ABOUT THE COUNCIL

The International Council on Human Rights Policy was established in 1998 following an international consultation that started after the 1993 World Conference on Human Rights in Vienna. It conducts practical research into problems and dilemmas that confront organisations working in the field of human rights.

The Council starts from the principle that successful policy approaches will accommodate the diversity of human experience. It co-operates with all that share its human rights objectives, including voluntary and private bodies, national governments and international agencies.

The Council's research agenda is set by the Executive Board. Members of the International Council meet annually to advise on that agenda. Members help to make sure that the Council's programme reflects the diversity of disciplines, regional perspectives, country expertise and specialisations that are essential to maintain the quality of its research.

To implement the programme, the Council employs a small Secretariat of seven staff. Based in Geneva, its task is to ensure that projects are well designed and well managed and that research findings are brought to the attention of relevant authorities and those who have a direct interest in the policy areas concerned.

The Council is independent, international in its membership and participatory in its approach. It is registered as a non-profit foundation under Swiss law.

How to order Council publications

All Council publications can be ordered through the Secretariat at:
ICHRP
48 chemin du Grand-Montfleury
CH-1290 Versoix
Geneva, Switzerland
Phone: +41 (0) 22 775 33 00
Fax: +41 (0) 22 775 33 03

All our publications can also be ordered through our web site at **www.ichrp.org** where they can also be accessed in PDF format.

For more information about the International Council and its work, please contact us at **info@ichrp.org**.